SPACE, TIME, AND PERVERSION

SPACE, TIME, AND PERVERSION

ESSAYS ON THE POLITICS OF BODIES

ELIZABETH GROSZ

Routledge   New York & London

Published in 1995 by
Routledge
29 West 35th Street
New York, NY 10001

Published in Great Britain by
Routledge
11 New Fetter Lane
London EC4P 4EE

Design: David Thorne
Printed in the United States of America on acid-free paper.

Library of Congress Cataloging-in-Publication Data

Grosz, E. A. (Elizabeth A.)
     Space, time, and perversion: essays on the politics of bodies / Elizabeth Grosz.
     p.   cm.
Includes bibliographical references and index.

ISBN 0-415-91136-2   —   ISBN 0-415-91137-0

     1. Feminist theory.   2. Body, Human—Social aspects.   3. Gender Identity.
     4. Lesbianism.   5. Homosexuality.   I. Title.

HQ1190.G758   1995   95-8699
306.4—dc20   CIP

CONTENTS

ACKNOLEDGMENTS

ONE CANNOT UNDERTAKE ANY EXTENDED research or writing project without the support of a whole network of friends, colleagues, and institutions. I hope I can adequately acknowledge all those who contributed in one way or another to this collection. My thanks to the Arts Faculty at Monash University for providing a most conducive and stimulating context for teaching, research, and writing. Here I would particularly like to single out Gail Ward for her continuing strength and wisdom. All the papers have been slightly, or in some cases, more drastically, modified since their original publication. Much of this occurred while I was moving between Monash and Johns Hopkins. My thanks also to the Humanities Center at Johns Hopkins University for helping provide time and resources for the final versions of these essays. More personally, I would like to single out Elizabeth Wilson, Cathryn Vasseleu, and Pheng Cheah for my very special thanks for reading the whole manuscript and for helping me to decide which essays to leave in and which to leave out: without their support, I think I would have abandoned the project in its early days as too complicated, and as too indulgent. My special thanks too to Linda Alcoff, who also shared short bursts of my agonizing over the selection of essays. To Teresa Brennan, Judith Butler, Drucilla Cornell, Dion Farquhar, Vicki Kirby, Teresa de Lauretis, Marshall Leicester, Jacqueline Reid, and Gai Stern, once again, my strongest gratitude for friendship, support, and stimulation of all kinds. I also owe my students, both in Australia and in the United States, a heartfelt thanks for their (sometimes involuntary) willingness to be the guinea pigs of much of this research, and for their level-headed openness in criticism. While it is common to thank publishers, in this case it is a real pleasure working with Maureen MacGrogan from Routledge, New York and Elizabeth Weiss from Allen and Unwin, Sydney. My particular thanks to Linda Dement for her stunning cover art, which continues to inspire me to think more about the strangeness of bodies; and to Valerie Hazel for her meticulous indexing. Finally, thanks to my loving family, for always being there, tolerating it all.

New York
October, 1994

A NOTE ON THE TEXT

I AM GRATEFUL TO HAVE PERMISSION TO reprint the following essays, which I have revised more or less drastically: "Bodies and Knowledges: Feminism and the Crisis of Reason" appeared in *Feminist Epistemologies*, edited by Linda Alcoff and Elizabeth Potter, New York: Routledge, 1993, 187–216; "Sexual Difference and the Problem of Essentialism" was written for *Feminist Theory. Critique and Construct*, edited by Sneja Gunew, London and New York: Routledge, 1990, 332–44; it was reprinted in *Inscriptions* No. 5, 1989; and in *The Essential Difference*, edited by Naomi Schor and Elizabeth Weed, Indiana University Press, 1994, 82–97. "Ontology and Equivocation. Derrida's Politics of Sexual Difference" will appear in *Feminist*

Interpretations of Derrida, edited by Nancy Holland, University of Texas Press; and *Diacritics* (Special 25th anniversary issue); "Space, Time and Bodies" originally appeared in *On the Beach*, No. 13, 1988: 13–27; it was reprinted in *Transition* 44/45, 1994: 74–103; "Bodies/ Cities" was published in *Sexuality and Space*, edited by Beatriz Colomina, Princeton Architectural Press, 1992, 241–54. "Women, *Chora*, Dwelling" appeared in *ANY*, January–February, 1994: 22–23, and was reprinted in *Postmodern Cities and Spaces*, edited by Sophie Watson and Katherine Gibson, Oxford: Blackwell, 1995, 47–58; "Architecture from the Outside" is forthcoming in *Society and Space*; and *ANYPlace*, edited Cynthia Davidson, New York: Rizzoli; "Lesbian Fetishism?" was originally published in *differences* (Special issue on 'Queer Theory' edited by Teresa de Lauretis), Vol. 3 No. 2, 1991: 39–54; and was reprinted in *Fetishism as Cultural Discourse*, edited by Emily Apter and William Pietz, Ithaca: Cornell University Press, 1993, 101–15; "Labors of Love. Analyzing Perverse Desire" is forthcoming in *differences*. "Refiguring Lesbian Desire" was published in *The Lesbian Postmodern*, edited by Laura Doan, New York: Columbia University Press, 1994, 67–84; a version of "Experimental Desire: Rethinking Queer Subjectivity" is in *The Subject*, edited by Joan Copjec, New York: Verso Press, 1994, 133–56; and "Animal Sex. Death and Desire" appeared in *Sexy Bodies: The Strange Carnalities of Feminism*, edited by Elizabeth Grosz and Elspeth Probyn, London and New York: Routledge, 1995, 278–99.

INTRODUCTION

BODIES HAVE BECOME THE OBJECTS OF intense cultural, philosophical, and feminist fascination within a remarkably short period of time. It seems as though 1980s culture exploded around a celebration of the body (-beautiful): the gym (or at least talk about it), body piercing, dance culture, and safe sex. Even the appeal of the Internet and cyberspace are part of the eighties' heritage that we will have to acknowledge, rethink, and work through. While presenting itself as a celebration of the body and its pleasures, this fascination bears witness to a profound, if unacknowledged and undiscussed, hatred and resentment of the body. The preferred body was one under control, pliable, amenable to the subject's will: the fit and healthy body, the tight body, the street-smart body, the body transcending itself into the infinity of cyberspace. A body more amenable, malleable, and more subordinate to mind or will than ever before. Just pick the body you want and it can be yours (for a price). Such a conception never questioned the body's status as an *object* (of reflection, intervention, training, or remaking), never even considered the possibiity that the body could be understood as subject, agent, or activity. This pliable body is what Foucault (1997b) describes as "docile," though with an unforeseen twist: this docility is no longer functions primarily by external regulation, supervision, and constraint, as Foucault claimed, but is rather the consequence of endlessly more intensified self-regulation, self-management, and self-control. It is no longer a body docile with respect to power, but more a body docile to will, desire, and mind.

It is not simply that in the past, bodies were ignored or considered uninteresting; on the contrary, many recent histories of medicine and disease, or of sexuality and pleasure, have demonstrated that bodies have always been the objects of theoretical and pragmatic concern. The point is that it is only very recently that philosophical and feminist theory have developed terms complicated enough to do justice to the rich (and aporetically cultural and individual) complexity of bodies. The tools and techniques by which we can think corporeality in all its productivity are still in the process of being developed. Only very recently has the body been understood as more than an impediment to our humanity; and it is even more recently that feminists have come to regard women's bodies as objects of intense wonder and productivity, pleasure and desire, rather than of regulation and control. In many ways, *Space, Time, and Bodies* is a celebration of the (re)finding and (re)situating of the body in the mysterious—and perhaps ultimately abyssal—space between feminism and philosophy, cultural analysis, or critical thought. It is not, however, simply a celebration of bodies (which in themselves do not require academic celebration), but more an enjoyment of the unsettling effects that rethinking bodies implies for those knowledges that have devoted so much conscious and unconscious effort to sweeping away all traces of the specificity, the corporeality, of their own processes of production and self-representation.

This rethinking of the body has implications well beyond the disciplinary interests of philosophy: it implies that the ways in which we understand subjectivity, and its co-implicated terms—space and time, materiality, exchange, knowledge, power, pleasure, social and cultural production—must themselves be transformed. If what differentiates humans from each other, from other species, and other materialities is the specific configuration of bodies, if it is bodies in their morphologies, rather than the hidden or inferred depths of reason, the psyche or interiority that particularize women and men, then those knowledges—the humanities and social sciences—that take subjects as their object of investigation must also be reconsidered. This book does not even begin to undertake this huge task of the revaluation of knowledges. Instead, its task is more modest: to make some initial inroads into some of the key regions where the implications of corporeality have yet to be posited, some provisional forays into epistemic domains where the neutrality, transparency, and universality of the body are founding (if implicit) assumptions.

This book is a heterogeneous collection of essays I wrote over ten years, under highly varied and diverse conditions, with many aims in mind. Many were specifically written for conferences, seminars, and teaching purposes. Some were responses to invitations to contribute to specific volumes. I had no suspicion they could or should be put together; indeed, I still have some reservations.

Some of these essays now seem painfully, embarrassingly dated. In a sense, they are all dated, all responses to a highly particular field of questions and problems that will, sooner rather than later, shift in focus.[1] Nevertheless, I hope that the following essays will still be relevant. With hindsight, a broad picture emerges—perhaps more a mosaic or patchwork than a picture, which has the insinuation of a pattern, if you squint a little. While neither an anthology nor collection (a heterogeneous series that has no cohesive structure or one imposed only from without), nor a monograph, this text lies somewhere in between. Certain lines, directions, images, and movements emerged that I could not see as each essay was written, (for example, a movement from psychoanalytic discourses to discourses of exteriority and inscription; broadly, from Freud to Deleuze). Certain interests of mine appeared that I wasn't aware that I had possessed (an ongoing if untutored interest in spatiality, architecture, and the visual arts), certain obsessions (theorizing desire while refusing its domestication), and commitments (about defying the authority of 'shoulds' and 'oughts,' whether these are issued by the powers-that-be in analytic philosophy, the lure of conformity in continental philosophy, the imperatives of patriarchal discourse, or the morality of a self-righteous and self-certain feminist, queer, or leftist orthodoxy) kept reappearing.

What brings these essays together is both a certain thematic connection of a most oblique kind;[2] as well as a common set of foes or targets. I have both a negative concern with combating dominant presumptions and values, and a positive commitment to transforming the ways in which bodies are conceived to highlight the unthought productivity of those bodies in the disparate domains from which their traces have been excised. *Space, Time and Perversion* is divided into three thematically linked sections, each of which exhibits a movement from earlier to later writings. The first section, "Bodies and Knowledges," primarily focuses in positive terms on the epistemological implications of an acknowledgement of bodily differences, on the effects the sexual specificity of the knower, the writer, the reader have on our understanding of knowledge and its various connections to authentification, validation, and valuation. It aims to problematize received conceptions of knowledge and their relation to power, so that the political investments of *all* knowledges and discourses, as well as their content become objects of analysis and contestation. More critically, it takes on a complaisant and tokenistic feminism that is assured of its own certainty and correctness, that refuses to rethink, to reconsider the possibility or even likelihood of its own transformations.

The second section, "Space, Time, and Bodies," deals with the questions of space, spatiality and its accompanying 'arts'—architecture, urban planning, geography—and their relationship to subjectivity, corporeality, and thought. Here, rather than speaking as an expert, my work seeks to make a virtue out of incompetence: I write as an acknowledged outsider who has some interest in the question of space (and time), but whose interests are not those of the architect, planner, or geographer. I do not *criticize* physics, mathematics, architecture, or geography, but place some of their interests beside my own to see what contaminations and cross-fertilizations occur among them. This section focuses on the possibility of forging a non-hierarchical relation between philosophical theory and the arts (most notably, architecture), a relation of mutual enrichment rather than criticism or aesthetic evaluation. Here, my target is a smug and self-assured cadre of art and architecture critics who have never put their own work on the line, never dared to think that what they do is also a mode of messy, and basically corporeal, production, not altogether unlike the production of the artist or architect.

In the third and longest section, "Perverse Desire," I bring together a series of essays (written over a five-year period) that explore and interrogate the domain of perverse (primarily lesbian, but also to some extent, queer, masculine, and quirkily heterosexual) desire, to investigate a range of sexualities, pleasures, bodies, and desires that do not commonly figure in validated representations of desire. Here I explore the possibilities of thinking sexuality, sexual desire, otherwise, in terms other than though also related to those provided by the currently privileged discourses of sexuality—psychoanalytic, Foucaultian, feminist, and queer theory. I attempt to question and distance myself from the self-proclaimed transgressive status assumed by many representatives of the more vulgar positions within queer and lesbian theory, that witness representative theorists taking their own lives, pleasures, and desires as the standard of the radical, while designating others, even other lesbians and queers, as inherently straight by virtue of their difference; who posture or exhibit themselves as the most deviant, the most threatening, the most oppressed, the most hip, without rethinking the relations between articulation, discourse, and self-representation, without, that is, rethinking the effects of such a self-proclamation can only result in recuperation. Instead of a blatant, exhibitionistic lesbianism, certain of itself, clear in its constituency—in many ways the binary opposite of the representation of the lesbian as the victim of multiple, crippling oppressions—I was more concerned with how thought might accommodate a positive, joyous understanding of sexual pleasure in all its strange permutations, raising a series of questions rather than offering solutions, proclamations, or manifestos.

How to think knowledge without the presumption of the neutral interchangeability of the subject of knowledge? How to think space outside the constraints of this neutral subject's corporeal projections? How to think desire beyond the limits of castration and thus beyond the phallus, the subject's inherent masculinity? These are the simplified questions that are raised with increasing insistence throughout the essays that follow.

In bringing together these disparate texts, I had hoped to show both that there is, and must be, a place for the transgression of transgression itself: that there must be space, both conceptual and material, for (perpetually) rethinking and questioning the presumptions of radicality—not from a position hostile to radicalism or transgression (as the majority of attacks are) but from within. Not to show the superiority of my position over those I am challenging (it is not clear to me that 'a' 'position' as such emerges from this text: I would certainly prefer this book to be read as a series of temporary flashes or illuminations that light up a variety of objects, rather than as the articulation of a position). In this sense, I would hope this book may be read as an engagement with the presumptions and beliefs governing some positions—within philosophy, feminism, visual culture, spatiality studies, queer theory, and cultural studies—that seek validation in terms of their moral force rather their intellectual, political, or ethical weight. Avital Ronell describes this as a mode of policing (Ronell, 1994: xi). If systems of policing, the police, are everywhere, then the point is to make our own work, our practices, as free from such policing as possible, not because unrestrained thought or action is always right (quite the contrary) but because, under scrupulous policing, nothing new can be produced, except perhaps evasions. Indeed the right to make mistakes and to be wrong is just as important—perhaps more so—than the right to be accorded the status of knowledge. Instead, everything is scrutinized in ever more minute degrees. If something more positive than a common series of adversaries links these essays, perhaps it is a commitment to the notion that the new—whatever it might be (this much is certain now: we cannot know what it is)—needs its space. The task of these essays is not really to produce the new, but to clear the clutter, open up a space in the frenzied negotiations and compromises that constitute both thought and the academy that pays for the luxury of thinking, so that others may at least have their chance at the new.

While they cover a broad range of objects—"women's writing," traditional epistemology, the implications of knowledge in ethics, the functioning of specific modalities of spatiality, the operations of queer, nonnormative desire—"objects" that may seem to share little in common, these essays are all concerned with rethinking subjectivity in its various modalities, and with questioning the body-to-body connections between subjects and the epistemic, cultural, and interpersonal contexts into which they are cast. While I hope this book has some broad interdisciplinary appeal, I write from a specifically positioned disciplinary background in continental philosophy (a discipline that has sometimes been stripped of its specificity in its derogation and translation into the term "theory"). If this is yet another book "in" feminist or critical theory, if it deals with a series of interdisciplinary topics, it, nonetheless, comes from a certain (disciplinary and cultural) background which locate it off-center, that is, as feminist, Australian, and philosophical.

In refusing to seek answers, and in continuing to pose questions as aporias, as paradoxes—that is, to insist that they have no readily available solutions—is to face the task, not of revolution, i.e. the overthrow of the old (whether capitalism, patriarchy, binary oppositions, or prevailing models of radicality) but, less romantically or glamorously, endless negotiation, the equation of one's life with struggle, a wearying ideal but one perhaps that can make us less invested in any one struggle and more capable to bearing up to continuous effort to go against the relentless forces of sameness, more inventive in the kinds of subversion we seek, and more joyous in the kinds of struggle we choose to be called into.

(PART ONE)

BODIES AND
KNOWLEDGES

FEMINISM AFTER THE DEATH OF THE AUTHOR

SEXUAL SIGNATURES

> *The "subject" of writing does not exist, if we mean by that some sovereign solitude of the author. The subject of writing is a **system** of relations between strata.... In order to describe the structure, it is not enough to recall that one always writes for someone; and the oppositions sender-receiver, code-message, etc., remain extremely coarse instruments. We would search the "public" in vain for the first reader: i.e., the first author of a work. And the 'sociology of literature' is blind to the war and the ruses perpetrated by the author who reads and by the first reader who dictates, for at stake here is the origin of the work itself. The **sociality** of writing as **drama** requires an entirely different discipline.*
>
> —Derrida, 1978: 226–27

THERE IS A VEXING PROBLEM THAT TODAY seems to be at the heart of many feminist, literary, and philosophical texts, a problem related to their modes of self-representation and self-understanding. After more than twenty-five years, feminist theory has gained a measure of academic and social legitimacy, as well as political and cultural weight. The time has come for it to reflect on and critically understand its own methods and assumptions, its objects of investigation and tools of research. This entails a critical awareness of both its various techniques, its "raw materials," data, or contents, and the ways it transforms these materials—in short, its particular theoretical modes of production. It is thus surprising, and a little disconcerting, that feminist theory tends to be committed to a notion of textuality and, consequently, a mode of politics, which commonly goes unexamined. It is crucial that feminists—and not just those working in the fields of literature and language—now turn to the question of the status and nature of textuality, if feminism is to understand not only what a feminist text is but, as significantly, what constitutes a patriarchal text, what the possible (and actual) relations between them are, as well as what the political investments feminism itself has in trying to set up a clear-cut and definitive separation between its products and those of the patriarchal orthodoxy it seeks to undermine.

By what criteria can we say that a text is feminist, or feminine? How is a feminist text to be distinguished from the patriarchal or phallocentric mainstream within which we locate it and where it finds its context? What is distinctive about it such that we can say that it is subversive or transgressive of its representational milieu? These questions not only raise the methodological and political issue of the ways in which feminist theory is different from (or even better than?) the traditional or patriarchal knowledges it attempts to criticize and displace, but also of its status as a mode of policing, a mode of intellectual self-regulation, that adjudicates what gets included as feminist and what does not. The same sorts of questions that were once directed by (white, usually middle-class) feminists to traditional male texts and masculine disciplines can now, perhaps more alarmingly and disappointingly, be raised about feminist theory's own intellectual and political self-representations and policing tactics. [1]

Many of the more common and self-evident answers to these questions do not hold up well under critical scrutiny. However, some suggestions posed by Derrida in his writings on signature, and Benveniste in his account of the relations of subjectivity in language,[2] might well prove useful in elaborating this complex set of issues so vital for feminist conceptions of textuality, for feminist political and cultural interventions into knowledge, writing, and production of all kinds.

Here I wish to explore some possible answers to the question of what distinguishes a feminist from a patriarchal text, drawn from feminist literature, to critically evaluate their merits and problems, and to raise the question of alternatives. In doing so, I do not speak as literary or cultural theorist, but rather as one trained in one of the most text-phobic of disciplines, philosophy. Nevertheless, I hope that my scattered remarks may prove relevant to those working in a number of disciplines (and interdisciplines) constituting the broad field of feminist theory. The question of the status and categorization of feminist texts is central to how feminists proceed in their various strategic battles within the university and its peripheral apparatuses, as well as in cultural studies. I hope to show that many of the more conventional positions regarding the categorization and assessment of feminist (and patriarchal) texts are problematic in feminist terms; yet, at the same time, following the hints posed by many post-structuralist thinkers,[3] I also hope to move beyond critique and formulate new conceptions of textual production and reception that may help to explain the ways in which political judgements about the textual and sexual positioning of theories and texts may be possible. My goals are both methodological and political: I am interested in how, from what positions, and with what effects we are able to judge statements and discourses, and how we are able to use statements and discourses to do things, to effect changes, to challenge prevailing and problematic norms governing textuality. In short, my goal will be to examine and pose the question of the materiality of texts and the relations between this materiality and the materiality that comprises subjects, the subjects of writing, and reading practices.

Before proceeding, I would like to explain, at least in a preliminary way, how I will be using two concepts central to my arguments. By "texts" I mean the products of any kind of discursive practice, whether poetic, literary, philosophical, scientific, visual, tactile or performative—that is, any tangible network of signs that exhibits a "grammar" and "syntax," and finds its context or milieu in other texts within a broadly similar sign-system. I will not privilege one mode of textuality over another, for example, the verbal or linguistic over the visual or the performative. And when I refer sometimes to "feminist texts," sometimes to "feminine texts," and sometimes to "women's texts," I am purposely being vague. Exploring the relations between "women's texts" (texts written by women, largely for women), "feminine texts" (those written from the point of view of feminine experience or in a style culturally designated as feminine), and "feminist texts" (those which self-consciously challenge the methods, objects, goals, or principles of mainstream patriarchal canons) is precisely my purpose here. I hope that by linking the question of textual production to conceptions of the sexually specific signature and the sexually specific body, if not to answer the question of what is a feminist or feminine text, then at least to provide some grounds on which positions may be possible.

What, then, enables us to describe a text as feminist or feminine? In the feminist literature surrounding this question, there seem to be four broad types of answers to this question: 1) the sex of the author; 2) the content of the text; 3) the sex of the reader; and 4) the style of the text.

None of these crude answers seems satisfactory. I will look briefly at each in turn, indicating what I find problematic. Nevertheless, the grounds for a possible answer may well be developed using insights and clues provided from the ways in which each of these approaches have analysed the feminism or femininity of feminist texts.

The sex of the author. The assumption that the sex of the author is some indication, if not guarantee, of the text's position as feminist or feminine is a common one, made by many feminists in the 1970s and 1980s, and remains a commitment of many today who adopt what I would call the "women and..." approach, or maintaining a radical separation between the representation and its "real" referent (here I include such diverse thinkers as Dale Spender, Patricia Meyers Spacks, Elaine Showalter, Sandra Gilbert, and Susan Gubar, and, in perhaps a more sophisticated form, Evelyn Fox Keller, Sandra Harding, Nancy K. Miller, Nancy Fraser, Rosi Braidotti, Lois McNay, and Susan Bordo), who may share little in common besides subscribing to a rupture or gulf between textual representations and that which they represent, between the textual representations of women, and "real women."[4] In spite of varying degrees of sophistication, and a number of extremely important insights developed by this rather diverse body of thinkers, there is an assumption that knowing the sex of the author—a real individual situated outside of and beyond the text she produces—enables us to say that the texts she produces are feminist. A text's feminine status depends on *who* writes it. Spacks, for example, asks the crucial question: "So what is a woman to do, setting out to write about women? She can imitate men in her writing or strive for an impersonality beyond sex, but finally she must write as a woman: what other way is there?" (Spacks, 35). She compiles a list of female authors in order to examine what they have in common, which she calls "the female imagination." Miller, to take another more recent example, wants to claim that one's reading of a text depends on empirical information about the author as concrete sexed subject, a "real" man or woman, in a sophisticated resurrection of the correspondence between the real and its representation.[5] In taking women *per se* as her object of investigation, whether as authors, creators, or agents—a project with which I have no disagreement in certain contexts[6]—this kind of approach nevertheless leaves *texts* largely unexplained.[7] I will list some of the more disturbing problems I see with this approach.

Perhaps the most relevant counterbalance to the privileging of the author is Roland Barthes's well-known proclamation of the "death of the author" (Barthes, 1977), and Foucault's materialist analysis of what he calls "the author function" (Foucault, 1977a); that is, their claim that judging a text in terms of its author's intentions, wishes, biography, historical location, sociological position, and so on is an attempt to fix and control the meaning and inherent ambiguity of a text, what Foucault describes as the "ponderous, awesome materiality" of texts, their explosive potential. The author is postulated to provide an explanation of the origins of a text, and to ensure its unity and homogeneity. Barthes argues:

> The Author, when believed in, is always conceived of as the past of his own book: book and author stand automatically on a single line divided into a *before* and an *after*. The Author is thought to *nourish* the book, which is to say that he exists before it, thinks, suffers, lives for it, is in the same relation of antecedence to his work *as a father to his child*. In complete contrast, the modern scriptor is born simultaneously with the text, is in no way equipped with a being preceding or exceeding the writing, is not the subject with the book as its predicate; there is no other time than that of enunciation and every text is eternally written *here and now*. (Barthes, 1977: 145, emphasis added)

The author's intentions, emotions, psyche, and interiority are not only inaccessible to readers, they are likely to be inaccessible to the author herself. For Barthes and Foucault, as for Derrida, a text cannot be the expression of an individual's interior, nor simply the representation of some social exterior, for it is as *an act of writing*, the material manipulation of signs, discursive structures, textual elements, an act of inscription, with its own protocols, modes of constraint, and regulation. The author's signature, as Derrida argues, is not a full presence that somehow stands outside the text, while finding itself reflected inside the text as a mark of the author's propriety, ownership over, or singular connection with the text.[8] Neither quite outside the text nor at home within it, the signature is a trace resonating and disseminating the textual exterior with its interior. The relation between exterior and interior is not a mapping or correspondence of the kind that Spacks, and others, seek. There is no carry-over—or at least no *simple* carry-over—of the *person writing the text*, the author, and what she writes within the text. The signature, as preeminently forgeable, transformable, iterable, recontextualizable, provides no guarantee of authenticity, no residue of the full presence of the subject's politics. In short, the signature signs on/as the subject as much as it signs the text in the subject's proper name.

Paradoxically, the signature is the possibility of the infinite repetition of what is unique and irreplaceable: "The drama that activates and constructs every signature is this insistent, unwearying, potentially infinite repetition of something that remains, every time, irreplaceable." (Derrida, 1984a: 20). The signature is not self-contained and given, cannot be a presence-to-itself, for it always requires a counter-signature, a reception, an other to sign for it.[9]

Perhaps most importantly, as Spacks herself half-acknowledges, and in a way that Miller doesn't adequately address, a text can readily have a female author who nonetheless writes "as a man"; that is, who writes according to prevailing patriarchal norms, in a mode of sexual neutrality, sexual indifference. It is, then, not simply a matter of *being a woman* that guarantees that an author produce a feminist text. Nor is it simply a matter of being, outside, in "everyday life," a feminist. Whatever attitudes women may have to their status as women, this psychological and sociological designation is quite independent of a woman's authorial status. One could be a committed feminist activist, for example, and *intend* to produce a feminist text without succeeding in doing so. Conversely, it seems to me plausible that a man, or a male-identified woman, could in principle, even if rarely in fact, produce a feminist text. This depends less on what they do extra-discursively, "in real life," than what of their masculinity they put at risk in their texts. The status, and sex, or the "gender identifications" of the author have little, if any, direct relation to the status of the texts produced.

The content of the text. If the author's sex or gender identifications do not provide an index to a text's feminist (or non-feminist) status, then perhaps it is the "content" of the text, what the text is "about," what it refers to, what its object of reflection, description or speculation might be, that provides some indication of its feminist or feminine status. The question thus becomes: Is there a distinctively feminist or feminine set of objects, contents, in feminist texts? Is there a series of preferred themes, preoccupations or concerns that feminist texts share in common? This way of formulating it makes the proposal circular: is there in fact a common set of contents to feminist texts? If there is not, what enables them to be classified as feminist? If there is, isn't this already presumed in designating such texts as feminist?

Many feminists have posited what might be understood as a "distinctive set of preoccupations" in feminist or women's writing and creativity. Once again, Spacks can be taken as representative here. She claims that the feminist or feminine text reflects the distinctive interests occupying women's lives:

> …for readily discernible historical reasons, women have characteristically concerned themselves with matters more or less peripheral to male concerns, or at least slightly skewed from them. The differences between traditional female preoccupations and roles and male ones make a difference in female

writing. Even if a woman wishes to demonstrate her essential identity with male interests and ideas, the necessity of making the demonstration, contradicting the stereotype, allies her initially with her sisters. And the complex nature of the sisterhood emerges in the books it has produced. (Spacks, 7)

The female or feminine novel is the one that reflects women's often contradictory, patriarchal roles: the production of the domestic novel, the realist portrait, and the play of manners are reflections and effects of the pre-twentieth-century social confinement of women's experience to domesticity. The kinds of concerns that preoccupy the majority of women—or perhaps, those forbidden to women—might be the very ones which serve to characterize women's writing. Perhaps, it is argued, their shared experience of sequestration means that many women share a common "sensibility." Variations of this position are not confined to literary studies. This position has, through the writings of Nancy Chodorow and other feminist object-relations theorists, formed the basis of feminist epistemology. Evelyn Fox Keller and Sandra Harding claim, among other things, that there is a distinctively feminine approach to the production of knowledge.

There are as many problems as with the preceding category. This second category also depends on the notion of the female author in specifying and opening up to empirical investigation what the major objects of women's writing actually are. Perhaps most striking is the assumption that women are a largely homogeneous group who share a number of experiences and perspectives that they make the basis for representations. On the one hand, it seems unlikely to me that women, as culturally, geographically, politically, and historically diverse as they are, do in fact share common experiences (whether based on early childhood or any other life stage)—women's experiences are as varied as men's. And on the other hand, to claim that women write only on the basis of their experience, and to claim that these experiences are only the result of women's *patriarchal* subordination (no others count), is to impose a preset limit on women's writing: it must always remain reactive, a writing tied to oppression, based on *ressentiment*.

There is no special set of objects or topics that define women's writings or interests: it is perfectly plausible that *any* object or content, ranging from nuclear physics to stock market fluctuations, could be dealt with in a feminist manner. In any case, whenever one does specify a distinctive set of "women's issues"—even those most intimately tied to women's experiences, there is nothing to prevent men not only from speaking about this experience, but also becoming experts regarding it. From the moment it has some kind of textual or material existence, no object remains sacred, of access to only one sex or group. As material object, the text is available for anyone to use in any way, within extremely broad limits. This is an important principle for feminists to accept, since it amounts to a refusal on women's part of their traditional exclusion from esoteric discourses. But it also implies the abandonment of any attempt to create a special or identifying type of discourse that is only of concern or available to women. There can be no such thing as an inherently secret code, a private language. Any discourse is repeatable, useable, transformable.

The sex of the reader. More recently, focus has shifted from the text and its production to the question of the text's reception, and thus the position of the reader. This is one of the implications of Barthes's position. Many feminists within this category will readily accept the notion of the author's death, and will even celebrate the demise of textual integrity, the abandonment of the search for a singular meaning or a received interpretation, and revel in the multiplicity and ambiguity of all texts, their perpetual openness to re-interpretation, which Derrida calls "grafting" or "iterability." Barthes's proclamation of the death of the author heralds the birth of the reader, or rather, *readers.* In place of the singular origin of the text presumed by subsuming it as the author's property, Barthes evokes a plural destination.

The elevation of (multiple) reader(s) to the position of textual creator has had a number of liberating effects for feminist theory. For one thing, it has opened up a whole history of patriarchal discourses to feminist appropriations and recontextualizations. Any text, however patriarchal it may have been at its outset and in its author's intentions, can be read from a feminist point of view. This may explain why, over the last two decades or more, the most privileged and analyzed texts were those written by men—and often recognized as phallocentric by the feminists working with them: for example, the writings of the likes of Marx, Freud, Lacan, Levi-Strauss, etc.—avowedly non-feminist, if not anti-feminist, writers. *Any* text can be read from a feminist point of view, that is, from the point of view that brings out a text's alignment with, participation in, and subversion of patriarchal norms.

There are also major problems, not unrelated to the death of the author, with this third category. One of the most contentious presumptions of author-based interpretations is the presence of a knowing, controlling consciousness, a rational, intentional subject for whom language is simply a means of expression of ideas. The presumption of the active productive reader, so strongly advocated by Barthes, simply shifts the position of the sovereign subject from sender to receiver, while still relying on a problematic communicational model of language and the notions of self-presence it presumes. While perhaps decentering the sovereignty of the singular author, the multiplication of reading subjects remains governed by the norms of sovereignty. This becomes clear when the notion of the "ideal reader" replaces that of the multiplicity. As Derrida suggests, the reader is as dead as the author (if death admits such relativity!): "To be what it is, writing must, therefore, be capable of functioning in the radical absence of every empirically determined receiver in general." (Derrida, 1988a: 8).

Reader-based theories must also recognize the material constraints the text imposes on the range of possible readings or interpretations: while there may be no singular or correct interpretation of a text, there *can* be inappropriate or incorrect interpretations. The text's materiality exerts a resistance, a viscosity, not only to the intentions of the author but also the readings and uses to which it can be put by readers. In this sense, the text is liable to never arrive at its destination.

The style of the text. If neither the author, the reader, nor the content of a text explains how we are able to designate it as feminist, or patriarchal, perhaps there is a distinctively feminist style of writing. It may not be *what* is written but *how* it is written that indicates a text's feminist position. Women's writing would have its own, anti-patriarchal, style or styles, ways of writing and representing. Many critics in this category would claim that certain stylistic and structural conventions—in the early days of feminist theory these were identified with the norms governing narrative closure, or the forms of the realist film or novel—are either to be avoided, or parodied and exceeded. What is feminist, or perhaps, more recently, queer, is that which performs its own parody, its own excesses (Butler, 1990; 1993) Prevailing norms governing grammar and syntax have been designated as phallic or symbolic, while an emphasis on the text's materiality is seen as feminine and subversive. Fluid, ambiguous, experimental writing is commonly advocated by many theorists in this category.

As appealing as it may be, this position does not spell out necessary and sufficient conditions. There are many clearly feminist texts which do not question the norms and ideals of grammar, logic, or coherence, yet deserve the appellation "feminist." Moreover, the kinds of experimentation and opening up implied in this position are by no means the privileged domain of women or feminists. The avant garde is largely male dominated; clearly, many male writers, artists, painters, and filmmakers also advocate subversions of textual norms. The avant garde has a long and accepted place as the tolerable boundary of coherence for the mainstream, a safety valve for handling its own excesses.

Admittedly, seeing "style" as an index of the text's political position has advantages over the other three types of explanation insofar as it does not rely on a communicational model to enshrine the notion of the self-conscious (Cartesian) subject, no presumption of unified coherent forms of meaning-producing subjectivity, and no fixed notion of the text as a set of stable contents or conceptual issues. Unlike these alternatives, it provides no link between transgressive textual practices or experiments, and feminist politics, or even women. The avant garde can be allied with feminism only insofar as they share a common enemy—the rule-governed operations of a phallocentric symbolic order. But this in no way makes avant garde writing, in itself, necessarily feminist.

If the attribution of a female author is not enough to ensure the feminist status of a text; if there is no privileged content that is uniquely feminist; if there is no mode of reception or interpretation that represents a feminist point of view or mode of understanding; and if, finally, there is no distinctively feminist style of writing or representation, does this mean we must abandoned such taxonomies? Or are there other criteria that we might use to distinguish between feminist and mainstream texts? What is at stake in such a classification?

I have two contrary attitudes or inclinations: on the one hand, I am curious about why we want or need a clear-cut distinction between feminist and non-feminist texts, what is invested or at stake in this distinction, and who wants the distinction to be drawn. This is a Foucauldian anxiety about what power is invested in providing definitive categories. In proposing a dividing line, a rigid or *a priori* schema or mode of classification, personal and political agendas are put into action without acknowledgment of what values and commitments they honor. It might be a worthwhile strategy to admit that there isn't really a clear-cut distinction between feminist and mainstream texts and that, moreover, one and the same text can, in some contexts, be regarded as feminist and in other contexts, as non- or anti-feminist. On the other hand, although the four positions I have outlined are all problematic, there is nonetheless a way of proposing a femininity for texts that takes some elements from each position but also deals with what each leaves out, with what I would call "discursive positioning," a complex relation between the corporeality of the author, that is, the author's textual residues or traces, the text's materiality, and its effects in marking the bodies of the author and readers, and the corporeality and productivity of readers.

This concept follows the work of Benveniste on subjectivity in language and Derrida's work on the signature. Benveniste distinguishes between the author (the person outside the text who puts pen to paper) and the "I" of the text in his discussion of the relations between the *énoncé* and the *énunciation*, the utterance and the act producing the utterance. Benveniste claims that the "I" of the utterance is necessarily different from the "I" producing the utterance. This is the same distinction as that between the author and the (implicit or overt) narrational position. Benveniste's claim is twofold. On the one hand, we cannot presume an identity between the "I" of the *énoncé* and the "I" of the *énunciation*, even in the case of autobiography: the "I" who speaks cannot be identified with the "I" spoken about. On the other hand, these two terms cannot be definitively separated, for the processes of the production of the utterance are always inscribed in the utterance itself. Although the author cannot control the text—every text exceeds its author—and although we can't make inferences about the text through a knowledge of the author (nor of the author through a knowledge of the text), nonetheless there remains a process of inscription, some trace of the process of production on the text.

This trace, a track from the outside or borderline of the text to its inside and, correlatively, from its interior to its edge or border is precisely what Derrida refers to in his discussion of the operations of the signature. Derrida distinguishes three modalities of signature:

> The one that we call the signature is the proper name, articulated in a language and readable as such: the act of someone not content to write his proper name (as if he were filling out an identity card), but engaged in authenticating (if possible) the fact that it is indeed he who writes…. The second modality, a banal and confused metaphor for the first, is a set of idiomatic marks that a signer might leave by accident or intention in his product. These marks would have no essential link with the form of the proper name as articulated or read 'in' a language…. We sometimes call this the style, the inimitable idiom of a writer, sculptor, painter, or orator…. Thirdly, and it is more complicated here, we may designate as general signature, or signature of the signature, the fold of the placement in abyss where, after the manner of the signature in the current sense, the work of writing designates, describes, and inscribes itself as act (action and archive), signs itself before the end by affording us the opportunity to read: I refer to myself, this is writing, I am a writing, this is writing—which excludes nothing since, when the placement in abyss succeeds, and is thereby decomposed and produces an event, it is the other, the thing as other, that signs. (Derrida, 1984a: 52–54)

The first modality of the signature presumes something like the author function: the living being testifies to *his* authenticity by signing with the proper name, the name which is proper insofar as it has a definite and clear-cut place, an identity which can be confirmed by self-verification. The second modality, derived as it is from the first, is what I have referred to above as style—the marks of individuality, idiosyncrasy, distinctiveness, that tie an individual not to the text's border or frame (as does the first) but to its interior. The third modality, much closer to Benveniste's understanding of the paradoxical and divided position of the subject in and beyond the text, involves the necessary and irreducible trace of the one in the other, the implication of the text's outside with its inside, and of its inside with establishing its borders and thus its outside, in short, its fundamentally folded, "invaginated" character.

As both inside and outside the text, the signature is not simply the author's proper name, but the citation or iteration of a name. Neither a noun nor a part of language available for anyone to use, it functions more as a form of spacing or dissemination, a textual space; rather, in Derrida's understanding, a double line or bind that he sometimes refers to as a "double band" (punning on *bander*: i.e., "to have a hard-on," as well as to bind or band) in the sense that it links itself both to a unique, singular individuality, irreducibly specific, and, at the same time, it is always capable of being reduced from proper name to common noun, becoming the content of an utterance. Rather than the name of the author, it infuses the text's interior, making impossible any definitive or final separation between them:

(20)

> In the form of the whole name, the inscription of the signature plays strangely with the frame, with the border of the text, sometimes inside, sometimes outside, sometimes included, sometimes overthrown. But it is still included when thrown overboard and always eminent when drunk in by the surface of the text. (Derrida, 1984a: 120)

The trace of the signature, then, cannot simply be identified with the proprietary mark of the author; instead, it is an effect of the text's mode of materiality, the fact that as a product the text is an effect of a *labor*, a work on and with signs, a collaborative (even if hostile) labor of writing and reading.

Although Benveniste does not develop the political and social implications of his distinction between the subject of the utterance and the subject of the act producing the utterance. Although Derrida does not examine the notion of the signature as sexually differential (after all, as Nancy K. Miller has recognized, it is only man who has a "proper name," one that belongs to him alone, his label for life; at best, women have the proper name only on loan or provisionally, borrowing it from the father or the husband, always potentially exchangeable for another name), their work has implications for feminists who, in the wake of the death of the author, are searching for a way of tying sex and politics to textuality. The sex of the author has, I would contend, no direct bearing on the political position of the text, just as other facts about the author's private or professional life do not explain the text. Nevertheless, there are ways in which the sexuality and corporeality of the subject leave their traces or marks on the texts produced, just as we in turn must recognize that the processes of textual production also leave their trace or residue on the body of the writer (and readers). This indeed seems the point of Judith Butler's understanding of the "discursive limits of sex" (1990; 1994). One's sexuality, whatever it might be, is not a function of pregiven nature or fixed materiality but is rendered possible through its discursive production and iteration; the repetition and possible subversion of this discursive production makes it more amenable to transformation: bodies *and* discourses produce and transform each other. But as Jean-Luc Nancy makes clear, this is not a matter of naming or labelling the body and its parts, for there is also always a mismatch between representation and corporeality (Nancy, 1993). The text and the writer/reader are neither in a relation of exteriority nor interiority relative to each other. The text is not inhabited by an authorial presence, in whatever form, nor is the author simply the subject who, independent of writing, exists outside of and autonomously from the text. The relations between text and author/readers is more enfolded, more mutually implicating than either realism or expressivism can recognize.

The signature not only signs the text by a mark of authorial propriety, but also signs the subject as the product of writing itself, of textuality; it functions as a double mark, a hinge, folding together (or separating) the author/reader or producer and the text or product. The signature cannot authenticate, it cannot prove, it cannot make present the personage of the author; but it is a remnant, a remainder of and a testimony to both a living past and a set of irreducible and inelimimable corporeal traces. It is not that author/reader and text are entirely other to each other: the otherness of the other is also the condition of the self-consolidating subject. The subject is necessarily implicated in the other's otherness, even when this other is a text. I am interested in the ways in which the author's corporeality, an always sexually specific corporeality—not the author's interiority, psyche, consciousness, concepts, or ideas—intrudes into or is productive of the text.

On the analogy with painting, the text cannot be conceived simply as an intentional effect, but can also be seen from the point of view of its production and the labor that always leaves its marks in its product. I am not suggesting that one can infer the sex of the author in any direct or guaranteed way, just as one *may* guess at the sex of the painter from the shape, height, or direction of the brushstrokes but may be liable to error. In paying attention to the production of the text (including that production which is commonly subsumed under the text's reception), we are perhaps able to see more clearly how the question of sexuality—that is, sexual specificity—is relevant to the question of textuality.

The necessarily excessive, superabundant traces of corporeality involved in every mode of textual production carry with them certain implications, for example: an emphasis on the corporeality of the author, and its relation to the production of the text as material object entails an acceptance of the notion of Nietzschean perspectivism. Perspectivism implies that one has a finite and limited view of or grasp over the context and object of speculation. Perhaps more relevant for our purposes here, a perspectivism must take into account the specificities and positionality of the speaking/writing/reading subject, not only the position he or she occupies in textual production, but also the *way* in which the authorial position is occupied. This may help bring us back to the question of the criteria necessary for the evaluation of a text's feminist—or patriarchal—status.

Now, to draw together these various strands. The personality, individuality, attitudes, and beliefs of the author do not seem to me to provide relevant information regarding the political status of a text. It is problematic to see a text on a communicational model in which it functions as a message directed from an author to a reader. A text is not a form of communication, nor a neutral mode of transmission of information; it is not an embodiment of ideas or perceptions. A feminist text has no distinctive subject matter, nor a distinctively feminine style. Indeed, it seems that there is no one characteristic which could ensure a text's feminist status. Rather, judgements about the political status of the text are a more complex and contextual matter. Among the more relevant relations that need to be taken into account, I would suggest the following.

First, the relations between a text and the prevailing norms and ideals which govern its milieu (the way it affirms, extends or problematizes existing paradigms of textuality) must be explored. For the text to be regarded as feminist, it must render the patriarchal or phallocentric presumptions governing its contexts and commitments visible. It must question, in one way or another, the power of these presumptions in the production, reception, and assessment of texts. This may involve major stylistic developments and upheavals, but it need not; or it may involve developing new objects of discussion or new methods of assessment. No one kind of upheaval is privileged over any other. Whether stylistic, content-based or both, any form of commitment to feminist principles and politics involves some degree of challenge to phallocentrism.

Second, while independent of the author as an external individual, texts nevertheless always retain a trace of their (singular or collective) production. A feminist text does not, strictly speaking, require a feminist author; but it must, in some way or other, problematize the standard masculinist ways in which the author occupies the position of enunciation. In this sense, a text's having a female author in itself carries a certain probability of shaking up or unsettling the phallocentric equation of masculinity and humanity, but no guarantee. Moreover, it implies that where men's occupation of the authoritative position of knower is challenged, there may also be a "feminist" subversion of the patronym. One can produce an authorial position aware of its limitations, its specific position, and the sexual coding of this position perhaps more easily if one is a woman (women have less to lose), but being a man does not preclude this possibility either.

And third, a feminist text must not only be critical of or a challenge to the patriarchal norms governing it; it must also help, in whatever way, to facilitate the production of new and perhaps unknown, unthought discursive spaces—new styles, modes of analysis and argument, new genres and forms—that contest the limits and constraints currently at work in the regulation of textual production and reception.

While there is a signature of one kind or other, while the reader(s) countersign(s), the signature never ties the text to its origin nor provides it with a definite destination, a fixed and settled context or a controllable audience. The signature is the condition for a text's endless repeatability, its perpetual openness to repositioning, its capacity to be continuously re-read, rewritten, its capacity to slip into—and out of—feminist interests and contexts, its fundamental plasticity and its material contingency regarding its own political status and effectiveness. While I may not have adequately answered the question of what makes a feminist text, and while it seems there can be no clear-cut and uncontentious criteria, it is nonetheless necessary to understand that no text wears its political status as a nameplate or label, no text can be classified once and for all as wholly feminist or wholly patriarchal: these appellations depend on its context, its place within that context, how it is used, by whom and to what effect. These various contingencies dictate that at best a text is feminist or patriarchal only provisionally, only momentarily, only in some but not in all its possible readings, and in some but not all of its possible effects.

$\left(2\right)$ FEMINISM AND THE CRISIS
OF REASON

BODIES AND KNOWLEDGES

If the skin were parchment and the blows you gave me were ink...

—William Shakespeare, *The Comedy of Errors*[1]

MY AIM HERE IS TO EXACERBATE RATHER than dissolve what is commonly regarded as "the crisis of reason." This crisis has threatened to infect all knowledges, particularly in the humanities and social sciences, although the natural sciences are not immune to its implications, either. This crisis has methodological, epistemological, and political implications for metatheoretical conceptions of knowledge and its production; it entails reconceiving the sources, aims, and goals of knowledges. I intend to outline one of the strategies of attack available to feminist theory in its challenge to many of the founding presumptions and methodological criteria governing knowledges by examining some recent (re-)explorations of the body and drawing out some implications of accepting the role the body plays in the production and evaluation of knowledge.

This crisis of reason is in part a consequence of the historical privileging of the purely conceptual or mental over the corporeal; that is, of the inability of Western knowledges to conceive their own materiality and the conditions of their (material) production. These knowledges must simultaneously rely on and disavow the role of the body. If the body is an un- or an inadequately acknowledged condition of knowledges, then the sexual specificity of bodies must be a relevant factor in the evaluation of these knowledges This chapter addresses the *explicit sexualization of knowledges* in order to draw out some of the effects that a concept of *sexed corporeality* may have on relations between knowers and objects known, as well as on the forms, methods, and criteria of assessment governing knowledges.

In working though the meaning and many ramifications of this crisis in twentieth-century reason, I am not articulating a new concern, but echoing an often-voiced anxiety, one which perhaps originated with scepticism in ancient Greece and which reemerges in distinctively modern terms in the writings of Descartes, considered by many to be the "father" of modern philosophy.

More recently, in *The Crisis of European Sciences and Transcendental Phenomenology*, Husserl formulated the crisis as a confrontation between a Galilean mathematization of nature (a tendency toward mathesis) and a Cartesian concern for the knowing subject (a phenomenological tendency). Through a reading of the history of modern philosophy, *The Crisis* attempts to reinsert the Cartesian emphasis on the subject into the realm of the objectivity sought by Galileo and the empiricist tradition. On Husserl's argument, the clash of "transcendental subjectivism" and "physicalist objectivism" is the principle of the "unity of history." Others, such as Heidegger, Habermas, Lyotard, Rorty, Jameson and, in quite different terms, Foucault, Derrida, and Deleuze, have formulated the crisis in *very broadly* similar terms—the mismatch, conflict, or displacement between "objectivity" and "subjectivity." This crisis is one of self-validation and methodological self-justification, formulated in different terms within different disciplines and periods, the crisis of reason's *inability to rationally know itself*, to enclose and know itself from the outside: the inadequation of the subject and knowledge.

THE CRISIS

The following are what seem to me the fundamental assumptions within various systems of contemporary knowledges that have been brought into question by the crisis of reason.

1. There is the underlying presumption in the humanities and social sciences that reason and knowledges based upon it are *methodologically appropriate* to their object of investigation, the human subject. The procedures of socially legitimated knowledges are assumed to be *transparent and neutral* conceptual tools which contribute to the growth of knowledges but are unproblematically disposable by them. They are tools whose influence or productive contributions can be calculated and distinguished from their objects. This instrumentalization of methods is not restricted to realist approaches to knowledge but characterizes any position according a recalcitrance to reality, the object of knowledges. (It may well be that methodological procedures do have largely instrumental value, but this value resides in their relations to goals, ideals, or strategies, not in their representative relations to reality). The question, "How does this knowledge, this method, this technique, constitute its object?" cannot be raised or answered. If methods of knowing are indeed transparent and neutral, being either mere tools that could be replaced by others (and thus not integral to knowledge, merely convenient for it) or *a priori* necessities, we are assured that knowledges do not distort, manipulate, or constrain their objects. Instead, they describe and/or explain them without loss or residue. In other words, what is in question here is the adequacy of methods, axioms, and criteria of evaluation in knowledges relative to their objects of investigation, the presumption of the transparent neutrality of ways of knowing to the objects known.

2. There is a presumption about the boundaries, scope, and limits of knowledges, in other words, their disciplinary organization. The disciplines are effects of concrete, dynamic historically and culturally specific relations of power.[2] Although the boundaries between disciplines are not immutable, enabling some cross-fertilization and major historical interactions, nevertheless each defines and is defined by both a mainstream or core of accepted texts, methods and presumptions, and a periphery or margins, which contain the residues of and rejects from the mainstream. These margins and the *spaces between disciplines* cannot be theorized in the terms of the core—that is, within any discipline. Interdisciplinary, as much as disciplinary, practices may be analyzed from *within* a discipline, but the spaces of exclusion between disciplines must remain untheorized by the disciplines themselves.[3]

3. There are presumptions about the criteria by which such knowledges are judged valid and/or true. Clearly, criteria of truth and validity vary enormously from one discipline to another, but it is not clear that truth is relevant at all for the more "interpretive" disciplines, such as lit-

erature, psychoanalysis, cultural studies, or film theory. Lacan, for example, actively affirms the radical cleavage of knowledge from truth.[4] There are a number of assumptions, including clarity, precision, the capacity to be verified or falsified, parsimony, communicability, and translatability, which all those knowledges in the institution share. Underlying these is a belief that the object of investigation—whether a text, human behavior, or social interactions—exists independently of knowledge of it, presuming a "reality" resistant to false or invalid methods, misinterpretation, or misrepresentation. There is, in other words, the presumption of a rift between the object of knowledge and knowing such that knowledges can be judged in terms of their adequacy to this object.

4. There is the presumption of the atemporal and transgeographic value and validity of knowledges by its most uncritical supporters. Although knowledges are produced at specific times and places, their genesis is considered largely irrelevant (except perhaps for historical purposes) to the information they produce. These processes of production leave no trace in their product. Theories and knowledges are produced in their transparency as *eternally true* or valid, independent of their origins. Knowledge is outside of history, capable of being assessed and reevaluated independently of the space and time of its production. Knowledges do not carry the index of their origins.

5. Knowledge is considered *perspectiveless*. If it represents a particular point of view, this point of view is accessible to anybody, insofar as they are suitably trained. This process of "suitable training," rather than the regularity of the objects investigated, helps produce the regularity and repeatability of results, which is a necessary criterion for objectivity.

If the subject of knowledge is a "blind spot" in knowledge production and assessment, then all knowledge is necessarily contaminated by an irreducibly arational component at its core. The knower who utilizes and relies upon the principles of reason is not *him*self capable of being included in terms of the reason *he* utilizes. The epistemic and cultural crisis faced by theory today must be located in a number of tendencies and commitments produced within this intellectual tradition. Even many so-called radical theories actively participate in a process of salvaging or resuscitating reason. If I can be permitted to merely indicate these tendencies and commitments in point form, this should suffice to recognizably characterize the tradition.

1. There is a notable breakdown of confidence in modes of "objectivist" inquiry even among its proponents. The criteria constituting objectivity are subject to stringent criticisms from within even the most "objective" of knowledges—particularly theoretical physics (since

Heisenberg, Einstein, and the principle of uncertainty or, more recently and in a different way, chaos theory). Kuhn, Lakatos, and Feyerbend, among others, question this aspiration to unmediated objectivity. If objectivity means unprejudiced, observer-independent knowledge, some physicists and epistemologists challenge the belief that observers face "facts" directly, in a manner unmediated by theories, presumptions, or values. They deny the prevailing belief in facts, "raw data," and information as being somehow independent of and unaffected by the presence of the observer. Objectivity implies a monolithic world that is posited as external to and autonomous from subjects.

2. In spite of an occasionally recognized limit to the value of objectivity within the natural sciences—or at least in their most developed forms—part of the current crisis faced by the humanities and social sciences is dependent on their aspiration towards a natural science model of knowledge, which is impossible for them to achieve and which has dire consequences for the types of knowledge they produce. This produces a positivist version of the "Sciences of Man" which reduces its object—humanity—to the status of measurable object: behavioral psychology, statistical sociology, and positivist historiography provide recognizable examples. The crisis faced by pseudo-scientific approaches to the human subject is that utilizing objective, verifiable, and formalizable techniques, ignores the specificities, the singularities of the subject.[5]

3. The humanities and social sciences have been increasingly confronted by the problem, outlined in logic by Gödel, of the impossibility of reason's self-knowledge. If reason is not self-inclusive, then there must be an irrational or nonrational kernel within rationality that subverts its claims to provide methods and systems of judgment for knowledges. I have already suggested that reason's blind spot can be located in its inability to know the knower. This has had particularly traumatic effects on the social sciences insofar as their object and subject are avowedly similar. Kristeva locates the problematic limits of linguistic and literary theory in their failure to conceptualize adequately *the speaking subject;* Lacan admonishes psychology and psychiatry for effacing the *subject of desire;* and Merleau-Ponty locates philosophy's impasses in its failure to understand the nature of a *subjectivity that perceives, thinks, and acts.* All of these shortcomings highlight a particular dilemma for the humanities. A discipline whose object is man is necessarily incomplete unless it can include its own production as a discipline *within* the knowledges it produces.

4. Knowledges lack the means to understand their own self-development as knowledges. They lack the means by which to understand their

own historicity and materiality. Indeed, the history of knowledges is explicitly excluded as irrelevant to the contemporary forms of these knowledges. This absence has major strategic effects. If knowledges are not marked by the various, often widely disparate kinds of events that construct them into and as disciplinary forms, they are unaffected by a *political investment in knowledge*; they remain, in a certain ironic sense, "value-free." The political investment of knowledges remains external to knowledge and can be seen to be an effect of *external impingements*, the application or technologization of knowledges, rather than their being located within knowledges themselves—as the distinction between "pure" and "applied" knowledges or between science and technology that enables knowledges to protect themselves from political scrutiny. Foucault has argued convincingly that the relations between power and knowledge must be considered *internal* to knowledges, providing their condition of possibility and guiding their material effects.

5. Because of the elision of the presumed subject of knowledge and the (historical) processes of production of knowledges, prevailing intellectual paradigms face a crisis of "perspectivism." They cannot acknowledge their partial and limited access to objects of investigation. To admit that knowledges are but perspectives—points of view on the world—is to acknowledge that other, quite different positions and perspectives are possible. This opens up a multiplicity of vantage points or positions in fields that, up to now, have been governed by a singular, exclusive, and privileged access to true representations and valid methods of knowing reality. To accept these limits and their own partisan nature amounts to relinquishing their claim to objective, true, singular, transhistorical, and transgeographic value. Moreover, it is to accept a heterogeneous series of influences—some rational, some not, some universal, some highly particularized—in the production and nature of knowledge.

6. Finally, the crisis of reason consists in the impossibility of rationally deciding between competing methods and paradigms produced from different positions. One certainly makes decisions within disciplines about which theories to rely upon, which methods to use, and which basic premises to assume; these are not based on reason alone but are the products of a variety of psychological, social, political, and epistemological forces. This adherence to positions and values that cannot be rationally justified and that compete with each other for supremacy within disciplines is not a function of incommensurable theories: although it may be true that some discourses and paradigms have no basis of comparison or common grounds, it is also true that most actively compete with each other (at any given time) around a cluster of shared

issues. Nor am I here affirming a relativism that asserts the equal value of all theories and all positions or perspectives. Relativism amounts to an abdication of the right to judge or criticize a position—any position—and a disavowal of any politics insofar as all positions are rendered equivalent. On the contrary, it is only through a perspective that the criticisms of other perspectives are possible.

Although I have suggested that this crisis is based on an inability to know the subject of knowledge, this can now be understood as a *crisis of specificity*, a crisis of the limits or the particularity of knowledges—a crisis in status and at the level of self-representations of the (sexual) specificities at play in the production of knowledges.

FEMINISM AND THE BODY
Although feminists have frequently struggled around issues involving women's bodies—abortion, contraception, maternity, reproduction, self-defence, body image, sexuality, and pornography, to name a few—there is still a strong reluctance to conceptualize the female body as playing a major role in women's oppression. Few concepts have been as maligned or condemned within feminist theory, with monotonous charges of biologism, essentialism, ahistoricism, and naturalism continuing to haunt those who use it. More recently, few concepts seem so readily embraced while at the same time undergoing a process of sanitization or neutralization—that is, a strange de-corporealization—by those feminist and cultural theorists who insist on the *discursivization* (if I may so name it) of bodies as a mode of protecting themselves from their materiality. Analyses of the *representation* of bodies abound, but bodies in their material variety still wait to be thought.

However understandable the charges of essentialism and ahistoricism may be (in the context of patriarchal reductions of women to natural passivity, maternity, dependence, and so on), they presume that *only* anatomical, physiological, or biological accounts of bodies are possible, obscuring the possibility of *sociocultural* conceptions of the body and ignoring the transformations and upheavals that may transform biological accounts. Nonbiologistic, nonreductive accounts of the body may entail quite different consequences and serve to reposition women's relations to the production of knowledges.

How and why, then, are bodies, in the stuff of their corporeality, relevant to feminism and the structure of prevailing knowledges? The following outline presents some possible reasons:

1. Given the prevailing binarized or dichotomized categories governing Western reason and the privilege accorded to one term over the other

in binary pairs (e.g., mind over body, culture over nature, self over other, reason over passions), it is necessary to examine the subordinated, negative, or excluded term *body* as the *unacknowledged condition* of the dominant term, *reason.*

2. Because these binary pairs function in lateral alignments, which are cross-correlated with other pairs—particularly the distinction between male and female—the body has been and still is closely associated with women and the feminine, whereas the mind remains associatively and implicitly connected to men and the masculine. Exploring these phallocentric alignments is prerequisite to transforming the presuppositions underlying prevailing knowledges.

3. If the notion of a radical and irreducible *difference* is to be understood with respect to subjectivity, the specific modes of corporeality of bodies in their variety must be acknowledged. These differences must in some way be inscribed on and experienced by and through the body. Sexual differences, like those of class and race, *are* bodily differences, but in order to acknowledge their fundamentally social and cultural "nature," the body must be reconceived, not in opposition to the culture but as its preeminent object. Any attempt to create a representation of "the human" must take a specific mode of corporeality as its ideal: it is doomed to erase difference, to convert difference to variation.

4. If we take antihumanist critiques of personal identity seriously, feminists can meaningfully talk about women as an oppressed group or a site of possible resistance only by means of specifying the female body and its place in locating women's experiences and social positions. As pliable flesh, the body is the unspecified raw material of social inscription that produces subjects as *subjects of a particular kind.*

5. Power can thus be seen to operate directly on bodies, behaviors, and pleasures, extracting from them information necessary for the emergence of the knowledges that constitute the social sciences and humanities. Knowledges require the interaction of power and bodies; correlatively, power requires knowledges of bodies and behaviors in order to remain effective and "in play." The disciplines (including psychology, criminology, sociology, psychiatry) are, as Foucault argues, formed through the interaction of disciplinary regimes and institutions—prisons, asylums, clinics, doctor's surgeries, the psychoanalyst's couch—with their concomitant knowledges to inscribe bodies in distinctive ways. Bodies are thus essential to accounts of power and critiques of knowledge. Feminist conceptions of the body are unlike those of their male counterparts (e.g., Nietzsche, Freud, Lacan, and Foucault) insofar as the bodies and pleasures of individuals and groups are always *sexually specific*

and may well entail different regimes of power and their associated knowledges.[6]

THE BODY AS SURFACE OF INSCRIPTION

Two broad kinds of approach to theorizing the body can be discerned in twentieth-century radical thought. One is derived from Nietzsche, Kafka, Foucault, and Deleuze, which I will call "inscriptive"; the other is more prevalent in psychology, especially psychoanalysis and phenomenology. I will refer to this second approach as the "lived body." The first conceives the body as a surface on which social law, morality, and values are inscribed; the second refers largely to the lived experience of the body, the body's internal or psychic inscription. Where the first analyzes a *social*, public body, the second takes the body-schema or imaginary anatomy as its object(s). It is not clear to me that these two approaches are compatible or capable of synthesis. Nevertheless, each may provide some of the theoretical terms necessary to problematize the major binary categories defining the body—inside/outside, subject/object, active/passive, fantasy/reality, and surface/depth.

The body can be regarded as a kind of *hinge* or threshold: it is placed between a psychic or lived interiority and a more sociopolitical exteriority that produces interiority through the *inscription* of the body's outer surface. Where psychoanalysis and phenomenology focus on the body as it is experienced and rendered meaningful, the inscriptive model is more concerned with the processes by which the subject is marked, scarred, transformed, and written upon or constructed by the various regimes of institutional, discursive, and nondiscursive power as a particular kind of body. In this section I will explore the inscriptive model of corporeal subjectivity and in the next, the notion of the lived body, the body as it is experienced.

In *The Genealogy of Morals*, Nietzsche outlines a basic account of corporeal inscription. At the horizon of culture, he argues, social morality and memory are not inscribed by man's unique reason, compassion, or morality, but by mnemotechniques—methods of branding or permanently etching the body. A genealogy of morals reveals a history of corporeal cruelty:

> The worse man's memory has been, the more fearful has the appearance of his customs; the severity of the penal code provides an especially significant measure of the degree of effort needed to overcome forgetfulness and a few primitive demands of social existence as present realities upon the slaves of momentary affect and desire (Nietzsche, 1969: 61)

For Nietzsche, economic equivalence, the capacity to exchange and to make contracts, does not derive from a sense of social justice, because justice itself derives from a primitive notion of "corporeal compensation," a kind of originary social violence by which damages are retrievable from the body of the guilty party. Debt is ultimately expiated by flesh and blood. Civilization carves meanings onto and out of bodies; it does not, as it professes, "enlighten the masses" by reason and education but instead ensures its cohesion through coercion and cruelty. All cultures, all modes of civilization practice a kind of ritualized body-inscription that is no more or less painful or primitive than in our own forms of initiation ceremonies. Scarring, tattooing, circumcizing, exercising, excizing, and remaking parts of the body by surgical means, through processes of stretching, marking, and distorting the lips, teeth, ears, necks, breasts, feet, genitals, acculturate the body and its parts. The body is adorned with color, mud, feathers, or stones and marked by processes securing, at least ideally, its social integration. Inscriptions mark the surface of the body, dividing it into zones of intensified or de-intensified sensation, spreading a libidinal concentration unevenly over the written-and-erotic living surface.

(34)

Ritualistically inscribed scars and incisions become the marks of one's social location and position, creating a (provisional) fixity from the flux of the body's experiential intensities. As a receptive surface, the body's boundaries and zones are constituted in conjunctions and through linkages with other surfaces and planes: the lips connected with the breast in orality, possibly accompanied by the hand in conjunction with an ear, each system in perpetual motion and interrelation with the other; toes in connection with sand in the obsessional's fixation with his shoes and calluses. These linkages are assemblages that harness and produce the body as a surface of interchangeable and substitutable elements. They libidinize the body's capacity to form linkages with other bodies, animate and inanimate.[7] Libidinal intensifications of bodily parts are *surface effects*, interactions occurring on the surface of the skin and various organs. These effects, however, are not simply superficial, for they generate an interior, an underlying depth, individuality, or consciousness. This *depth* is one of the distinguishing features marking out the modern, Western capitalist body from other kinds. Western body forms are considered expressions of an interior, of a subjectivity. By constructing a soul or psyche for itself, the "civilized body" forms libidinal flows, sensations, experiences, and intensities into needs, wants, and commodified desires that can gain a calculable gratification. The body becomes a text, a system of signs to be deciphered, read, and read into. While social law is incarnate, "corporealized," correlatively, bodies are textualized, "read" by others as *expressive* of a subject's psychic interior. A storehouse of inscriptions and messages between its internal and external boundaries, it generates or constructs the body's movements into "behavior," that then has interpersonally and socially identifiable meanings and functions within a social system.

Foucault outlines various systems for the normalization of bodies within a regime of disciplinary control. As procedures of punishment developed, there was a transition from a macropolitics of spectacular display (a kind of intimidatory and exemplary, or ostentatious, power) to a microphysics of intricate bodily supervision and surveillance. Punishment remains coupled with knowledges—either those produced by legal "proofs," confessions, and expert opinions, or those originating in the minds and behaviors of the spectators of punishment. Disciplinary normalization, Foucault's description of contemporary power, culminates in an increasingly medicalized discourse: health, well-being, clinical supervision, and surgical intervention become ever more crucial to legal, juridical, and political domains. These are agencies for regimenting, observing, and inspecting "delinquent bodies" (those of the sick, insane, or criminal); through them, the normalized body is surveyed as well. Epistemic and coercive relations create what Foucault describes as the "modern soul," the psychological interior or subjectivity so central to the "Sciences of Man."

The increasing medicalization of the body, based on processes of removal (incision, cutting, removing, and reduction) or addition (inlaying, stitching, and injection), demonstrate a body pliable to power, a *machinic* structure in which "components" can be altered, adjusted, removed, or replaced. The body becomes increasingly regarded as functional, composed of parts capable of mechanical/cybernetic duplication. Correlatively, there is an ever more insistent inscription by cultural object-signs on the surface of the body. Clothing, jewelery, makeup, cars, living spaces, and work all function to mark the subject's body as deeply as any surgical incision, binding individuals to systems of significance in which they become signs to be read (by others and themselves). Food, dieting, exercise, and movement provide meanings, values, norms, and ideals that the subject actively ingests, incorporating social categories into the physiological interior. Bodies speak, without necessarily talking, because they become coded with and as signs. They speak social codes. They become intextuated, narrativized; simultaneously, social codes, laws, norms, and ideals become incarnated.[8]

If bodies are traversed and infiltrated by knowledges, meanings, and power, they can also, under certain circumstances, become sites of struggle and resistance, actively inscribing themselves on social practices. The activity of *desiring, inscribing bodies* that, though marked by law, make their own inscriptions on the bodies of others, themselves, and the law in turn, must be counterposed against the passivity of the inscribed body.[9]

LIVED, SEXED BODIES

Sexual differences demand social representation insofar as social roles and procreative functions are not governed by instincts or "nature" but are socially required, produced, and regulated. Sexually differential biological processes—menstruation, pregnancy, childbirth, lactation, and sexual maturation in women and phallic maturation, erection, paternity, and emission in men—must be signified in all cultures. These differences ensure that even if the text to be written seems the "same" one, the body's positive contribution to the "text" produced ensures that the inscribed message will be different. The inscribed surface is not neutral but may require different typographical procedures and result in very different kinds of meanings, depending on the type of (sexed) materiality to be inscribed.

On a psychic level, according to the preeminent discourse of lived bodies, psychoanalysis, the pre-Oedipal child may not experience its body as *different from the other* (sex), but whether it exercizes this comparative faculty or not, the social and psychical significance of sexual differences are signified to it long before the oedipus complex. Its body is *always already* sexually coded in terms of the meanings each sex has for the parental generation, and for a given cultural situation (which includes class, race, and historical factors). The child's body means different things according to its sex. The parental-social meaning of the child's body is not externally imposed but is actively incorporated by means of its narcissistic identifications with others and their formative role in the establishment of the ego. Although psychoanalysis suggests that sex makes a difference to the kind of body image and subjectivity available for the subject, this difference is explained in terms of a binary structure of active and passive, presence and absence that grants primacy to male sexuality. If women are to be granted a position *congruous* with but independent of men, the female body must be capable of autonomous representation. This demands a new use of language and new forms of knowledge capable of articulating femininity and women's specificity in ways quite different from prevailing alternatives. Biological sciences, for example, would have to be drastically modified so that distinctively female processes are no longer considered passive *a priori* or by definition, in opposition to the activity attributed to men's biological processes. Female characteristics are often considered aberrations of the male norm. It is significant that in listing some of the defining characteristics of the two sexes earlier, I had to specify only the female; this is not surprising, given the presumption that men provide the ideal by which women are judged.[10] They also require transformations in social practices and exchange relations—sexual or otherwise—between men and women, so that women's bodies are no longer treated as inert, passive, incapable, and dependent, but in terms relevant to women's specificity.

If bodies are objects of power and sites of social inscription that are densely inhabited by psychic and social meaning, what effect is an understanding of the *sexually differential* forms of body going to have on our understanding of power, knowledges, and culture? What is the effect of acknowledging *autonomous differences* between kinds of human bodies on our understanding of subjectivity and the epistemological presumptions governing theory development?

KNOWLEDGE AND SEXUAL DIFFERENCE

Knowledges are not purely conceptual nor merely intellectual; they are not governed by a love of truth or a will to comprehension. The self-images of knowledges have always been, and remain today, bereft of an understanding of their own (textual) corporeality. Knowledge is an activity; it is a *practice* and not a contemplative reflection. It *does things*. As product or thing, it denies its historicity and asserts its indifference to questions of politics in such a way that it functions as a tool directed to any particular purposes its user chooses. Knowledges are effects of a drive for mastery, a visceral force or impulse to appropriate and subdue, a will to power:

> (a) sort of malicious destruction of the valuations by which men live, an unsatisfied soul that feels the tamed state as a torture and finds voluptuous pleasure in a morbid unravelling of all bonds that tie it to such a state. (Nietzsche, 1968: 461)

Knowledges are a product of a bodily drive to live and conquer. They misrecognize themselves as interior, merely ideas, thoughts, and concepts, forgetting or repressing their own corporeal genealogies and processes of production. They are products of bodily impulses and forces that have mistaken themselves for products of mind.

Like others I have cited, however, Nietzsche is guilty of abstracting and reducing the body to a singular masculine model. Along with Foucault, Freud, Lacan, and others, he assumes the corporeality of knowledge production, evaluation, and use; yet the corporeality invoked is itself not concrete or tangible, but ironically, "philosophical." Once the universal is shown to be a guise for the masculine and knowledges are shown to occupy only one pole of a (sexual) spectrum instead of its entirety, the possibility of other ways of knowing and proceeding—the possibility of feminine discourses and knowledges—reveals itself. Only through developing alternative modes of representational and inscriptional etching of female bodies can the singular domination of the universal by the masculine be made explicit. Conversely, it is only through a careful reading of phallocentric texts and paradigms that the rifts, flaws, and cracks within them can be utilized to reveal spaces where these texts exceed themselves, where they say more than they mean, opening themselves up to a feminine (re) appropriation.

The masculinity or maleness of knowledges remains unrecognized as such because there is no *other knowledge* with which it can be contrasted.[11] Men take on the roles of neutral knowers only because they have evacuated their own specific forms of corporeality and repressed all its traces from the knowledges they produce. In appropriating the realm of mind for themselves, men have nonetheless required a support and cover for their now-disavowed physicality. Women thus function as *the* body for men—correlative with the effacement of the sexual concreteness of their (womanly) bodies. If women are represented as the bodily counterparts to men's conceptual supremacy, women's bodies, pleasures, and desires are reduced to versions or variants of men's bodies and desires. Women are thus conceptualized as castrated, lacking, and incomplete, as if these were inherently qualities (or absences) of their (natural) bodies rather than a function of men's self-representations.

Women's reduction to the status of "neutral" bodies for men is an effect of the male sexualization of knowledges, a projection of men's sexualized bodies onto the structures of knowledges and, conversely, of the power of inscription that knowledges, discourses, and representational systems impose on bodies to constitute them as such. This correspondence between prevailing discursive models and forms of male sexuality and corporeality, described by Irigaray in terms of isomorphism, is not the result of a male conspiracy to create knowledges in their own image; rather, the hierarchical organization of men's bodies under the dominance of the phallus is the result of marking social meanings, values, and knowledges on the boy's body. This correspondence is a function of the systems of representation that traverse and constitute both men's bodies as such and the criteria for the evaluation of knowledges. Women's bodies are also represented and inscribed by the same systems.

Instead of seeing man as the active creator of discursive and epistemic values, the male body must be seen as an inscribed product of the intervention of meanings into the way men live their bodies. It is not really a question of blaming men but of understanding that certain perspectives are particular to their social and corporeal interests. These may not be relevant to women except insofar as they find these interests oppressively imposed on them. Many features of contemporary knowledges—knowledges based on the presumption of a singular reality, preexistent representational categories, and an unambiguous terminology able to be produced and utilized by a singular, rational, and unified knowing subject who is unhampered by "personal" concerns—can be linked to man's disembodiment, his detachment from his manliness in producing knowledge or truth.

FEMINISM AND THE CRISIS

Feminism has a complex relation to this crisis in contemporary knowledges. Its unprecedented development over the last twenty years is both a product of and a response to the dilemmas such a crisis poses for current knowledges. Feminist theory is implicated in this crisis in sometimes unrecognized ways. I will attempt to outline some of the major factors involved in this complex interaction.

For the purposes of my argument feminist theory could be divided into two broad categories. The first is committed to the introduction, analysis, and affirmation of "women" and "the feminine" as viable objects of knowledge. It aims to include women in those domains where they have been hitherto absent. It aspires to an ideal of a knowledge adequate to the analysis or representation of women and their interests, and exhibits varying degrees of critical distance from the male mainstream. What distinguishes this group from the second are its interests in focusing on woman or femininity as *knowable objects*. This must be distinguished from a second type of feminist theory, concerned with articulating knowledges that take woman as the *subject* of knowledges.

The first category of feminism is committed to the basic precepts and indeed implicit values governing mainstream knowledges and disciplines (or interdisciplines). To somewhat crudely characterize their views, their major contention with mainstream knowledges lies in the neglect or active exclusion of issues related to women and the feminine. This means that their works are largely ameliorative, confined to rewriting and supplementing existing knowledges, adding and suitably altering, say, history, sociology, or literary theory, where these leave out the contributions of women. This is no easy task, for it soon becomes clear that it

(39)

does not merely involve adding a neglected "object" to knowledges that are already more or less methodologically complete. It is not merely rectifying an oversight, but involves a more thorough questioning of the theoretical frameworks and intellectual ideals governing knowledges. It is simply not possible to supplement knowledges by adding women to an otherwise neutral or objective knowledge: knowledges have not just "forgotten" women, their amnesia is strategic and serves to ensure the patriarchal foundations of knowledges. This was an early, memorable lesson in feminist scholarship, the fundamentally patriarchal or phallocentric, rather than neutral, orientation of knowledges. Many recognized that if knowledges were to encompass women and femininity without reduction to male interests, they must be submitted to a thorough and critical overhaul. Their patriarchal investments needed to be understood and challenged if feminism was to adequately *know woman*.

Feminist attempts to supplement existing knowledges were nevertheless extremely fertile, particularly during the 1970s. Mitchell's work on "reading" psychoanalysis, the project of socialist or marxist feminists to utilize marxist categories of economic production and historical materialist analysis of class relations, and the work of women within academic disciplines such as history—in which both "forgotten women" and women's unrecognized contributions to historical events were being unearthed—serve as some examples of this remarkable productivity.

Yet many such projects are implicated in the challenge posed by the crisis of reason. The degree of commitment of mainstream knowledges to reason is an index of the extent to which feminist contributions to knowledges are themselves put into crisis. Where feminist theory questions mainstream knowledges either to augment them; to replace them with competing, feminist knowledges; or to dispense with them altogether, reverting to an anti-theoretical, anti-intellectual reliance on "experience" or "intuition," it remains unresolved relative to this crisis. In other words, where feminism remains committed to the project of knowing women, of making women objects of knowledge, without in turn *submitting the position of knower or subject of knowledge to a reorganization*, it remains as problematic as the knowledges it attempts to supplement or replace. A structural reorganization of positions of knowing, their effects on the kinds of object known, and our pregiven ways of knowing them is necessary for recognition of the implications and effects of the crisis of reason. If reason is an effect, not of reason itself, but of something unreasonable (i.e., power), then adhering to even an altered, modified reason is no solution. Nor is the abandonment of knowledges and the reversion to experience or (women's) common sense. These are the two poles around which this questioned reason oscillates—an unbridled "irrationalism" that verges on a celebration of ignorance and entrapment in what is (sociopolitically) given, and a project of ever-improving progress towards perfection, both of which are equally unacceptable.

A second broad approach within feminist theory grew out of this disillusionment, the recognition that knowledges cannot be neutral or objective. Adherents can be distinguished from the first category in several ways:

1. They attempt to create new subject positions as well as new objects to know.

2. They seem more prepared to reject existing models of knowing without attempting a "correction" or "supplementation."

3. They subject the methodological and criteriological commitments of knowledges to scrutiny and reject their claims to completion, universality, and in some cases, even their limited relevance. Yet they do not scorn theory production nor shirk from dealing with patriarchal or phallocentric knowledges.

Instead of taking women and the feminine as the object of their analyses, feminists within this second category take patriarchal knowledges as their objects and starting point. What distinguishes their work from the mire of competing male theories, each of which attempts a critique of the prevailing norm, is that these feminists have had to develop altogether different forms and methods of knowing and positions of epistemological enunciation, which are marked as *sexually* different from male paradigms.

Arguably the most developed—and neglected—example of this second category is Luce Irigaray. Although I cannot do justice here to the richly complex work she has written regarding questions of epistemology, nonetheless I would like to conclude with a broad outline of those elements of her work that seem to me to accommodate the problems posed by the crisis of reason. She champions one among many possible strategies that feminists may develop and utilize in rethinking knowledges as the products of sexually specific bodies.

1. Irigaray takes as her critical object of investigation neither "Woman" nor women. Instead, she examines key examples of phallocentric knowledges—psychoanalysis and the history of idealist philosophy (from Plato through Descartes, Kant, Hegel, and Rousseau to Merleau-Ponty and Levinas). Yet she does not simply analyze these objects neutrally or indifferently. Her readings of philosophical texts demonstrate not simply male "bias" or "domination" at the level of theory—such terms imply the possibility of a corrected, "purified," unbi-

ased knowledge—but the deeper implications of their phallocentrism—their representations of women and femininity in terms that are chosen by and affirm masculinity. Phallocentrism, however, is not limited to men's representations of women but must also include the elision of any *maleness* or masculinity in the perspectives and enunciative positions constitutive of knowledges, an isomorphism of theory with male (socio-historical) bodies.

2. She spells out how the supposedly neutral, sexually *indifferent* or universal status of knowledges or truths hides the specifically masculine interests that produce them. If men have in part rationalized their domination of the production of knowledges by claiming their interests are universal or sexually neutral, this is only because they rely upon a culturally inscribed correlation of men with the category of mind and of women with the category of body. Men are able to dominate knowledge paradigms because women take on the function of representing the *body, the irrational, the natural,* or other epistemologically devalued binary terms. By positioning women as *the* body, they can project themselves and their products as *disembodied,* pure, and uncontaminated. Irigaray's project consists in part in returning the male body to its products.

3. This implies that knowledges must be seen as *perspectival, partial,* limited, and contestable products, the results of historically specific political, sexual, and epistemological imperatives. Prevailing knowledges, in being recognized as male and as representing men's perspectives, are not thereby rendered redundant or useless (though this may be the effect on some) but are instead limited to a narrower, more constricted position—as partial views, commensurable or incommensurable with other perspectives and possible perspectives. This challenges the dominant positions accorded to masculine or phallocentric knowledges, and enables women to learn from them and from their various crises in developing different positions.

4. Irigaray's work thus remains critical of such traditional values as "truth" and "falsity" (where these are conceived as correspondence between propositions and reality), Aristotelian logic (the logic of the syllogism), and accounts of reason based upon them. This does not mean her work could be described as "irrational," "illogical," or "false." On the contrary, her work is quite logical, rational, and true in terms of quite different criteria, perspectives, and values than those dominant now. She both combats and constructs, while strategically questioning phallocentric knowledges without trying to replace them with more inclusive or more neutral truths. Instead, she attempts to reveal a *politics* of truth, logic, and reason.

5. To be more explicit, she does not present a more encompassing knowledge, but rather a *less* encompassing knowledge, one committed to the struggles in and around specific texts and debates, not a new eternal truth or a final answer. In other words, her texts are openly acknowledged as historical and contextual, of strategic value in particular times and places, but not necessarily useful or valid in all contexts. Knowledges, however, do not simply *reflect* the social and historical contexts out of which they were developed; rather, they help to actively inscribe or engender the meaning of the social.

6. She works strategically from a borderline or marginal position that is both within and beyond the bounds of existing theory. Only from such a tenuous and ambiguous position can she both challenge patriarchal texts at their most fundamental levels and, at the same time, prevent the co-option and integration that patriarchal systems use to transform serious threats to their operations. She aims to subvert the readymade boundaries between knowledges—not by ignoring them or pretending they do not operate but by strategically harnessing precisely the most tension-ridden and contrary disciplines so that the presuppositions of each are challenged.

Irigaray has demonstrated that there is a plurality of possible techniques, procedures, and methods within knowledges. She shows that there are always *other ways* of proceeding, other perspectives to be occupied and explored, than those contained within our history. The fact that a single contested paradigm (or a limited number) governs current forms of knowledge demonstrates the role that power, rather than reason, has played in developing knowledges. This power, although not as clearly visible as other forms of patriarchal coercion, is nonetheless integral to women's containment within definitions constituted by and for men. Unlike phallocentric and patriarchal models, her work is openly proclaimed as partial, partisan, and motivated. It is a political intervention into a politically unacknowledged field of intellectual warfare. Her tactics are hit-and-run: strategic forays into the "enemies' camp," the camp defined by male theory; skirmishes involving the use of the enemies' own weapons against them seems to be her goal. For her, the crisis of reason does not represent an impasse, but rather a path for women to explore and judge for themselves. Her work is a facing up to the implications of this crisis to know (as woman, as other) the knower (as man has been and woman is now becoming). Her work poses the question of the partiality, that is, the sexualization of all knowledges. It entails an acknowledgment of the sexually particular positions from which knowledges emanate and by which they are interpreted and used.

(3)

SEXUAL DIFFERENCE AND THE PROBLEM OF ESSENTIALISM

FEMINIST THEORY IS NECESSARILY IMPLI-
cated in a series of complex negotiations
between tense and antagonistic forces. On the
one hand, it is a self-conscious reaction to the
overwhelming masculinity of historically
privileged knowledges, and acts as a kind of
counterweight to the imbalances resulting
from the male monopoly over the production and reception of knowledges. On the
other hand, it is a response to the broad political aims and objectives of feminist struggle.
Feminist theory is thus bound to two kinds
of goals, two commitments or undertakings
that exist only in an uneasy and problematic
relationship. This tension means that feminists have had to tread a fine line either
between intellectual rigor (as it has been

defined in male terms) and political commitment (as feminists see it)—
that is, between the risks posed by patriarchal recuperation and those
posed by a conceptual sloppiness inadequate to the long-term needs of
feminist struggles—the tension between seeking acceptance in male
terms and retaining a commitment to women's struggles.

The ways in which feminists have engaged in the various projects of
constructing or fabricating a knowledge appropriate to women—while
keeping an eye on male academic traditions as well as on feminist politics—have left many open to criticism from both directions. From the
point of view of masculine conceptions of theory evaluation, including
notions of objectivity, disinterested scholarship, and intellectual rigor,
feminist theory is accused of a motivated self-interest, of developing a
"biased" approach, in which pregiven commitments are simply confirmed rather than objectively demonstrated;[1] and from the point of
view of (some) feminist "activists," feminist theory is accused of playing
male power games, of participating in and contributing to the very forms
of male dominance feminism should be trying to combat. It is not altogether surprising that underlying both criticisms is a common demand
for a purity of position—an intellectual purity in the one case (a purity
from social, personal, and political factors that may mitigate or interfere
with the goals of scholarly research), and a political purity in the other
(from the influence of patriarchal and masculinist values). Male-dominated theories require the disavowal of the sociopolitical values implicit in the production of all knowledges and the creation of a supposedly
value-free positioning of knowing, while feminist political purists require
the disavowal of the pervasive masculinity of privileged knowledges and
social practices, including those adopted by some or many feminists.

In spite of the sometimes puerile and often naïve extremism of both
types of objection, they do nevertheless articulate a real problem for feminist theory, highlighting an untheorized locus in its self-formation: By
what criteria are feminists to judge not only male theory but also feminist theory? If the criteria by which theory has been judged up to now
are masculine, how can new criteria be formulated? Can such criteria
adequately satisfy the dual requirements of intellectual rigor and political engagement? Is it possible to produce theory that compromises neither its political nor its intellectual credibility? In what ways is feminist
theory to legitimize itself in theoretical and political terms? These questions are neither idle nor frivolous. They are of direct relevance to the
ways in which feminist theory is assessed, and may help to clarify a number of issues that have polarized it in unproductive ways.

I would like to use a major dispute between feminist theorists—the debate between so-called feminisms of equality and feminisms of difference—to raise the question of the dual commitments of feminist theory and the need to devise appropriate criteria for its assessment. Is the concept of sexual difference a breakthrough term in contesting patriarchal conceptions of women and femininity, or is it a reassertion of the patriarchal containment of women? Is the concept essentialist, or is it an upheaval of patriarchal knowledges?

ESSENTIALISM AND ITS COGNATES

Feminists have developed a range of terms and criteria of intellectual assessment, over the past twenty or so years, that aim to affirm, consolidate, and explain the political goals and ambitions of feminist struggles. These terms have tended to act as unquestioned values and as intellectual guidelines in assessing both male-dominated and feminist-oriented theories. Among the most frequent and powerful of these terms are those centered around the question of the nature of women (and men)—essentialism, biologism, naturalism, and universalism. While these terms are closely related, sharing a common concern for the fixity and limits that define women, it is also important to be aware of the subtle differences between them in order to appreciate the ways in which they have been used by and against feminists. Patriarchal discourses commonly use the terms to justify women's social subordination and their secondary positions relative to men in patriarchal society.

Essentialism, a term that is rarely defined or explained explicitly in feminist contexts, but which has a long and illustrious history within the development of Western philosophy, refers here to the attribution of a fixed essence to women. Women's essence is assumed to be given and universal and is usually, though not necessarily, identified with women's biology and "natural" characteristics. Essentialism usually entails biologism and naturalism, but there are cases in which women's essence is seen to reside not in nature or biology but in certain given psychological characteristics—nurturance, empathy, support, non-competitiveness, and the like. Or women's essence may be attributed to certain activities and procedures (which may or may not be dictated by biology) observable in social practices—intuitiveness, emotional responses, concern and commitment to helping others, etc. Essentialism entails the belief that those characteristics defined as women's essence are shared in common by all women at all times. It implies a limit on the variations and possibilities of change—it is not possible for a subject to act in a manner contrary to her essence. Her essence underlies all the apparent variations differentiating women from each other.

Essentialism thus refers to the existence of fixed characteristics, given attributes, and ahistorical functions that limit the possibilities of change and thus of social reorganization.

Biologism is a particular form of essentialism in which women's essence is defined in terms of biological capacities. Biologism is usually based on some form of reductionism: social and cultural factors are the effects of biological causes. In particular, biologism usually ties women closely to the functions of reproduction and nurturance, although it may also limit women's social possibilities through the use of evidence from neurology, neurophysiology, and endocrinology, or at least through their popularizations. Biologism is thus an attempt to limit women's social and psychological capacities according to biologically established limits. It asserts, for example, that women are weaker in physical strength than men; that women are, in their biological natures, more emotional than men. Insofar as biology is assumed to constitute an unalterable bedrock of identity, the attribution of biologistic characteristics amounts to a permanent form of social containment for women.

Naturalism is also a form of essentialism in which a fixed nature is postulated for women. Once again, this nature is usually given biological form, but this is by no means invariant. Naturalism may be asserted on theological or ontological rather than biological grounds. For example, it may be claimed that women's nature is derived from God-given attributes that are not explicable or observable in biological terms. Or, following Sartrean existentialism or Freudian psychoanalysis, there are ontological invariants that distinguish the two sexes in, for example, the claim that the human subject is somehow free or that the subject's social position is a function of his or her genital morphology. More commonly, however, naturalism presumes the equivalence of biological and natural properties.

While also closely related to essentialism, biologism, and naturalism, universalism need not be based on innate or fixed characteristics. It is usually justified in terms of some essential or biological characteristics, but universalism may be conceived in purely social terms. Here, it refers to the attributions of invariant social categories, functions, and activities to which all women in all cultures are assigned. These may be the result of biology or ontology, but just as frequently they may reflect universal social or cultural requirements, such as the sexual division of labor or the prohibition of incest. Unlike essentialism, biologism, or naturalism, in which not only the similarities but also the differences between women may be accounted for (race and class characteristics can also be explained in naturalist, biologist, or essentialist terms), universalism tends to suggest only the commonness of all women at all times and in all social contexts. By definition, it can only assert similarities, what is shared in common by all women, and what homogenizes women into a category.

These four terms are frequently elided. Each has commonly served as a shorthand formula for the others. In charging theories with these conceptual commitments, feminists assert that they are necessarily complicit in reproducing patriarchal values. In claiming that women's current social roles and positions are the effects of their essence, nature, biology, or universal social position, these theories are guilty of rendering such roles and positions unalterable and necessary, thus providing them with a powerful political justification. They rationalize and neutralize the prevailing sexual division of social roles by assuming that these roles are the only, or the best, possibilities, given the confines of the nature, essence or biology of the two sexes. These commitments entail a range of other serious problems: they refer to necessarily ahistorical qualities; they confuse social relations with fixed attributes; they see these fixed attributes as inherent limitations to social change; and they refuse to take seriously the historical and geographical differences between women—differences between women across different cultures as well as within a single culture. (49)

It is not surprising that these terms have become labels for danger zones or theoretical pitfalls in feminist assessments of patriarchal theory. One could be sure that the theories one analyzed were tinged with patriarchal values whenever a trace of them could be discerned. They are the critical touchstones of assessment, self-evident guidelines for evaluating patriarchal theories and residues or adherences of feminist theories. These terms seem unquestionably problematic; they indicate, at least at first glance, a rare harmony between the principles of feminist politics and those of intellectual rigor, for they are problematic in both political and theoretical terms. Yet their value as criteria of critical evaluation for feminist as well as patriarchal theory is not as clear as it might seem.

SEXUAL IDENTITY/SEXUAL DIFFERENCE

Among the most contested issues in contemporary feminist theory are the terms in which women's social, sexual, and cultural positions are to be understood. This kind of question is, moreover, crucially positioned at the heart of the conflict between feminist politics and the requirements of patriarchal knowledges. Are women to be attributed an identity and sociocultural position in terms that make it possible for them to be conceived as men's equals? Or are women's identities to be conceived in terms entirely different from those associated with and provided by men? These questions imply two other related questions: Are the frameworks of prevailing patriarchal knowledges capable of bestowing on women the same basic capacities, skills, and attributes posited for men? If so, are these frameworks adequate for characterizing not only what women share in common with men (what makes both sexes "human") but also what particularizes women and distinguishes them from men?

The positions of a number of pioneers in the history of second wave feminism, including Simone de Beauvoir, Betty Friedan, Eva Figes, Kate Millett, Shulamith Firestone, and Germaine Greer, could be described as egalitarian. Broadly speaking, they claim that the liberation of women from patriarchal constraints entails an opening up of social, economic, political, and sexual positions previously occupied only by men. These theorists in different ways believed that women have been unfairly excluded from positions of social value and status normally occupied by men. Women in patriarchy were regarded as socially, intellectually, and physically inferior to men as a consequence of various discriminatory, sexist practices that illegitimately presumed women were unsuited for or incapable of assuming certain positions. This belief was fostered not only by oppressive external constraints but also by women's own compliance with and internalization of patriarchal sexual stereotypes.

Egalitarian feminists—among whom we should include, in spite of their differences, liberal and socialist feminists—were reacting to the largely naturalistic and biologistic presumptions on which much of social and political theory are based. If it is in women's nature to be passive, compliant, nurturing, this is a "natural" index, guide, or limit to the organization of society. Defenders of patriarchal social order assume that social and cultural relations should conform with and be conducive to "(human) nature." The goal is not an augmentation and reorganization of "nature," but simply its confirmation. The divisions and inequalities between the sexes were seen as the effects of a nature that should not be tampered with. This provides a ready-made justification for the most conservative and misogynist of patriarchal social relations: they are treated as if they were the effects of a pure and inert nature.

Egalitarian feminists claimed that women are as able as men to do what men do. The fact that women were not regarded as men's equals was not, they claim, the result of nature but of "patriarchal ideologies," discriminatory socialization practices, social stereotyping, and role-playing. Women's social roles were, in other words, the result of culture not nature, of social organization rather than biological determinants, and were thus capable of being changed. Indeed, if women's social roles are dictated by nature, feminism itself becomes impossible, for resistance to nature is, in one sense at least, impossible. Feminism is founded on the belief that women are capable of achievements other than those recognized and rewarded by patriarchy, other than those to which women's "nature" has hitherto confined them.

As a category, women were consistently underrepresented in positions of social authority and status and overrepresented in socially subordinate positions. Girls systematically underachieve and are inadequately prepared for social success, while boys' social roles tend to maximize their social potential. Feminism began largely as a struggle for a greater share of the patriarchal pie and equal access to social, economic, sexual, and intellectual opportunities. The early feminists of equality were bound up in what Kristeva has called "the logic of identification," an identification with the values, norms, goals, and methods devised and validated by men. In its beginnings, the women's movement, as the struggle of suffragists and of existential feminists, aspired to gain a place in linear time as the time of project and history. While this movement aspired to a universalized humanism, it also committed to questions of social and civic reorganization. The political demands of women—the struggles for equal pay for equal work, for taking power in social institutions on an equal footing with men; the rejection, when necessary, of the attributes traditionally considered feminine or maternal insofar as they are deemed incompatible with the insertion in that historical context—are part of the logic of identification with certain values: not with the ideological (these are combated, and rightly so, as reactionary), but rather, with the logical and ontological values of a rationality dominant in the nation-state.[2]

In place of the essentialist and naturalist containment of women, feminists of equality affirm women's potential for equal intelligence, ability, and social value. Underlying the belief in the need to eliminate or restructure the social constraints imposed on women is a belief that the "raw materials" of socialization are fundamentally the same for both sexes: each has an analogous biological or natural potential that is unequally developed because the social roles imposed on the two sexes are not equivalent. If social roles could be readjusted or radically restructured, if the two sexes could be resocialized, they could be rendered equal. The differences between the sexes would be no more significant than the differences between individuals. These feminist arguments for egalitarian treatment of the two sexes were no doubt threatening to patriarchs insofar as the sex roles the latter presumed were natural could be blurred through social means: women could become "unfeminine," men "unmasculine"; the sovereignty of the nuclear family, monogamy, and the sexual division of labor could be undermined. Where it was necessary to recognize the changeable nature of sex roles and social stereotypes, as feminists of equality advocated, this was not, however, sufficient to ensure women's freedom from sexual oppression. The more successful egalitarian programs became, the more apparent it was that the political agenda entailed a number of serious drawbacks:

1. The project of sexual equality takes male achievements, values, and standards as the norms to which women should also aspire. At most, women can achieve an equality with men only within a system whose overall value is unquestioned and whose power remains unrecognized. Women strive, then, to become the same as men, in a sense, "masculinized," produced within the terms of men's identities and self-representations.

2. To achieve an equality between the sexes, women's specific needs and interests—what distinguishes them from men—must be minimized and their commonness or humanity stressed. (This may, for example, explain the strong antipathy to maternity amongst a number of egalitarian feminists,[3] a resistance to the claim that women's corporeality or sexuality makes a difference to the kinds of consciousness or subjectivity they attain.)

3. Policies and laws codifying women's legal rights to equality—antidiscriminatory and equal opportunity legislation—have tended to operate as much against women as in their interests. For example, men have been as able as women to use antidiscrimination or equal opportunity regulations to secure their own positions.

4. In this sense, equality becomes a vacuous, or rather, a formal concept insofar as it reduces all specificities, including those which serve to distinguish the positions of the oppressed from those of the oppressor. One can be equal only insofar as the history of the oppression of a specific group is effaced.[4]

5. Struggles for equality between the sexes are easily reduced to struggles around a more generalized and neutralized social justice. This has enabled a number of men to claim that they too are oppressed by patriarchal social roles, and are unable to express their more "feminine" side. The struggles of women against patriarchy are too easily identified with a movement or reaction against a general "dehumanization" in which men may unproblematically represent women in struggles for greater or more authentic forms of humanity.

6. The project of creating equality between the sexes can be socially

guaranteed, if at all, only in the realm of public and civic life. Even if some kind of domestic equality were possible, an equality at the level of sexual, and particularly reproductive, relations seems impossible insofar as these are untouched by egalitarianism.

7. Most significantly, even if the two sexes behave in the same ways, perform the same duties and play the same roles, the social meanings of their activities remain unchallenged. Until this structure of shared meanings is problematized, equality in anything but a formal sense remains impossible.

Try as it may, a feminism of equality is unable adequately to theorize sexual and reproductive equality. This, in turn, results in its inability adequately to theorize women's specific positions within the social and symbolic order. Kristeva makes clear the link between sexual and symbolic functioning:

> Sexual difference—which is at once biological, physiological, and relative to reproduction—is translated by and translates a difference in the relation of subjects to the symbolic contract which is the social contract: a difference, then, in the relationship to power, language and meaning. The sharpest and most subtle point of feminist subversion brought about by the new generation will henceforth be situated on the terrain of the inseparable conjunction of the sexual and the symbolic, in order to try to discover, first, the specificity of the female, and then, in the end, that of each individual. (Kristeva, 1981: 21)

In contrast to egalitarian feminism, a feminism based on the acknowledgment of women's specificities and oriented to the attainment of autonomy for women emerged during the 1980s. From the point of view of a feminism of equality, feminisms of difference seem strangely reminiscent of the position of defenders of patriarchy: both stress women's differences from men. However, before too readily identifying them, it is vital to ask how this difference is conceived and, perhaps more importantly, who defines this difference and for whom. For patriarchs, difference is understood in terms of inequality, distinction, or opposition, a sexual difference modeled on negative, binary, or oppositional structures within which only one of the two terms has any autonomy; the other is defined only by the negation of the first. Only sameness or identity can ensure equality. In the case of feminists of difference, however, difference is seen not as difference *from* a pregiven norm, but as *pure difference*, difference in itself, difference with *no identity*. Difference, viewed as distinction, implies the pre-evaluation of one of the terms from which the difference of the other is drawn; pure difference refuses to privilege either term.[5] For feminists, to claim women's difference from men is to reflect existing definitions and categories, redefining oneself and the world according to women's own perspectives.

The right to equality entails the right to be the same as men, while struggles for autonomy imply the right to either consider oneself equal to another, or reject the terms by which equality is measured and to define oneself in different terms. It entails the right to be and to act differently. The concept of difference is used by a number of contemporary feminist theorists, including Luce Irigaray, Jane Gallop, Hélène Cixous, and Naomi Schor. It implies, among other things, the following:

1. Difference suggests major transformation of the social and symbolic order that, in patriarchy, is founded by a movement of universalization of the particular (white, heterosexual male) identity. Difference cannot be readily accommodated in a system that reduces all difference to distinction and all identity to sameness.

2. Difference resists the homogenization of separate political struggles insofar as it implies not only women's differences from men, and from each other, but also women's differences from other oppressed groups. It is not clear, for example, that struggles against racism will necessarily be politically allied with women's struggles or, conversely, that feminism will overcome forms of racist domination. This, of course, does not preclude the existence of common interests shared by various oppressed groups, and thus the possibility of alliances over specific issues; it simply means that these alliances have no prior necessity.

3. Struggles around the attainment of women's autonomy imply that men's struggles against patriarchy, while possibly allied with women's in some circumstances, cannot be identified with them. In acknowledging their sexual specificity, men's challenge to patriarchy is necessarily different from women's, which entails producing their own sexual specificity.

4. The notion of difference affects women's definitions not only of themselves but also of the world. This implies not only that social practices must be subjected to feminist critique and reorganization, but also that the very structures of representation, meaning, and knowledge must be subjected to a thoroughgoing transformation of their patriarchal alignments. A politics of difference implies the right to define oneself, others, and the world according to one's own interests.

THE DIFFERENCE THAT MAKES A DIFFERENCE

Feminists involved in the project of establishing women's sexual differences from men have been subjected to wide-ranging criticisms coming from both directions. They face the same general dilemma confronting any feminist position that remains critical of patriarchal knowledges yet must rely on their resources. From the point of view of traditional, male-governed scholarly norms, their work appears utopian, idealistic, romantic, polemic, fictional—but above all, without substantial content or solid evidence and justification. From the point of view of other forms of feminism it may appear essentialist and universalist. In the one case, these feminists are accused of straying too far from biological and scientifically validated information; and in the other, of sticking too closely to biological evidence. It seems that both these criticisms misunderstand the status of claims made by many feminists of difference, judging them in terms inappropriate to their approach.

Charges of essentialism, universalism, and naturalism are predictable responses on the part of feminists concerned with the idea of women's social construction. Thus, any attempt to define or designate woman or femininity is in danger of relying on commitments that generalize on the basis of the particular, and reduce social construction to biological pre-formation. Any theory of femininity, any definition of woman in general, any description which abstracts from the particular historical, cultural, ethnic, and class positions of particular women verges perilously close to essentialism. Toril Moi provides a typical response to a feminism of difference in her critique of Irigaray's notion of women or the feminine. (55)

> …any attempt to formulate a general theory of femininity will be metaphysical. This is precisely Irigaray's dilemma: Having shown that so far femininity has been produced exclusively in relation to the logic of the same, she falls for the temptation to produce her own positive theory of femininity. But, as we have seen, to define "woman" is necessarily to essentialize her. (Moi, 1985: 139)

This, however, leads to a paradox: if women cannot be characterized in any general way, if all there is to femininity is socially produced, how can feminism be taken seriously? What justifies the assumption that women are oppressed *as a sex*? What, indeed, does it mean to talk about women as a category? If we are not justified in taking women as category, what political grounding does feminism have? Feminism is placed in an unenviable position: either it clings to feminist principles that entail its avoidance of essentialist and universalist categories (in which case its rationale as a political struggle centered around women is problematized); or it accepts the limitations patriarchy imposes on its conceptual schemas and models and abandons the attempt to provide autonomous, self-defined terms in which to describe women and femininity. Are these the only choices available to feminist theory—an adherence to essentialist doctrines, or the dissolution of feminist struggles into localized, regional, specific struggles representing the interests of particular women or groups of women?

Posed in this way, the dilemma facing feminists involves a conflict between the goals of intellectual rigor (avoidance of the conceptual errors of essentialism and universalism) and feminist political struggles (struggles directed toward the liberation of women as women). But is this really a choice feminists must face? Is it a matter of preference for one goal over the other? Or can the linkages between theory and political practice be understood differently so that the criteria of intellectual evaluation are more "politicized" and the goals of political struggle more "theorized"?

Gayatri Spivak sums up this dilemma well in her understanding of concepts and theoretical principles, not as guidelines, rules, or blueprints for struggle but as *tools* and *weapons* of struggle. It is no longer a matter of maintaining a theoretical purity at the cost of political principles, nor is it simply a matter of the ad hoc adoption of theoretical principles according to momentary needs or whims. It is a question of negotiating a path between always impure positions—seeing that politics is always already bound up with what it contests (including theories)—and that theories are always implicated in various political struggles (whether this is acknowledged or not):

> You pick up the universal that will give you power to fight against the other side, and what you are throwing away by doing that is your theoretical purity. Whereas the great custodians of the anti-universal are obliged therefore simply to act in the interest of a great narrative, the narrative of exploitation while they keep themselves clean by not committing themselves to anything.... [T]hey are run by a great narrative even as they are busy protecting their theoretical purity by repudiating essentialism. (Spivak, 1984/1985: 184)

The choice, in other words, is not between maintaining a politically pure theoretical position (and leaving the murkier questions of political involvement unasked) and espousing a politically tenuous one which may be more pragmatically effective in securing social change. The alternatives faced by feminist theorists are all in some sense "impure" and implicated in patriarchy. There can be no feminist position that is not in some way or other involved in patriarchal power relations; it is hard to see how this is either desirable or even possible, for a purity from patriarchal "contamination" entails feminism's incommensurability with patriarchy—thus the inability to criticize it. Feminists are not faced with pure and impure options. All options are in their various ways bound by the constraints of patriarchal power. The crucial political

questions are: Which commitments, despite their patriarchal alignments, remain of use to feminists in their political struggles? What kinds
of feminist strategy do they make possible or hinder? What are the costs
and benefits of holding these commitments? In other words, the deci-
sion about whether to "use" essentialism or to somehow remain beyond
it (even if these extremes are possible) is a question of calculation, not a
self-evident certainty.

In challenging the domination of patriarchal models that rely on
essentialism, naturalism, biologism, or universalism, egalitarian feminists have pointed to the crucial role these assumptions play in making
change difficult to conceive or undertake: as such, they support, rationalize, and underpin existing power relations between the sexes. But in
assuming that feminists take on essentialist or universalist assumptions
(if they do, which is not always clear) in the same way as patriarchs,
instead of attempting to understand the ways in which essentialism and
its cognates can function as unavoidable and therefore possibly strategically useful terms, this silences and neutralizes the most powerful of
feminist theoretical weapons, the ability to use patriarchy and phal-
locratism against themselves, to take up positions ostensibly opposed to
feminism and to use them for feminist goals.

> ...I think it is absolutely on target to take a stand against the discourses of
> essentialism, universalism as it comes to terms with the universal—of classi-
> cal German philosophy or the universal as the white upper-class male...etc.
> but strategically we cannot. Even as we talk about feminist practice, or privi-
> leging practice over theory, we are universalising. Since the moment of essen-
> tialising, universalising, saying yes to the onto-phenomenological question, is
> irreducible, let us at least situate it at the moment; let us become vigilant about
> our own practice and use it as much as we can rather than make the totally
> counter-productive gesture of repudiating it.... (Spivak, 1984/1985: 184)

In other words, if feminism cannot maintain its political purity from
patriarchal frameworks, methods, and presumptions, its being implicated by them needs to be acknowledged instead of being disavowed.
Moreover, this (historically) necessary binding by patriarchal terms is
the very condition of feminism's effectivity in countering and displac-
ing the effects of patriarchy: its *immersion* in patriarchal practices
(including those surrounding the production of theory) is the condition of its effective critique of and movement beyond them. This immersion provides not only the conditions under which feminism can become
familiar with what it criticizes, but also the very means by which patriarchal dominance can be challenged.

**ONTOLOGY AND
EQUIVOCATION**

THE POLITICS OF EQUIVOCATION

Only a political or theoretical commitment
that can confront its own internal paradoxes, its inherent or constitutive inconsistencies,
and its necessary if changeable limits can be
said to have come of age. I believe that, after
considerable struggle, and often great reluctance, feminist theory has finally reached the
stage when it can not only defend itself from
outside incursions and external criticism—
from positions committed to anti-feminism,
phallocentrism, patriarchalism—but is also
prepared to speak up against some of its own
commitments, some of the stages and positions that were perhaps historically necessary
for its current forms but to which it can now
no longer adhere. This entails that feminist

theory must be prepared to accept that any position has its limits; no position can encompass the entire field. To present a position, to provide a strategy, to make specific claims, is always to exclude, to deny and to problematize other, competing positions.

As part of its maturation, feminism (and indeed any political movement with theoretical aspirations and commitments) must be prepared as it were, to air dirty laundry, to make public as well as private criticisms of other feminists, to be seen to disagree with other feminists or feminisms. This may well prove confusing, unsettling, and disappointing to outsiders (who may like to believe in generally agreed upon base issues and platforms and may be shocked that feminists can disagree with each other at least as strongly as they may disagree with phallocentric or male positions), but it is something that most feminists themselves have probably long recognized and that many have evaluated as one of the positive strengths of feminist politics—its diversity, its commitment to multiplicities and specificities, its nonunified functioning.

Postmodern theory in general and Derridean deconstruction in particular have posed a series of the most difficult challenges to the self-conception of feminist theories, challenges—not simply critiques or objections—that have raised serious questions about the status of subversion, the position of subordination, and the possibilities of transgression, transformation, and upheaval that feminism must address if it is to remain a viable and effective political force into the twenty-first century. The general suspicion that many feminists have of that work now most easily categorized as postmodern,[1] the wariness of different projects to decenter subjectivities, sexualities, agencies, political platforms, and revolutionary goals has caused many feminists to cling steadfastly to humanist and enlightenment values, or to naturalist and essentialist commitments that may ultimately harm more readily than help various feminist aims and strategies. In this chapter I hope to provide something of a feminist revaluation of some of the writings of Jacques Derrida that will function as a mode of criticism of both those feminists who have resolutely attacked deconstruction (often in the name of postmodernism) without any familiarity with his writings, and those feminists who have actively struggled with his texts only to reject his work as outside of or hostile to feminist concerns. My purpose here, though, is not to criticize other feminists (though I no longer want to shy away from this necessity when it occurs); it is to demonstrate that feminist demands for a clear-cut position, for answers, for unequivocal boundaries and divisions, and for certainties in political judgement can afford to learn much from deconstruction.

I do not want to suggest that Derrida's works are feminist in themselves; nor the contrary claim that his writings are anti-feminist in any straightforward sense. His position defies ready-made categories and clear-cut characterizations. It is perhaps this apparently *slipperiness*, this refusal to stay within a singular definitive frame, more than anything else, that may explain the suspicion his work seems to arouse among feminists and political activists of various kinds. Although his work cannot be assigned a definitive position on one side or the other of a divide separating feminist from anti-feminist positions—indeed, it problematizes this very dividing line—and although his work is not easily assimilable into a kind of feminist appropriation that would or could reread his works to absorb or ingest them, nonetheless I believe that deconstruction provides a series of challenges and insights that may serve to make feminist theory more self-critical of its conceptual and political investments and their costs, and thus more incisive in its struggles. Moreover, deconstruction provides a way of rethinking our common conceptions of politics and struggle, power and resistance by insisting that no system, method, or discourse can be as all-encompassing, singular, and monolithic as it represents itself. Each is inherently open to its own undoing, its own deconstruction (deconstruction is not imposed from outside a discourse or tradition but emerges from that discourse's own inner dynamics). It is for this reason that, rather being construed as a system of critique, of destruction, Derrida insists over and over that deconstruction must be understood as a mode of affirmation, indeed as a mode of double affirmation.[2]

(61)

In a feminist context this means that discourses influenced by or in some way involved with deconstruction are committed to *both* an affirmation, a saying-yes to patriarchy (the gesture of phallocentrism), *and* an affirmation of feminism, of the overcoming of patriarchy. The first affirmation is perhaps the one many feminists wish were unnecessary, that they can simply and resoundingly say no to patriarchy. Yet the inherited nature of feminist discourse, which is not or not yet a discipline, and its location within "patriarchal" institutions, knowledges, and languages; the ways in which feminist self-help projects and equal opportunity commitments must negotiate with patriarchal institutions of the capitalist state for funding, the implication of Western feminism in neocolonialism—indeed, the very investment of all of us in the West in a cannibalization of the other—illustrate our *necessary*, constitutive immersion in the very systems from which we seek to distance and against which we seek to position ourselves. Without both moments in this affirmative investment, however, feminism remains in danger of repeating and being unable to recognize the very implications it believes it has repudiated.

Derrida does not question the errors or false assumptions of feminist theory, as some philosophers have attempted to do without much success.[3] He is not interested in how to correct or improve any particular theory (indeed, such a notion presupposes that deconstruction somehow knows what a theory means to say and can say it better, more rigorously or more accurately than the theory it corrects, a commitment that Derrida acknowledges is necessarily bound up with notions of teleology and truth in ways that he himself has problematized). Rather, his work raises difficult, possibly unresolvable questions regarding the internal and essential implications of feminist theory and practice in an often unrecognized complicity with the very forces feminists have commonly identified as outside of feminism itself—patriarchy, phallocentrism, racism—forces from which feminists have, they believe, separated themselves in order to see feminism as beyond or outside their sphere of influence. Derrida is not addressing an error that, by ingenuity or careful rethinking, could somehow be rectified, but a constitutive binding, the *always already* implication of feminism or any oppositional mode of political struggle in the law it undertakes to subvert or displace. He poses the necessary implication of feminism in phallogocentrism, of antiracism in racism, of philosophical texts (most particularly Nietzsche's, Heidegger's, and de Man's, no less than his own) in Nazism and fascism, of the "revolution" in what it revolts against—possibly the most unsettling and disquieting charge that can be levelled at any political position that strives to transcend given situations and power relations. This is *not* the claim that feminism is doomed from the start, that it cannot hope to accomplish its aim, but is rather the more limited claim that feminism can only hope to succeed insofar as it is implicated in and part—admittedly a recalcitrant part—of patriarchy itself.

This question of complicity is probably the most forceful and disturbing challenge—I cannot call it a critique, because there can be no correction, no truth, no superceding of this complicity—that can be posed for any discourse or practice that regards itself as oppositional: the claim that one's struggles are inherently *impure*, bound up with what one struggles against, that one reaffirms its power even as one struggles. This assertion of complicity, while it is not a claim of a conscious collusion, nonetheless refuses the idea of a space beyond or outside, the fantasy of a position insulated from what it criticizes and disdains. If feminism does not occupy a space outside of patriarchy and phallocentrism, if it is implicated in the interstices of patriarchal functioning, then the security of its identity, the definitiveness of its borders as other than and outside of patriarchy, its very self-representations as a bounded position separable from patriarchy, are problematized. I do not see this as an anti-feminist gesture, but as a measure of the maturity of feminism to accept its internal limits and to use them in enabling and productive ways.

In this chapter, I will explore a number of feminist positions regarding Derrida's work, most of which remain highly critical of his various interventions into and speculations on femininity. I propose to defend Derrida against common feminist reactions to and resistances of his deconstructive strategies, by showing that they have misunderstood and misrepresented his position. I do not want to suggest that Derrida's work is *simply* misread; but that part of this misreading is systematic and structurally related to his equivocal position regarding feminism. I will then examine his account of the ontology of sexual difference, with the aim of showing what a more positive feminist relation to deconstruction may look like.

FEMINISMS WARY OF DECONSTRUCTION

With the exception of only very few feminists (Drucilla Cornell, Avital Ronell, Gayatri Spivak, Barbara Johnson, Vicki Kirby, Nancy J. Holland, Peggy Kamuf, among them), Derrida's work has been regarded almost uniformly with great suspicion even by those feminists who find themselves attracted to other postmodern discourses and commitments. While only rarely is open hostility expressed, his work remains ambiguous in status. However, it may be this very ambiguity that offers feminists something of value.

Rosi Braidotti may in this context serve as representative of a more general feminist hostility towards Derrida's work—a hostility she directs to Derrida along with a number of other (male) "postmodernists." She claims that Derrida is part of a tendency within contemporary theory to use the metaphor of woman to question the status of truth, knowledge, and subjectivity at the expense of women's concrete social struggles. Woman has become the metaphor for the undoing of truth, knowledge, and subjectivity, while never herself being accorded access to these deemed social goods. Braidotti sees Derrida as part of a general tendency within postmodernism to borrow from femininity while effacing its specificity and its links to "real" women. This opposition between (male) representations of women and femininity, and "real" women seems both oversimplified and assumes what it needs to argue. I am not suggesting that men's representations of women necessarily accord with or refer to "real" women without residue or resistance: on the contrary "real" women are themselves the products and effects of discursive practices that cannot be confined simply to misogynist (mis)representations. "Real" women are as much an effect of women's discourses as men's, especially seeing that the dividing line between feminist discourses and patriarchal ones cannot be drawn with any *a priori* certainty. At the same time, however, it is also the case that any assumption of the independent existence of "real" women outside of or before representation, able to rise against it, must be invested in certain unnegotiable essentialisms. I am not claiming that there are no real women, but that real women are the consequences or effects of systems of representation and inscription.

> The zero value of the feminine in the system of representation is confirmed [in Derrida's work]; but in this instance, the feminine is used by the (male) thinker so as to avoid confronting the problem of the reality of women and their relation to truth, both of which have been declared fluid and indefinable.... Not only is woman undefinable, but she becomes, besides, the sign of unrepresentability itself; definitively other than the system of truth.... Historically,...truth has become woman at the moment when philosophy can only survive in the becoming woman of the idea, that is in the affirmation of the non-truth of truth, in the acceptance of its lack. (Braidotti, 1991: 103)

Elsewhere, she questions the timing of what she (mistakenly) sees as a Derridean revelling in the fragmentation and destabilization of identities provoked by postmodernism: at precisely the moment that women for the first time in history are about to claim an identity, a voice, a politics, a series of positions as their own, men such as Derrida find ever more devious ways of robbing women of these new-found gains:

> Well may the high-priests of postmodernism preach the deconstruction and fragmentation of the subject, the flux of all identities, based on phallocentic premises; well may they keep reading into feminism the image of the crisis of their own acquired perceptions of human consciousness. The truth of the matter is: one cannot deconstruct a subjectivity one has never been fully granted; one cannot diffuse a sexuality which has historically been defined as dark and mysterious. In order to announce the death of the subject one must first have gained the right to speak as one; in order to demystify metadiscourse one must first gain access to a place of enunciation. (1989a: 237)

A self-righteous tone is usually an index of the degree to which one has projected outwards, in anger, the very points of uneasiness one feels in one's own position. My point here is Braidotti invokes a certainty, a clarity, and definitive position that she must elsewhere and in other terms deny or disavow. One cannot simply adjudicate the matter by stating what "the truth of the matter" is. Is it unequivocally "the truth of the matter" to claim that women *do not* have a subjectivity, a position of enunciation, a sexuality? If this were simply "the truth of the matter," feminism itself, including Braidotti's position, would not be possible. It is only if women are ambiguously *both* subjects *and* deprived of a socially recognized subjective position, are *both* speaking beings *and* beings whose words have not been heard; and beings who have a sexuality, but whose sexual specificities are ignored, denied, or covered over that women can undertake feminist politics. In a certain sense, women must be accredited with precisely the qualities patriarchal practices attempt to deprive them of in order to account for the very possibility of feminism, of women overcoming these patriarchal constrictions. Braidotti seems to criticize Derrida for the kinds of claims he himself criticizes: she mistakes his position as an affirmation rather than a contestation. This is quite striking in her discussion of *Spurs* (Derrida, 1979). For Derrida, there is no question of simply decentering the subject once and for all,[4] or simply moving beyond metaphysics or logocentrism into a somehow pure deconstructive space; there is no question that deconstruction, rather than being beyond logocentrism, always remains implicated in it. Braidotti accuses Derrida of attempting to eliminate the very attributes feminists have so long sought for women, when in fact he questions the very possibility of such an elimination.

Braidotti is not the only feminist to raise such objections. Although Alice Jardine is considerably more careful in her analysis of Derrida's texts, she too seems to share Braidotti's suspicions of Derrida's appropriation of the radicality of feminist theory and politics:

> Might there be a new kind of desire on the part of (Modern) Man to occupy all positions at once (among women, among texts?) Are we here only brushing up against a new version of an old male fantasy: that of escaping the laws of the fathers through the independent and at the same time dependent female? Are men projecting their own "divisions" onto their primordial interlocutors—women? Do they hope to find a way of depersonalizing sexual identity while maintaining the amorous relation through women?
>
> How can we emphasize the political stakes of those questions without betraying the necessity of asking them knowingly—even "academically"? (Jardine, 1985: 207)

Jardine implies that the danger of deconstruction is its attempt to be pervasive, to occupy all specific positions—to speak as woman, as man, as decentered, as centered—opportunistically seeking any position momentarily or strategically while remaining committed to none. This signals a kind of disavowal of his position as masculine that Braidotti

(65)

has also suggested, a refusal to be located, to make a definite statement, being evasive when he should be straightforward.

Significantly, Margaret Whitford accuses Derrida of precisely the opposite maneuvre: not of disavowing the masculinity of his position, for she claims that "he makes it possible to address the question of the *maleness* of the speaking subject/ the subject of philosophy"; on the contrary, Whitford is concerned with what he does not do, which is "to make it possible to address the question of how one might be a woman speaking subject/ philosopher" (1991: 129.)

For Whitford, Derrida does not adequately speak "in his own voice," he hides his own position behind a web of quotations and readings of other texts. She describes his position as "elusive," "feminine," difficult to locate, for he does not own up to any position:

> Discourse is citation; meaning is ultimately elusive (feminine). Where is Derrida's place of enunciation if he is always quoting someone else? In a sense he wants to make his position impregnable, ultimately undecidable, ultimately "feminine." Deconstruction enables him to speak indefinitely, to hold the floor…. [H]e "masters" feminist discourse by speaking about it. (Whitford, 1991: 130)

Several questions arise for me here. Surely a position of enunciation is not simply hidden behind the apparent neutrality of all citation. It has been Derrida who has claimed that an enunciative position, the possibility of (provisional or temporary) contextualization, of a parergonal framing of any utterance, is always a matter, not simply of citation, but also of a citation-situating activity, which is itself amenable to other citations and thus other resituatings (as Whitford herself demonstrates in critically repeating/reframing Derrida's work in the context of the Irigarayan affirmation of sexual difference). And far from hiding behind a system of citationality which makes his position "impregnable" (the implication being that he hides his "real" position behind citations; that there is a discourse, concept or view-point "hidden," but logocentrically "present," like the signified, behind mere words), his position only emerges as such within the structure of citationality or iteration, as one provisional destination of the cited text. In any case, there seems to be no attempt on his part to "master feminist discourse," because feminist discourses do not provide the texts he cites and are not the objects of his investigations. These are usually derived from what are often considered the most misogynist of male writers—Nietzsche, Heidegger, Levinas, Freud.[5] Derrida cannot naïvely pretend to master feminist discourse through a careful reading of Nietzsche, *et. al.*, largely because they are

(66)

not themselves feminist texts.

These represent some typical, well-worn objections to or reservations about the relevance of deconstruction for feminist theory. They are merely the tip of a veritable iceberg of criticisms generally directed at the incursions of postmodern thought on the "authenticity" and political efficacy of feminism. While not wishing to engage too much in the general demeaning of postmodern thought in the works of a number of feminists,[6] it is probably worthwhile nonetheless to outline in schematic form a few of the more common and serious objections that may be and have been levelled at Derrida by feminists and other political activists.

1. Derrida speaks in the name of/for/as a feminine subject in a mode of male appropriation of women's right to speak. Just at that moment in history when speaking as a woman finally has some political and theoretical credibility, Derrida, along with Deleuze and others, wants to occupy the very speaking position that women have finally produced for themselves. This is a claim Irigaray articulates very clearly:

> What I am able to say without any hesitation is that when male theoreticians today employ women's discourse instead of using male discourse, that seems to me a very phallocratic gesture. It means: "We will become and we will speak a feminine discourse in order to remain the master of discourse." What I would want from men is that, finally, they would speak a masculine discourse and affirm that they are doing so. (Irigaray, quoted in Whitford, 1991: 132)

While this plea is an understandable one, it rests on two problematic assumptions: first, that one can, through a conscious avowal, acknowledge what one's position is. This seems to be a basic assumption in much of what is presently called "identity politics," which commonly functions in a publicly confessional mode, and in anti-racist calls for an authentic native voice, a voice that can speak only for and as it is. Can one *admit* what one's position is? Is a position definitively present, not only to a subject's self-representation, but for all others to avow and accept? Does any subject or position have the stability to definitively state what-it-is? It seems that texts, speaking positions, identities cannot anchor themselves so readily in a definite moment of articulation where their "consciousness" exactly coincides with their existence. Secondly, the assumption exists that there is a clear-cut distinction between talking as a man and talking as a woman. We may be able to presume (possibly without clear-cut justification) a ready distinction between men and women; but even if we do, it is not clear how any one can contain men and women to speak only in their own voice or as their sex. This is to ignore or misunderstand that language itself is the endless possibility of speaking otherwise.

2. Derrida has placed deconstruction in a position oppositional to feminism, a position of structural domination over feminist concerns, able to adjudicate the merits and radicality of feminism without in turn being judged by it. This is a claim that Whitford makes explicitly:

> ...there is in practice a "violent hierarchy" at work in which deconstruction is the privileged term. In the opposition which he sets up between deconstruction and feminism, there is no question for Derrida of privileging the subordinate term, since it could leave him without a place to speak. (Whitford, 1991: 130)

This seems to misunderstand the commitment Derrida has to undermining oppositional thought and structures precisely through the assertion of difference. The relations between deconstruction and feminism cannot be regarded as oppositional: deconstruction does not affirm what feminism denies; feminism is not the denial or negation of deconstruction, because their relations do not occupy the same intellectual space.[7] It is only on the basis of an acceptance—not of an oppositional relation, but of a possibly antagonistic or possibly allied set of struggles, this outsideness—that any *relation* between deconstruction and feminism may be possible.

3. A number of those openly committed to political activism—Ryan, Braidotti, Fraser, Brodrib—claim that while deconstruction may help to problematize certain philosophical and intellectual practices, it remains both elitist and unrelated to power struggles that function in more mundane and everyday terms. Ryan, for example, in agreement with a number of feminists, claims that Derrida's work is limited by the absence of any social, political, or economic understanding of the more "real," pressing issues of day-to-day struggle. This is not unrelated to a common lament of those who discuss Derrida's position without having read or having badly read his works: it is too textually bound, it is too enclosed within language, it is hermetically sealed from the real world and real politics.

This often-remarked claim seems to miss the point entirely. Only two kinds of response are possible here: the first is to point out, as has been done many times before by Derrida and others, that this objection too closely identifies writing, and textuality, with the book—with writing in its vulgar sense—as the opposite of speech. Derrida talks of the writing of a world, the production of reality by the trace, by difference. Such a notion of writing cannot be understood literally (though it is no mere metaphor either) for it makes the world, objects, and relations possible and structures and gives this world and its contents meaning and value. Writing cannot be confined to the safe pages of formal texts, but must be seen to underlie and exceed the very structure of oppositional thought—whether "real" (the male/female opposition) or "textual" (e.g., the pervasive functioning of oppositional forms within the history of Western philosophy). Indeed the notion of writing Derrida develops underlies this very opposition that activism relies on to distinguish itself—the opposition between the real and the text. A second response, again developed by Derrida himself, is to problematize the presumed finality and givenness of what qualifies as politics, to ask what presumptions have already been made about what politics is and must be, to position politics as somehow outside of, beyond or other than deconstruction (and equally, what presumptions about deconstruction have set it up as somehow apolitical).[8] Deconstruction is a preeminently political set of maneuvres, capable of taking as its object the primary political concerns of the present—nuclear arms, the environment, the reorganization of Europe, the struggles of indigenous peoples, women, lesbians and gays—as any discourse, even if one does not always necessarily agree. Disagreement is itself a mode of political engagement.

If these represent serious misunderstandings of the deconstructive project associated with Derrida's name, it is perhaps now time to turn more directly to a couple of Derrida's central texts on the question of the ontological status of sexual difference, to see more precisely what he has to offer feminist theory and to what extent the general feminist nervousness surrounding his position is justified.

(69)

THE ONTOLOGY OF SEXUAL DIFFERENCE

The question of the ontological status of sexual difference is one of the most central issues facing feminist theory today. It provides probably the broadest way of raising the more "regional" questions of the status of the "given" in feminist thought, whether this is conceived in terms of the status of the female body, the origins of patriarchy, or the power of phallocentric discourses. To take the body as a particular example,[9] in other recent work I have asked the question that seems central for any corporeal feminism: what is the ontological status of the sexed body? Is the sexed body (a body presumably given by biology) the raw materials of modes of social inscription and production? Or do modes of social inscription produce the body as sexually specific? Which comes "first"— sexed bodies or the social markers of sexual difference? If feminists take patriarchy as a given term in feminist analysis, the question can always be asked—what is the origin or source of patriarchy? Is it men's natural strength, aggression, and competitiveness that produced a system of patriarchal domination over women; or did a system of patriarchal domination produce men's strength, etc., as the relevant explanatory factor in the devaluation of women's attributes? How could such questions be resolved? It is these constitutive types of feminist question that Derrida's analysis of the ontology of sexual difference may help to resolve or at least understand.

Derrida deals with the question of sexual difference largely indirectly, through his readings of various texts in which woman, femininity, or sexual difference function either as invisible but traceable supports (Heidegger) or as the explicit objects of secondarization or derision in a philosophical system (Levinas, Nietzsche). He does talk more directly about contemporary feminist movements, admittedly rather reluctantly and evasively, in some interviews.[10] His position must be teased out, for it resists any reading that seeks to place him firmly on either side of a divide between a pure, a- or pre-sexual ontology and an ontology that takes sexual difference as its first presumption or defining characteristic. In what follows, I will present a highly selective reading of some of Derrida's key texts on the ontology of sexual difference.

In his elaboration of Heidegger's relation to the question of sexual difference in "*Geschlecht*. Sexual Difference, Ontological Difference" (1983), one purpose is to raise the question "How do you think by those words [sexual difference] or through them?" (66), what does it mean, for example, to say that Heidegger speaks little (less than other philosophers) of sexual difference? How is one to recognize what it means to speak of sexual difference, especially if sexual difference is not reducible to the sexual identities of male and female? What is its referent if it is difference and not identity that is articulated? If Heidegger does not speak of sexual difference as such, it may nonetheless pervade his text, in spite of his attempts to keep it contained and beyond the scope of *Dasein*, despite his ambition to render *Dasein* neutral, clean, unbounded with the complications of sexuality and anthropological specificity. Basically, Heidegger seems committed to two positions that sit uneasily together, and whose tension will provoke a reexploration and reinterpretation of both.

On the one hand, Heidegger insists that *Dasein* is a neutral term, a term that must be stripped of its humanist, egoist, anthropomorphic associations and characteristics in order to be understood in terms of fundamental ontology, in terms prior to any concrete specification, at the origin of any particularity:

The peculiar *neutrality* of the term "Dasein" is essential, because the interpretation of this being must be carried out prior to every factual concretion.... Neutrality is not the voidness of an abstraction, but precisely the potency of the *origin*, which bears in itself the intrinsic possibility of every concrete factual humanity. (Heidegger, 1984: 136–37)

Dasein is thus construed as outside or beyond the reach of sexual difference, preceding it. It is being minus its sexual, cultural, historical, ethical, and political determinations, a pure relation, involving nothing but *Dasein*'s relation to itself: "This neutrality also indicates that *Dasein* is neither of the two sexes" (136).

On the other hand, in making *Dasein* the origin of things, of every concrete existence, including the human, through a kind of scattering or dispersion, in insisting that *Dasein* is not a negativity or abstraction, but is itself capable of corporeality, facticity, concreteness, Heidegger acknowledges for *Dasein* its inherent openness to sexual specificity and the centrality of sexual difference to *Dasein* in its very neutrality. Heidegger affirms that *Dasein* is the well or source of all concreteness, the "intrinsic possibility of every factual humanity" (137):

Neutral *Dasein* is never what exists; *Dasein* exists in each case only in its factical concretion. But neutral *Dasein* is indeed the primal source of intrinsic possibility that springs up in every existence and makes it intrinsically possible.... *Dasein* harbors the intrinsic possibility for being factically dispersed into bodiliness and thus into sexuality.... As factical, *Dasein* is, among other things, in each case disunited in a particular sexuality. (137)

Dasein in its neutrality, free of any predetermination, in its "pure" relations to itself, is nonetheless implicated in the dispersion or dissemination that comes to constitute the specificity, determinacy, and sexual coding of any (human) being. Sexual difference cannot spring from nothing; it is not an artificial imposition from outside, which, like logocentrism itself, can have no outside. *Dasein* contains within itself the very possibility of its dispersion into multiplicity, the very condition of the attribution or acquisition of any qualities or properties, including a sexual specification. *Dasein* is both what neutralizes all determination—including that implied by sexual difference—while at the same time providing the precondition and possibility of the sexual determination of things, humans. Derrida suggests that *Dasein* is not simply *neuter*, without trace of sexual markings, but rather that it *neutralizes* a prior sexual marking, that of the oppositional or binarized model of sexuality.

Derrida is very careful, in a number of texts, to distinguish (as he or

(71)

we may not in fact be capable of doing as clearly as he suggests) between sexual opposition and sexual difference, between a binary structuring of the relations between the sexes in term of presence and absence, positive and negative, and a non-binarized *differantial* understanding of the relations between the sexes, in which no single model can dictate or provide the terms for the representation, whether negative or positive, of all sexes. His reading stresses that Heidegger (and presumably also Derrida) actively distances himself from the model of sexual binarity, through the neutralizing activity of *Dasein*:

> Whether a matter of neutrality or asexuality, the words accentuate strongly a negativity.... By means of such manifestly negative predicates there should become legible what Heidegger doesn't hesitate to call a "positivity," a richness, and, in a heavily charged code, even a power. Such precision suggests that the a-sexual neutrality does not desexualize, on the contrary, its *ontological* negativity is not unfolded with respect to *sexuality itself* (which it would instead liberate), but on its differential marks, or more strictly on *sexual duality*...asexuality could be determined as such only to the degree that sexuality would mean immediate binarity or sexual division.... If *Dasein* as such belongs to neither of the two sexes, that doesn't mean that its being is deprived of sex. On the contrary, here one must think of a predifferential, rather a predual, sexuality—which doesn't necessarily mean unitary, homogeneous or undifferentiated. Then, from that sexuality, more originary than the dyad, one may try to think to the bottom a "positivity" and a "power...." (Derrida, 1983: 71–72)

In short, Derrida wants to claim that there is a sexuality more primordial than the binarized opposition between the sexes, a sexual difference that is neutral with respect to the sexes as they are currently or have been historically represented, a "raw material" out of which, through dispersion and splitting, sexual difference is rendered concrete and specific. This primordial sexuality *is*, as it were, *Dasein*, an order before sexual determination that is in itself sexual. There is, on the one hand, the indebtedness of sexual opposition to a neutral *Dasein*; and on the other hand, *Dasein* is the primordial status of sexuality before its determination in concrete form:

> There is not properly a sexual predicate: there is none at least that does not refer, for its sense, to the *general* structures of *Dasein*. So that to know what one speaks of, and how, when one names sexuality, one must indeed rely upon the very thing described in the analytic of *Dasein*. Inversely, if this be allowed, that disimplification allows the general sexuality or sexualization of discourse

to be understood: sexual connotations can only mark discourse, to the point of immersing it in them, to the extent that they are homogeneous to what every discourse implies.... (Derrida, 1983: 82)

The same sort of interests and concerns that appear in "*Geschlect*" are also evident in Derrida's reading of Levinas in "At This Very Moment in This Work Here I Am" (1991). Here he again interrogates the relations between a foundational concept—no longer *Dasein* but now the Levinasian absolute Other as articulated in *Totality and Infinity*—with the question of sexual difference. The same sorts of questions remain appropriate in this new context: is the absolute Other beyond or before sexual determination, or is sexual determination part of the very establishment of the concept of the Other (the Other as feminine)? Is sexual difference and femininity (and even the collapsing of sexual difference into femininity, as if only the feminine side of the opposition can represent difference) primary or secondary? As with his analysis of Heidegger, Derrida's goal is not to criticize or punish the Levinasian double-take on the question of sexual difference, but to show its unacknowledged reliance on precisely that which his model must refuse, deny, or cover over.

While on the one hand, unlike virtually an entire history of Western philosophy, Levinas seems prepared to write as masculine, as a man, an "I-he" as Derrida describes it, to sign (with) his masculine signature, to own up to the position of authority and articulation usually unmarked as male, but occupiable only by men; on the other hand, he participates in a certain effacement of the question of sexual difference, a certain investment in the phallocentric covering of women under the generic human: (73)

> I interrogate the link, in E.L.'s work, between sexual difference—the Other as the other sex, otherwise said as otherwise sexed—and the Other as wholly other, beyond or before sexual difference. To himself, his text marks its signature by a masculine "I-he".... His signature thus assumes the sexual mark, a remarkable phenomenon in the history of philosophical writing, if the latter has always been interested in occupying that position without re-marking upon it or assuming it, without signing its mark. But as well as this, E.L.'s work seems to me to have always rendered secondary, derivative, and subordinate, alterity as sexual difference, the trait of sexual difference, to the alterity of a sexually non-marked wholly other. (Derrida, 1991: 40) [11]

Derrida recognizes in the well-known gesture of neutralization, or humanization, the ruses of a masculine domination that leaves itself unmarked as such. The emptying out of particular determinations is a prerogative of the masculine position: where one says "it doesn't matter if it is he or she," the he is always already privileged as unmarked, a mode of prior determination of the she. Derrida raises what seems to me one of the central questions of feminist theory: "How can one mark as masculine the very thing said to be anterior, or even foreign, to sexual difference?" (1991, 40) Elsewhere he reformulates this question as one of the relation of primacy between sexual difference and difference: "Must one think 'difference' 'before' sexual difference or taking off 'from' it? Has this question, if not a meaning (we are at the origin of meaning here, and the origin cannot 'have meaning') at least something of a chance of opening up anything at all, however im-pertinent it may appear?" (Derrida and McDonald, 1985: 172.)

It is never clear, Derrida claims, if Levinas is simply commenting on or affirming certain biblical passages, such as those that claim that "woman," *Ichah*, is derived from "man," *Iche*. This equivocation runs through the whole of Derrida's reading: is there a clear-cut division between description and affirmation? Levinas *describes* (let us for the moment give him the benefit of the doubt) the attribution of a secondariness to woman. Man is prior to and generic—before the division of

the man-human from the woman-human—not of woman, but rather of sexual difference itself, which woman now comes to represent. Humanity in general, before its division into the two sexes, is sexually neutral, i.e., masculine. With the later advent of sexual difference comes woman. But like Heidegger's gesture of removing all trace of sexual difference from *Dasein* only to restore a (different) notion of sexual difference, so too Levinas both removes all traces of sexual specificity from his ontology, while at the same time seeking to retain an ontological base that is the ground of sexuality:

> Levinas indeed senses the risk factor involved in the erasure of sexual difference. He therefore maintains sexual difference: the human in general remains a sexual being. But he can only do so, it would seem, by placing (differentiated) sexuality beneath humanity.... That is, he simultaneously places...masculinity in command and at the beginning, on a par with the Spirit. This gesture carries with it the most self-interested of contradictions. (Derrida and McDonald, 1985: 178)

If the wholly Other is beyond all determination, then the wholly other cannot identify with the other sex, with femininity. The indifference of the relation with the Other, the relation that, for Levinas, precedes ontology and founds the domain of ethical difference—is prior to and the precondition of sexual difference. On the one hand, this gesture of the neutralization of the domain of the other is perhaps a necessary condition for the very existence of an ethics. Can there be an ethics between men and women that does not rely upon or presume a common or neutral ground, a ground that the sexes (or races) share, a ground that ethics fills? Does it even make sense to talk of an ethics for women and an ethics for men as different projects if one of the implications of an ethics is that it regulates relations between the different sexes? (This is indeed the kind of ethics Irigaray seeks: she is not looking for a women's ethic, a feminist ethic, a set of principles or prescriptions governing women's behavior, because such an ethics leaves women's relations to men, and men's relations to each other and to women completely untouched; instead, she is seeking an ethics of sexual difference, an ethics cognizant of the specificity and autonomy of each sex, one that can attain symbolic status.)

On the other hand, the attribution of the masculine pronoun to mark the wholly Other, to mark the domain of the ethical, is clearly an attempt to master and control, not simply the terms by which sexual difference is thought but the very conceptions of the feminine and of woman, which now have to take their place under the label of the "he." The problem here is not simply that Levinas encloses the feminine in a masculine/universal model, but that even the masculine subject has effaced the wholly other status of the Other, the fundamental openness to alterity that he also attributes to the masculine. In defining the Other in the terms of the masculine, Levinas in effect reduces this otherness, converting it into a version of the same, thus obliterating the very possibility, in his terms, of an ethics.[12]

A different version of his analysis of the relations between sexual binarity and sexual difference has also marked Derrida's much observed and contested interviews on the question of femininity and feminism. Instead of, as some have been tempted to do, affirming women's specificity through some reference to a kind independent authenticity, or positing women's subversive powers and capacities in some inarticulable beyond of language (as psychoanalysis tends to), Derrida refers both to the historical tenacity of the binary dividing the sexes, which prioritizes the masculine at the expense of the feminine (the implication being that it is not so easy to dislodge the privileged masculine term in order to put the feminine in its place) and to the logical openness of our capacity to understand sexual difference in terms other than the binary type of model.

Drucilla Cornell seems to actively affirm Derrida's advocacy of a sexuality outside or independent of the sexual duality:

> [I will] argue that the deconstruction of the conventional structures of gender identity as either biologically necessary or as culturally desirable not only does not erase the "reality" of women's suffering, but demands instead the affirmation of feminine sexual difference as irreducible to the dominant definition of the feminine within the gender hierarchy as man's other or his mirror image. In other words, sexual difference and more specifically feminine sexual difference, is not being erased; instead the rigid structures of gender identity which have devalued women and identified them with the patriarchal conventions of the gender hierarchy are being challenged. (Cornell, 1991: 281)[13]

It seems to me that Derrida is indeed interrogating the very conditions under which women have been attributed a secondary social status on the basis of biological, natural, or essential qualities; he is suggesting a fundamental indeterminacy of sexuality before the imposition of sexual difference (and presumably he must also be committed to the claim that this indeterminacy is not quite captured by the sexual identities of males and females, that it exerts a kind of resistance to binary reduction). In doing so, he is not simply or straightforwardly speaking as a woman or appropriating women's right to speak. Unlike the vast majority of other male philosophers, particularly those labelled "postmodern,"[14] Derrida takes feminist issues seriously; he doesn't dismiss them as minor or regional problems reducible to or subsumable under the resolution of other problems. Neither does he provide solutions for these issues insofar as feminism is not resolvable through the acquisition of certain specific rights and values, or through the enactment of a program or specific path. Indeed, with and through his reading of Nietzsche in *Spurs* (1979), he remains generally critical of an egalitarian feminism in which women seek formal and legal equality with men. Such a feminism, as he rightly suggests, aspires to make women like men; it is inherently reactive. He is quite explicit about differentiating this, which aspires no further than the emulation of men's accomplishments and positions from other, more active and positive forms:

> Can one not say, in Nietzsche's language, that there is a "reactive" feminism and that a certain historical necessity often puts this form of feminism in power in today's organized struggles? It is this kind of "reactive" feminism that Nietzsche mocks, and not woman or women. Perhaps one should not so much combat it head on—other interests would be at stake in such a move—as prevent its occupying the entire terrain. (Derrida and McDonald, 1985: 168)

This is not however to suggest that Derrida's work should be accepted wholesale as feminist or as readily compatible with and amenable to feminism. Two factors make this a difficult assertion. First, it seems to me that Derrida has a good deal to offer feminist theory that does not generally appear in feminist works (except those who have been strongly influenced by him). His work mounts a productive challenge to many of the underlying assumptions, values, and methods in much feminist writing. Insofar as he provides insights into what might be called the "politics of representation," his work is both other than and useful for feminist theory. Second, perhaps more problematically, there remain residual feminist problems with Derrida's work that are less serious than those raised by the feminists I discussed earlier, but which nonetheless mitigate too easy an identification with and acceptance of his positions.

I have in mind here a certain strategic ambiguity in Derrida's use of the notion of an indeterminate or undecidable sexuality, a sexuality before the imposition of dual sex roles, that is somehow ontological but entirely without qualities and attributes. Derrida hovers between two uses of the notion of sexuality, sometimes using one to evade the implications of the other. It is clear that sexuality, in the sense of "pleasurable drive," could quite valuably be understood as a mode of prior indeterminacy that gains its specific form and qualities *a posteriori*, and largely as an effect of binary polarization. It is not so easy to see how sexuality—in the sense of sexed subjectivity, male and female—can be understood as indeterminate.[15] By this I do not want to suggest that a ready division can be made between these two conceptions, for they are clearly bound up with each other—how one lives one's sexuality in the first sense depends on how one is sexed in the second sense.

This is what I presume that the framework of sexual difference implies: that there is an irreducible specificity of each sex relative to the other, that there must be at least, but not necessarily only two sexes. In short, one lives one's sexual indeterminacy, one's possibilities for being sexed otherwise differently depending on whether one is male or female. This is not, however, to predetermine how one "is" male or female, but simply to suggest that there is an ineradicable rift between the two, in whatever forms they are lived.[16] Unless such a presumption is made, sexual difference remains in danger of collapsing into a sexual neutrality of precisely the kind Derrida problematizes in Heidegger and Levinas. Derrida's dream of a multiplicity of "sexually marked voices" seems to me worthy of carefully consideration, as long as the question of the limits of possibility of each (sexed) body is recognized. Each sex has the capacity to (and frequently does) play with, become, a number of different sexualities; but not to take on the body and sex of the other:

The relationship would not be a-sexual, far from it, but would be sexual otherwise; beyond the binary difference that governs the decorum of all codes, beyond the opposition feminine/masculine, beyond bisexuality as well, beyond homosexuality and heterosexuality which come to the same thing.... I would like to believe in the multiplicity of sexually marked voices. I would like to believe in the masses, this indeterminate number of blended voices, this mobile of non-identified sexual marks whose choreography can carry, divide, multiply the body of each "individual," whether he be classified as "man" or as "woman" according to the criteria of usage. (Derrida and McDonald, 1985: 184)

DECONSTRUCTIVE POLITICS

Derrida does not offer any political solutions for either feminism or any other politics. This has tended to evoke suspicion. If he does not offer any solutions, if his goal is to demonstrate the complex and paradoxical nature of any political commitment—or for that matter any conceptual commitment—then it is commonly and naïvely assumed that his work is non-political, apolitical, or, worst of all, produces quietism, and is thus aligned with the forces of conservatism or even fascism. What is usually not recognized is that his work has the effect of rethinking entirely the ways in which politics and theory have been considered. This does not amount to the creation of a new political theory or epistemology, but the reordering—or perhaps the disordering—of the ways in which politics and theory have been understood. Politics can no longer be understood in terms of clear-cut heroes and villains, the politically correct position and its incorrect alternatives; that is, on the polarized model of pro or contra that has dominated and continues to dominate so much of feminist and leftist politics. Instead, things are now murkier: saying no to a political or conceptual structure can no longer remain unequivocal, unilaterally opposed to any (conservative) yes. It is implicated in a yes, it is implicitly *also* a yes. One cannot say no to the law, to requirement, to history, to power, without being committed at the same time to affirmation of precisely that which one wishes to deny.

Derrida is concerned to complicate politics, to make it no longer simply readable as the setting out of a clear-cut, unambiguous, solid set of guarantees. This necessarily disturbs those who seek to be reassured of the rightness of their positions in all contexts and in all situations. Indeed, I suspect that this was precisely the appeal of a vulgar marxism or feminism which claimed to provide a perspective from which to judge other political positions and claims without accepting the right in turn to be judged by them, to submit to their perspectives, to be assessed in terms of their adequacy or relevance to the situation. This amounts, in effect and fundamentally, to a wish to end politics, to stop contestation, to have an answer which admits of no complications and ramifications.[17] To know, to be right.

Such a will to silence others, to prevent contestation, to adjudicate once and for all and with definitive status, the rightness, the appropriateness, the truthfulness or justice of any position cannot be readily repudiated. In claiming a position, one must remain committed to its ability to explain, enact, produce and outperform its alternatives; that is, in a certain sense, to its "rightness," its "truth," its value over and above others. This is what it is to have a position. Yet this will to overpower, to master, to control, must undermine itself, must remain bound up with the very disturbances, and to what is unsettling to, uncontainable by it, its others. The no is always committed to a (prior and stronger) yes. In turn, the yes always contains within it a maybe, a quivering of uncertainty, an acknowledgement that even as one commits oneself to a position (whatever it might be) at the same time one is also committed to its undoing and surpassing. Such a yes cannot be said once and for all, to make room for a later no but must remain continuous, an eternal return of/as the yes, even as one is inclined, propelled to repudiate it. (It is in this sense that Derrida openly acknowledges his responsibility for and implication in the views not simply of his acolytes and faithful followers, those who follow in his spirit, who remain within his orbit of influence, but also, and more significantly, for the misreadings generated by his work.)

His complication of the political thus involves not only the acknowledgement of the complexities and ambiguities of any position (this formulation still implies the possibility of resolving or at least clarifying these complexities) but of the aporias, the irresolvably contradictory tensions within each claim, the impossibility of assigning a singular assessment and a definitive and settled value. This may explain why those who have pretensions to any political certainty or having answers for political issues seem so hostile to what deconstruction may offer in rethinking the political. They see Derrida's work as an alternative that competes with their own positions without having anything commensurable to offer by way of political solutions. All he offers are complications, modes of unsettling.

To return, finally, to the question of the ontological status of sexual difference. To presume either the one or the other side of this question— that is, the claim that ontology is sexually neutral and thus precedes sexual difference and the claim that sexual difference is ontological—necessarily involves the implication of the one in the other. If ontology is claimed to be sexually neutral, then it has to be shown how, out of such a neutrality, it is nevertheless able to generate sexual difference; how, in short, there must be always already a trace of sexual difference even within the postulation of an indifference. Equally, if sexual difference is one, if not the, ontological bedrock, nonetheless it must also be clear that sexual difference takes the forms in which we recognize it today only through a later inscription or production (a binary ordering) that both contains and retranscribes it. The ontological status of sexual difference implies a fundamental indeterminacy such that it must explain its openness, its incompleteness, and its possibilities of being completed, supplemented, by a (later) reordering.

The question remains inherently undecidable, which is not to say that it is unintelligible. One cannot opt for one side of an opposition without at the same time (whether wittingly or not) remaining implicated in and complicit with its opposite. This does not mean one must accept both sides as equal in value, nor that one must abandon the opposition altogether and produce a middle or compromise path between them. None of the binary oppositions structuring logocentric and phallocentric thought can simply be avoided, and no compromise between them is possible. One must accept the tangible and singular irresolvability of oppositions in their concrete contexts, and in contexts to come. I believe that this remains one of the great strengths rather than a weakening of feminist theory: not its closure of certain positions with which it disagrees, but its openness to its own retranscriptions and rewritings.

(PART TWO)

SPACE, TIME, AND BODIES

(5)

SPACE, TIME, AND BODIES

BODIES

Many of those disillusioned with conventional forms of philosophy and theories of subjectivity have recently turned their attention towards long neglected conceptions of embodiment. This has characterized recent work within feminist as well as other radical forms of political and social theory. Given the overwhelming emphasis on *mind* within classical and even contemporary philosophy, and *consciousness* in political and social theory, this growing interest in the corporeal has been largely motivated by an attempt to devise an ethics and politics adequate for non-dualist accounts of subjectivity. Seeing that the subject's consciousness or interiority, its essential humanity or unique individuality, can no longer provide a foundation or basis for accounts of identity, it is appropriate to ask whether subjectivity, the subject's relations with others (the domain of ethics), and its place in a socio-natural world (the domain of politics), may be better understood in corporeal rather than conscious terms.

It is not enough to reformulate the body in non-dualist and non-essentialist terms. It must also be reconceived in specifically *sexed* terms. Bodies are never simply *human* bodies or *social* bodies. The sex assigned to the body (and bodies are assigned a single sex, however inappropriate this may be) makes a great deal of difference to the kind of social subject, and indeed the mode of corporeality assigned to the subject. It has been the task of the so-called "French feminists," sometimes described as "feminists of difference," to insist on recognition of the differences between sexes (and races and classes) and to question the assumed humanity and universality of prevailing models of subjectivity.

Kristeva, with her insistence on recognition of the receptacle, *chora*, as a debt that representation owes to what it cannot name or represent, to its maternal and spatial origins, and Irigaray's claims about the specificity of female morphology and its independence from and resistance to the penetration of masculine scrutiny, provide two of the earliest feminist explorations of conceptions of sexed corporeality, and the links between corporeality and conceptions of space and time, which may prove to be of major significance in feminist researches into women's experiences, social positions, and knowledges.

While providing a starting point for reconceiving the ways in which sexed subjects are understood, Kristeva and Irigaray have merely opened up a terrain that needs further exploration. If bodies are to be reconceived, not only must their *matter and form* be rethought, but so too must their environment and *spatio-temporal location*. This essay is a preliminary investigation of the space-time of bodies. At the same time, it may contribute to feminist interrogations of some of the guiding presumptions within the natural sciences—especially physics—and for the social sciences, insofar as they take the natural sciences as their epistemic ideal.

The exploration of conceptions of space and time as necessary correlates of the exploration of corporeality. The two sets of interests are defined in reciprocal terms, for bodies are always understood within a spatial and temporal context, and space and time remain conceivable only insofar as corporeality provides the basis for our perception and representation of them. The following is not written in the language of physics; rather, it is an attempt to assess conceptions of space/time from the point of view of the sexually specific embodiment of subjects.

PSYCHOANALYSIS AND CORPOREALITY

Psychoanalysis has a good deal to say about how the body is lived and positioned as a spatio-temporal being. The way the subject locates itself in/as a body is of major interest to psychoanalysis as it assumes that sexual drives and erotogenic zones of the body are instrumental in the formation of the ego and the positioning of the subject in the structure of the family and society as a whole. Freud is explicit in claiming that the (narcissistic) ego is the consequence of libidinal relations between the child and its erotic objects. The ego's identifications with others, particularly the mother, secure for it the illusion of a corporeal coherence that its own lived experience belies. Through its fantasized identity with others, it is able to take up the body as *its* body, to produce a separating space between it and others, between it and objects.

Freud claims that the ego's outline is a psychical map or project of the surface of the body, that provides the basis of the subject's assumption that it is coextensive with the whole of its body: "...for every change of erotogenicity of the organs, there might be a parallel change in the erotogenicity of the ego" (Freud, 1914: 84).

The form the ego takes is not determined by purely psychical functions, but is an effect of the projection of the erotogenic intensity experienced through libidinal bodily zones. He illustrates his claim with the metaphor of the cortical homunculus, the "little man" located in the cortex, as a map for the brain to control the body:

> The ego is first and foremost a bodily ego; it is not merely a surface entity, but is itself the projection of a surface. if we wish to find an anatomical analogy for it we can best identify it with the "cortical homunculus" of the anatomists, which stands on its head in the cortex, sticks up its heels, faces backwards and, as we know, has its speech area on the left-hand side. (Freud, 1923: 26)

To reiterate the nature of this corporeal contribution to the formation of the ego and consciousness, in a footnote added in 1927 to the above fragment, Freud expands:

> ...i.e., the ego is ultimately derived from bodily sensations, chiefly those springing from the surface of the body. It may thus be regarded as a mental projection of the surface of the body, besides...representing the superficies of the mental apparatus. (84)

While noting this peculiar interaction between body and mind—in which the mind can achieve psychical results only through the mediation of the body and in which the body finds its satisfactions in the fantasies

(85)

and scenarios of the psyche—Freud himself does little to develop this insight. It remains central to his understanding of narcissism and the narcissistic ego, but only through Jacques Lacan's work on the mirror stage (suggested by Freud's cortical homunculus metaphor) have corporeality and spatiality been related to the construction of personal identity, and the challenge to philosophical dualism undertaken head on.

Where Freud posits a schism between the information provided by visual and tactile perceptions in the young child (1923: 25), Lacan uses the opposition between tactile and kinaesthetic information (which yields the fragmented image of the body-in-bits-and-pieces) and visual perception (which provides the illusory unity of the image as an ideal model or mirror for the subject) to explain the genesis of an always alienated ego. The ego forms itself round the fantasy of a totalized and mastered body, which is precisely the Cartesian fantasy modern philosophy has inherited.

Lacan maintains that the infant's earliest identity comes from its identification with its own image in a mirror. The specular or virtual space of mirror-doubles is constitutive of whatever imaginary hold the ego has on identity and corporeal autonomy. The child's alienated mirror-image

> ...will crystallise in the subject's internal conflictual tension, which determines the awakening of his desire for the object of the other's desire: here the primordial coming together (*concours*) is precipitated into aggressive competitiveness (*concurrence*), from which develops the triad of others, the ego and the object, which, spanning the space of specular communion, is inscribed there.... (Lacan, 1977a: 19)

Lacan develops his understanding of the *imaginary anatomy* largely in his account of the mirror-stage. Like the homunculus, this too is a psychical map of the body, a mirror of the subject's lived experiences, not as an anatomical and physiological object, but as a social and psychical entity. This imaginary anatomy is an effect of the internalization of the specular image, and reflects social and familial beliefs about the body more than it does the body's organic nature:

> If the hysterical symptom is a symbolic way of expressing a conflict between different forces...to call these symptoms functional is but to confess our ignorance, for they follow a pattern of a certain imaginary anatomy which has typical forms of its own.... I would emphasise that the imaginary anatomy referred to here varies with the ideas (clear or confused) about bodily functions which are prevalent in a given culture. It all happens as if the body-image

had an autonomous existence of its own, and by autonomous I mean here independent of objective structure. All the phenomena we've been discussing seem to exhibit the laws of Gestalt.... (Lacan, 1953: 13)

Lacan explicitly refers to the work of Roger Caillois and Paul Schilder who, in quite different ways, analyze the effects of the image on the subject's acquisition of spatial comportment. I will turn to their work in a later section. Lacan himself asserts that the specular image with which the child identifies exhibits the characteristics of mirror reversal, made up as it is by "a contrasting size *(un relief de stature)* that fixes it and in a symmetry that inverts it" (Lacan, 1977a: 2). He stresses that the mirror *Gestalt* not only presents the subject with an image of its own body in a visualized exteriority, but also duplicates the environment, placing real and virtual space in contiguous relations. The mirror-image is thus indeed, as Lacan claims, "the threshold of the visible world" (1977a: 3).

The most psychical of agencies, the ego, is thus an unrecognized effect of the image of the body, both its own body and the bodies of others. Lacan returns to Freud's homunculus with his suspicion that "the cerebral cortex functions like a mirror, and that it is the site where the images are integrated in the libidinal relationship which is hinted at in the theory of narcissism" (1953: 13). The "cortical mirror" is a psychological rather than physiological or neurological postulate, although it is clear that Lacan's account owes much to the work of pioneers in neurological mappings of the body-image (Hughlings Jackson, Weir Mitchell, Head, Goldstein, Pick, and others). The body, lived in a "natural" or "external" space, must also find psychical representation in a purely psychical or conceptual space in order for concerted action and psychical reactions to be possible. Lacan never reduces psychological to physiological explanation.

Lacan gives no further details about the form and nature of this psychical map; he simply suggests that it is an integral factor in the acquisition of an ego, and in establishing a conception of space and time. He is clear about the crucial role the body-image plays in the subject's capacity to locate itself and its objects in space:

> ...we have laid some stress on this phenomenological detail, but we are not unaware of the importance of Schilder's work on the function of the body-image, and the remarkable accounts he gives of the extent to which it determines the perception of space. (1953: 13)

THE BOUNDARIES OF CORPOREALITY

Many of Lacan's key insights linking the ego to the structure of space through the mediation of an imaginary anatomy, are derived from or influenced by the astonishing work of the French sociologist, Roger Caillois. Caillois's work—which breaches the boundaries between the sacred and the profane, the sociological and the ethological, the human and the animal or even the inorganic, the inside and the outside—seems to entice Lacan, not merely because what Caillois suggests may be of indirect relevance to psychoanalysis, but perhaps more tellingly, because of Caillois's obsession with bringing together science and the uncanny, for pursuing projects verging on the eccentric or idiosyncratic with scientific rigor clearly parallel to, and to some extent anticipating, Lacan's fascination with psychoanalysis.

Caillois's research into the notion of spatiality occurs in the context of his analysis of the phenomenon of mimicry in the insect world. He presents a paradoxically sociological/entomological analysis of the behavior of insects in imitating either other insects or their natural environment. Mimesis is particularly significant in outlining the ways in which the relations between an organism and its environment are blurred and confused—the way in which its environment is not clearly distinct from the organism but is an active component of its identity. Caillois claims, in opposition to prevailing entomology, that mimicry does not serve an adaptive function by making recognition of the insect by its predators more difficult. Mimicry does not have survival value. In fact, most predators rely on smell rather than visual perception in seeking out their prey:

> Generally speaking, one finds many remains of mimetic insects in the stomachs of predators. So it should come as no surprise that such insects sometimes have other and more effective ways to protect themselves.
>
> Conversely, some species that are inedible and would thus have nothing to fear, are also mimetic. It therefore seems that one ought to conclude with Cuénot that this is an "epiphenomenon" whose "defensive utility appears to be nul." (Caillois, 1984: 24–25)

Caillois considers it an exorbitance, an excess over natural survival, inexplicable in terms of protection or species-survival. It is for this reason he abandons neurological and naturalistic explanations and seeks some kind of answer in psychology. Caillois goes on to argue that not only does mimicry have no particular survival value but may even endanger an insect that would otherwise be safe from predators:

We are thus dealing with a luxury and even a dangerous luxury, for there are cases in which mimicry causes the creature to go from bad to worse: geometer-moth caterpillars simulate shoots of shrubbery so well that gardeners cut them with their pruning shears. The case of the Phyllia is even sadder: they browse among themselves, taking each other for real leaves, in such a way that one might accept the idea of a sort of collective masochism leading to mutual homophagy, the simulation of the leaf being a provocation to cannibalism in this kind of totem feast. (Caillois, 1984: 25)

The mimicry characteristic of certain species of insects has to do with the distinctions and confusions it produces between itself and its environment, including other species. Mimicry is a consequence of the *representation* of space, the way space is perceived (by the insect and by its predators). Caillois likens the insect's ability for morphological imitation to the psychosis Pierre Janet describes as "legendary psychasthenia," that state in which the psychotic is unable to locate him- or herself in a position in space:

It is with represented space that the drama becomes specific, since the living creature, the organism, is no longer the origin of the coordinates, but one point among others; it is dispossessed of its privilege and literally *no longer knows where to place itself.* One can recognize the characteristic scientific attitude and, indeed, it is remarkable that represented spaces are just what is multiplied by contemporary science: Finsler's spaces, Fermat's spaces, Riemann-Christoffel's hyperspace, abstract, generalized, open and closed spaces, spaces dense in themselves, thinned out and so on. The feeling of personality, considered as the organism's feeling of distinctness from its surroundings, of the connection between consciousness and a particular point in space, cannot fail under these conditions to be seriously undermined; one then enters into the psychology of psychasthenia, and more specifically of *legendary psychasthenia,* if we agree to use this name for the disturbance in the above relations between personality and space. (Caillois, 1984: 28, emphasis in the original)

Caillois regards psychasthenia as a response to the lure posed by space for the subject's identity. For the subject to take up a position as a subject, he[1] must be able to situate himself as a being located in the space occupied by his body. This anchoring of subjectivity in *its* body is the condition of coherent identity, and, moreover, the condition under which the subject *has a perspective* on the world, becomes the point from which vision emanates. In certain cases of psychosis, this meshing of self and body, this unification of the subject, fails to occur. The psychotic is unable to locate himself where he should be; he may look at himself from

(89)

outside himself, as another might; he may hear the voices of others in his head. He is captivated and replaced by space, blurred with the positions of others:

> *I know where I am, but I do not feel as though I'm at the spot where I find myself.* To these dispossessed souls, space seems to be a devouring force. Space pursues them, encircles them, digests them in a gigantic phagocytosis. It ends by replacing them. Then the body separates itself from thought, the individual breaks the boundary of his skin and occupies the other side of his senses. He tries to look at *himself* from any point whatever in space. He feels himself becoming space, *dark space where things cannot be put.* He is similar, not similar to something, *but just similar.* And he invents spaces of which he is the "convulsive possession." (30)

Psychosis is the human analogue of mimicry in the insect world (which may thus be conceived as a kind of natural psychosis?): both represent what Caillois describes as the "depersonalization by assimilation to space." This means that both the psychotic and the imitative insect renounce their rights, as it were, to occupy a perspectival point, instead abandoning themselves to being spatially located by/ as others. The primacy of one's own perspective is replaced by the gaze of another for whom the subject is merely *a* point in space, and not *the* focal point around which an ordered space is organized. The representation of space is thus a correlate of one's ability to locate oneself as the point of origin or reference of space: the space represented is a complement of the kind of subject who occupies it.

Schilder, Guillaume, and Spitz confirm Caillois's assertions about the function of mimicry in insects, not by looking at psychosis, but by reflecting on the "normal," i.e., developmental, processes operating within the child's imitations of others, a central activity in its acquisition of a social and sexual identity. Imitation in children is an act of enormous intellectual complexity, for it involves both the confusion and the separation of the imitated acts of others and one's own imitative actions. It is so complex because, in the evaluation of whether one's own actions are the same as those being imitated, the subject would have to look at itself from the point of view of another. In assuming that it is *like* others, the child's identity is captured or assimilated by the gaze and visual field of the other. Imitation is conditioned by the child's acquisition of an image of itself, of an other, and a categorical assimilation of both to a similar general type. Guillaume makes explicit the connections between the child's imitative behaviour and its conceptions of space:

One may therefore conclude that the infant gradually constructs a visual image of his body and movements, even if he has never happened to contemplate them in a mirror. As the image becomes more specific, it will become assimilated with the objective perception of the human body, of others. Imitation therefore will be founded on assimilation that will be only a specific instance of the development of the idea of space. (Guillaume, 1971: 84)

Merleau-Ponty's researches in the phenomenology of lived space have strong affinities with Caillois's text, as well as with Lacan's account of the mirror-stage. He speculates that there must be a distinct stage in the infant's development in which the opposition between virtual and real space does not exist. It is only on this condition that it is able to identify with its mirror-image and, at the same time, to distinguish itself from the image, that is, recognize that the image is an image of itself.

The child knows well that he is where his introspective body is, and yet in the depth of the mirror he sees the same being present, in a bizarre way, in a visible appearance. There is a mode of spatiality in the specular image that is altogether distinct from adult spatiality. In the child, says Wallon, there is a kind of space clinging to the image. All images tend to present themselves in space, including the image of the mirror as well. According to Wallon, "his spatiality of adherence" will be reduced by intellectual development. We will learn gradually to return the specular image to the introspective body, and reciprocally, to treat the quasi-locatedness and prespatiality of the image as an appearance that counts for nothing against the unique space of real things.... An ideal space would be substituted for the space clinging to the images. It is necessary in effect, that the new space be ideal, since, for the child it is a question of understanding that what seems to be in different places is in fact in the same place. This can occur only in passing to a higher level of spatiality that is no longer the intuitive space in which the images occupy their place. (Merleau-Ponty, 1964: 129–30)

Within the first six months of its life, the child accedes to at least three different concepts of space: a spatiality based on the immediacy of its sensations, primarily tactile, oral, and auditory sense-perceptions; a spatiality based on the primacy of the information provided by sight; and, a spatiality that orders these experiences of space according to the hierarchical privilege of the visual, which is a unified manifold, an overarching space capable of positioning the tactile and the spatial within a single frame.

While he provides a detailed account of the subject's lived experiences of space—the subject's comportment in space, Merleau-Ponty is also interested in analyzing scientific judgements and theoretical paradigms that represent space. For him, the lived experience of space and the spatiality of science cannot be readily separated, insofar as the "objective space" of scientific speculation can only have meaning and be transmitted according to the subject's lived experience of space. In this sense, he affirms Bergson's philosophy of duration over Einstein's theory of relativity. Bergson attended Einstein's lecture, delivered to the Philosophical Society of Paris on April 6, 1922, and they disagreed about whether the theory of relativity implies that there is no single temporality within which multiple or fragmented forms of temporality are to be located. In opposition to Einstein, Bergson argued:

> ...there is a single time for everyone, one single universal time. This certainly is not undercut, it is even presupposed, by the physicist's calculations. When he says that Peter's time is expanded or contracted at the point where Paul is located, he is in no way expressing what is lived by Paul, who for his part perceives things from his point of view and has no reason whatsoever to experience the time elapsing within and around him than Peter experiences his. The physicist wrongly attributes to Paul the image Peter forms of Paul's time. He absolutizes the views of Paul, with which he makes common cause. He assumes he is the whole world's spectator.... He speaks of a time which is not yet anyone's time, of a myth. (Bergson, quoted in Merleau-Ponty, 1964: 195–96)

The subject's relation to space and time is not passive: space is not simply an empty receptacle, independent of its contents; rather, the ways in which space is perceived and represented depend on the kinds of objects positioned "within" it, and more particularly, the kinds of relation the subject has to those objects. Space makes possible different kinds of relations but in turn is transformed according to the subject's affective and instrumental relations with it. Nothing about the "spatiality" of space can be theorized without using objects as its indices. A space empty of objects has no representable or perceivable features, and the spatiality of a space containing objects reflects the spatial characteristics of those objects, but not the space of their containment. It is our positioning within space, both as the point of perspectival access to space, and also as an object for others in space, that gives the subject a coherent identity and an ability to manipulate things, including its own body parts, in space. However, space does not become comprehensible to the subject by its being the space of movement; rather, it becomes space through movement, and as such, it acquires specific properties from the subject's constitutive functioning in it.

For Merleau-Ponty, the subject's relation to its own body provides it with basic spatial concepts by which it can reflect on its position. Form and size, direction, centeredness (centricity), location, dimension, and orientation are derived from perceptual relations. These are not conceptual impositions on space, but our ways of living as bodies in space. They derive from the particular relations the subject has to objects and events; for example, its perceptions of sounds (sound is a better index of spatiality than sight insofar as it is detachable from its object, yet must, in a sense, be located "somewhere"). Their correlation with tactile and visual sensations forms the basic ideas of localization and orientation; place and position are defined with reference to the apparent immediacy of a lived here-and-now. These are not reflective or scientific properties of space but are effects of the necessity that we live and move in space as bodies in relation to other bodies.

THE SPACE-TIME OF PHYSICS
NEWTONIAN SPACE-TIME

The history of philosophy is strewn with speculations about the nature of space and time, which form among the most fundamental categories of ontology. Aristotle devised his theory of space and time in opposition to Plato. Plato identified time with movement, especially with the revolution of celestial bodies. Aristotle posed two major objections to this view: first, changes or processes are always located in space, but one is not entitled to say that therefore time is also located in space; second, he claimed that movement is fast or slow, while time itself has no speed, for it is itself the measure of the speed or movement of an object. Plato conceived of space as a kind of primordial matter, an original substratum. Aristotle interprets Plato to be equating space with a container or receptacle, chora: "Hence, Plato in the Timaeus says that matter and a receptacle are the same thing. For that which is capable of receiving and a receptacle are the same thing" (Aristotle, 1970 (Bk IV): 4).

For Aristotle, by contrast, space cannot be identified with matter, for it could not be a receptacle for any or all material things. Yet, if it is immaterial, it is not purely ideal or conceptual either, for space has magnitude and is amenable to measurement. For Aristotle, space has (at least) three essential characteristics—it is infinite (or at least infinitely extendable); it is empty, for it is only on this condition that it is capable of containing objects or things; and it is real, an extension that is uncreated, indestructible, and immobile. In analogous fashion, time is linked to motion: time is the measure of before and after with respect to motion (where space is the measure of the here or there of motion); like space, time is infinite or eternal and continuous, and is thus infinitely divisible in numerical terms; it too is real but, unlike space, its reality is linked to the possibility of counting. Finally, time is evenly distributed and an absolute reality, a reflection of the absolute regularity of the motion of heavenly bodies. Time's characteristics are thought in terms of the projection of those of space.

Aristotelian ontology is supported and confirmed by Euclidean geometry, which, until the nineteenth century, provided the most powerful and convincing model of the universality, regularity, and measurability of space and, by extension, time. Among the most appealing features of Euclidean geometry is its axiomatic method, which makes it a deductive system, guaranteeing validity independent of empirical confirmation. Its axiomatic form has in the past acted as a paradigm for scientific certainty, an ideal form of knowledge, which is self-contained, a coherent system in principle knowable, with a finite set of basic assumptions and rules for generating potentially infinite propositions, the closest measure of the dreamt-of "synthetic *a priori*." Using a few of these axioms or definitions, all the spatial conclusions are capable of being deduced through logical operations.

Since Euclid, geometry has been intimately connected to conceptions of space, and has at times considered itself a pure mathematical mode of representing space. Kant, strongly influenced by the way in which Euclid demonstrated that reason alone, independent of sense-perception, is capable of providing knowledge, used Euclid's postulates to show that we have a necessary knowledge of geometry prior to any experience.

For Kant, time and space are the pure forms of perception imposed on appearances in order to make them accessible to experience. Space and time are necessary structures, ideal rather than real, that are the conditions of possibility for the experience of objects. Euclidean geometry can be counterposed with Newtonian physics, and Kant's understanding correlates and counterparts their conceptions of knowledge.

Euclid's mathematization and axiomatization of space permitted space to be considered homogeneous, universal, and regular. Perhaps more importantly, Euclidean geometry enabled all the various conceptions of space (those, for example, prevalent in medieval or pre-perspectival space) to be represented according to a single, definitive model. This provided the conditions necessary for a generally agreed upon method of representation, through which a more "scientific" account of space might be possible—a Kuhnian paradigm shift at the threshold of modern science. Newton's laws of motion are an attempt to apply Euclidean geometry to mechanics, to the movement of bodies.

Like Euclid, Newtonian mechanics postulates an *a priori* system, governed by axioms or first principles, from which conclusions can be logically derived.[2] Like Euclidean geometry, it was not based on observation of empirical objects, for no empirical object could adequately represent the straightness of a geometrical line, the perfection of a geometric circle, nor the frictionlessness of the contact between Newtonian bodies. These are not scientific rules induced from a large number of observations, but self-contained rational principles, by which space and movement can be represented in their perfection.

Newtonian mechanics, like Euclidean geometry, reduces temporal relations to spatial form insofar as the temporal relations between events are represented by the relations between points on a straight line. Even today the equation of temporal relations with the continuum of numbers assumes that time is isomorphic with space, and that space and time exist as a continuum, a unified totality. Time is capable of representation only through its subordination to space and spatial models. Even if the linear temporality of Newtonian mechanics is disputed, more contemporary representations of time by topological closed curves still rely on geometrical and fundamentally spatial models for their coherence.

EINSTEINIAN CONCEPTIONS OF SPACE, TIME, AND RELATIVITY

Euclidean geometry's primacy as a mode of spatial representation was challenged by the advent of various non-Euclidean geometries that emerged during the eighteenth century. In 1764, Thomas Reid formulated a geometry based on the three-dimensionality of space, claiming that Euclidean geometry was relevant only to two-dimensional space. His privileged geometrical "object" was the sphere where, in a sense, Euclid's had been the triangle. Hyperbolic geometry (such as Reid, Gauss, Bolyai, and Lobachevsky developed) theorized about the nature of surfaces rather than flat spaces; from Gauss's theory of the geometry of surfaces, Reimann developed spherical geometry, which rejects the parallelism postulate of Euclid,[3] claiming that there is no line parallel to any other. Moreover, he postulated that any two lines have two distinct points in common, not one, as Euclid claimed.[4] Reimannian geometry enabled spaces of n-dimensions to be theorized, and this work enabled geometry to claim a much closer affinity to the production of empirical (rather than *a priori*) truths about the world, especially those theorized by physics. Reimann claimed that the geometrical properties of infinitely small bodies depend on the physical forces or fields (such as gravity), which provide their context.

Reimann defined space in terms of its dimensionality. For him, an n-dimensional space can be defined as one in which each position can be characterized by a set of coordinates. Such a space can be mapped, graphically and mathematically represented, defined in its particular qualities and attributes diagrammatically or formulaically. The assignment of coordinates reflects or can be redefined in terms of the topological properties of space.

For Newton, matter and its qualities are the determining factors in physics; for Einstein, in contrast, it is space that determines the presence of matter. Where Newton conceived of matter as located at points in space and time, Einstein's theory of relativity conceives of matter located within a space-time field. Einstein's theory was largely a physico-mathematical attempt to apply the principle of relativity to electromagnetic fields (Special Theory of Relativity), to gravitational and inertial movements (General Theory of Relativity), and to unify the mathematical expressions of electromagnetic and gravitational fields into one simple equation (Unified Field Theory). What Einstein rejects most forcefully of Newton's conception of space and time is its commitment to understanding space and time as separate and physically independent, autonomous entities.

Einstein, then, formulated a theory to describe the relationship of energy to mass, directly connecting mathematics to physics. In place of the Euclidean grid in which Newton's conjectures were developed, Einstein relied on topological representations of space in which shape is not relevant, where one shape can be transformed into another. The difference between a cube and a sphere are irrelevant:

> ...plane topology looks into whatever properties of figures would be unchanged if they were drawn on a rubber sheet which was then distorted in arbitrary ways without cutting the sheet or joining parts of it. (Nerlich, 1976: 87)

Boltzman, one of Einstein's predecessors, specifically linked space and time together in an indissoluble unity with his formulation of the principle of entropy. This principle implies that in physical processes, the movement of bodies is temporally irreversible. In themselves, the laws of mechanics do not entail the irreversibility of processes; they are indifferent to time. Space is said to be *isotropic* insofar as its relations are considered symmetrical. In the case of time, however, there is the common everyday belief in the "arrow of time," in time's directionality. Through the principle of entropy, time can be considered *anisotropic*, for the relations of before and after are regulated. The principle of entropy posits that self-contained systems of matter tend towards randomness, breaking down systematic connections over time. The thermodynamic entropy of a physical system confirms everyday conceptions of the progressivity of time: entropy increases over time. Entropy is the measure of the disorder of molecular particles and thus the increase of time corresponds with progressive disorder within the closed system.

In Einstein's reconceptualization, space, time and matter are interconnected and interdefined, relative terms. Space is n-dimensional, curved and relative to the objects within it. The mass or energy of objects is relative to their position within space (and in relation to other objects) at a certain time. While it is not within the frame of this paper to discuss the technical details or the relevance to physics of Einstein's work, it is worth signalling that through the development of non-Euclidean geometries and post-Newtonian physics, not only does our everyday understanding of space and time change, but a proliferation of different models of space-time, different kinds of space (and time) with different properties circulate. None have a universally accepted scope nor domination of the whole field of geometry or physics. Mathematical and scientific formulations of space-time become localized, relevant to the operations of specific types of object (subatomic particles, molecules, objects, etc.) and of specific properties (dimensionality rather than shape, space rather than lines, orientations rather than enclosed spaces). This rich pluralism of representations is not necessarily aligned to the primacy of the visual (as in Euclidean geometry), nor to the perception of matter, but enables a multiplicity of (sometimes) incommensurable models of space and time to be explored. This is not quite a situation of "anything goes," as Feyerabend suggests, but nevertheless, there is no final arbiter of which model will attain primacy.

(97)

SPACE, TIME, AND BODIES

The history of scientific, mathematical, and philosophical conceptions of space and time have witnessed a number of major transformations, some of which have dramatically effected the ways in which our basic ontologies are conceived. The kinds of world we inhabit, and our understanding of our places in these worlds are to some extent an effect of the ways in which we understand space and time. Two features of our historically determined conceptions of space and time are relevant to the concerns of this essay: the first is that representations of space have always had—and continue to have—a priority over representations of time. Time is represented only insofar as it is attributed certain spatial properties. The second is that there is an historical correlation between the ways in which space (and to a lesser extent, time) is represented, and the ways in which subjectivity represents itself.

First, then, the domination of time by space. This problem has no ready-made or clear-cut justification: space is no more "tangible" or perceptible than time, for it is only objects in space and time which can be considered tangible and amenable to perception. Space is no more concrete than time, nor is it easier to represent. The subject is no more clearly positioned in space than in time; indeed, the immediacy of the "hereness" of corporeal existence is exactly parallel to the "nowness" of the subject's experience. Phenomenology gives us no clear experiential preference for one dimension over the other. Perhaps it was the advent of geometry which conferred scientific and philosophical dignity on space at the expense of time. There was no analogous system to impose the rigors of method onto temporality.

Temporality is no less amenable to mathematical formulation; indeed, the phenomenon of counting provides the most pervasive of all notions of temporal duration and direction. Yet the formulation of principles and laws regarding the nature of time and its qualities occurs only when time is linked to space in a space-time continuum. Indeed, Bergson has frequently remarked on the subordination of temporality to spatiality, and consequently the scientific misrepresentation of duration. Time has been represented in literature and poetry more frequently and ably than in science. Questions about mutability and eternity are raised in philosophical speculation long before they were addressed scientifically, their stimulus coming from theology as much as from mechanics. The history of philosophy has thus far concentrated on two forms of temporality, one linear, progressive, continuing, even, regulated, and teleological (perhaps best represented by Hegel); the other circular, repetitive, and thus infinite (perhaps best represented by Nietzsche). The first form is best represented by a line, which can be divided into infinite units (recognizing time-measurement as arbitrary); the second, by a circle, which is capable of being traversed infinitely, in repetitions that are in some ways different, and in other ways the same.

In either case, temporality is defined as a relation of addition rather than one of order, in terms of numerical units rather than as a progression—as "1, 2, 3" rather than "first, second, third." It is considered as more psychical and somehow less objective than space. If Irigaray is correct in her genealogy of space-time in ancient theology and mythology, space is conceived as a mode (indeed God's mode) of exteriority, and time as the mode of interiority (Irigaray, 1993a: 18). In Kant's conception, too, while space and time are *a priori* categories we impose on the world, space is the mode of apprehension of exterior objects, and time a mode of apprehension of the subject's own interior. This may explain why Irigaray claims that in the West time is conceived as masculine (proper to a subject, a being with an interior) and space is associated with femininity (femininity being a form of externality to men). Woman is/provides space for man, but occupies none herself. Time is the projection of his interior, and is conceptual, introspective. The interiority of time links with the exteriority of space only through the position of God (or his surrogate, Man) as the point of their mediation and axis of their coordination.

This links the domination of conceptions of time by representations of space with the second point: that the representations of space and time are in some sense correlated with representations of the subject. This occurs both developmentally (as I argued in Part 2) and historically. Developmentally, the child perceives and is organized with reference to a series of spatial conceptions, from its earliest access to the "space of adherence" to the virtual space of mirror-images, the curved and plural spaces of dreams and the spatiality conferred by the primacy of vision. Historically, it can be argued (although I do not have the space to do so here) that as representations of subjectivity changed, so too did representations of space and time. If space is the exteriority of the subject and time its interiority, then the ways this exteriority and interiority are theorized will effect notions of space and time.

Le Doeuff, for example, argues that the kind of subject presupposed in the time of Shakespeare and Galileo is a notion divided between an absolute (and thus non-individualized) identity and a wholly particularized "personality" (Le Doeuff, 1986). The notion of subjectivity in which the subject reflects universal or cosmic affinities, as well as individualized particularities, is the correlative of the Galilean conception of time as it is formulated in the law of failing bodies, $V=dt$, (velocity = distance over time):

> The Galilean law supposes a capitalisation of the past, the falling body cumulatively acquiring degrees of speed, or undergoing a perpetual augmentation of speed.... Let us think of the way a loan with simple interest is defined (I am not speaking here of loans with compound interest, since that would involve exponentials): x per cent per annum on a one year loan; $2x$ percent on a two-year loan, etc. Labour hired by the hour obeys the same schema, as do all our practices of rent, hire, etc. It is not difficult to convince oneself that this social usage of time is strictly modern. (Le Doeuff, 1989: 42–43)

Le Doeuff's general point is the interdependence of scientific thought and prevalent social and cultural conceptions: she investigates how Galileo could have (correctly) formulated the law of failing bodies using time rather than space as a point of reference, when space seems more self-evident as a fixed reference point within the scientific context of his culture. Her point is that Galileo could not have formulated his law without relying on pre- and non-scientific notions of temporality. And in turn, the principles governing his law were able to be comprehended and understood by other scientists and educated non-specialists because they accorded with everyday notions of time.

The same could be said of Newtonian and Einsteinian conceptions of space: they accord with contemporary notions of subjectivity and social life. This correlation is, in all likelihood, dialectical: conceptions of the subject are projected onto the world as its objective features; in turn, scientific notions are internalized, if only indirectly, through their absorption into popular culture. The Kantian conception of subjectivity is a metaphysical correlate of Newtonian physics, and the decentered Freudian subject conforms to the relativity of an Einsteinian universe. Perhaps the postmodern subject finds its correlative in the virtuality of cyberspace and its attendant modes of respatialization. Such conceptions are both ways of negotiating our positions as subjects within a social and cosmic order, and representations that affirm or rupture pre-existing forms of subjectivity.

If, however, post-Euclidean and post-Newtonian conceptions are made possible during an historical questioning of the postulates and values of the Age of Reason and the era of the self-knowing subject, these have still, in spite of their conceptual distance from Euclid and Newton, confirmed the fundamental masculinity of the knower, and left little or no room for female self-representations, and the creation of maps and models of space and time based on projections of women's experiences. It is not clear that men and women conceive of space or time in the same way, whether their experiences are neutrally presented within dominant mathematical and physics models, and what the space-time framework appropriate to women, or to the *two* sexes may be. One thing remains clear: in order to reconceive bodies, and to understand the kinds of active interrelations possible between (lived) representations of the body and (theoretical) representations of space and time, the bodies of each sex need to be accorded the possibility of a different space-time framework.

To transform the castrated, lacking, inadequate representation of female corporeality, not only do the relations between the sexes and the dominance of masculine in the formulation of universal models need to be questioned, the overarching context of space-time, within which bodies function and are conceived also needs serious revision. The possibility of further alternatives must be explored. This investigation, in turn, must effect the nature of ontological commitments and the ways in which subjects (masculine as well as feminine) see themselves and are socially inscribed. This may amount to a scientific and conceptual revolution alongside sociopolitical transformations, but without questioning basic notions of space and time, the inherent masculinity of the "hard sciences" and of philosophical speculation will proliferate under the banner of the human. Women, once again, may be granted no space or time of their own.

(101)

SPACE, TIME, AND BODIES

(6)

BODIES-CITIES

FOR A NUMBER OF YEARS I HAVE BEEN involved in research on how to reconceive the body as socio-cultural artifact. I have been interested in trying to refine and transform traditional notions of corporeality so that the oppositions by which the body has usually been understood (mind and body, inside and outside, experience and social context, subject and object, self and other—and underlying them, the opposition between male and female) can be problematized. Corporeality can be seen as the material condition of subjectivity, and the subordinated term in the opposition, can move to its rightful place in the very heart of the dominant term, mind. Among other things, my recent work has involved a kind of turning inside out and outside in of the body. I have been exploring how the subject's exterior is psychically constructed; and conversely, how the processes of social inscription of the body's surface construct a psychical interior: i.e., looking at the outside of the body from the point of view of the inside, and looking at the inside of the body from the point of view of the outside, to reexamine the distinction between biology and culture and explore the way in which culture constructs the biological order in its own image. Thus, what needs to be shown is how the body is psychically, socially, sexually, and representationally produced.

One area that I have neglected for too long is the constitutive and mutually defining relations between bodies and cities. The city is one of the crucial factors in the social production of (sexed) corporeality: the built environment provides the context and coordinates for contemporary forms of body. The city provides the order and organization that automatically links otherwise unrelated bodies: it is the condition and milieu in which corporeality is socially, sexually, and discursively produced. But if the city is a significant context and frame for the body, the relations between bodies and cities are more complex than may have been realized. My aim here will be to sketch out the constitutive and mutually defining relations between corporeality and the metropolis.

It may be useful to define two key terms: body and city. By "body" I understand a concrete, material, animate organization of flesh, organs, nerves, and skeletal structure, which are given a unity, cohesiveness, and form through the psychical and social inscription of the body's surface. The body is, so to speak, organically, biologically "incomplete"; it is indeterminate, amorphous, a series of uncoordinated potentialities that require social triggering, ordering, and long-term "administration." The body becomes a human body, a body that coincides with the "shape" and space of a psyche, a body that defines the limits of experience and subjectivity only through the intervention of the (m)other and, ultimately, the Other (the language- and rule-governed social order). Among the key structuring principles of this produced body is its inscription and coding by (familially ordered) sexual desires (i.e., the desire of/for the other), which produce (and ultimately repress) the infant's bodily zones, orifices, and organs as libidinal sources; its inscription by a set of socially coded meanings and significances (both for the subject and for others), making the body a meaningful, "readable," depth entity; its production and development through various regimes of discipline and training, including the coordination and integration of its bodily functions so that not only can it undertake general social tasks, but also become part of a social network, linked to other bodies and objects.

By "city," I understand a complex and interactive network that links together, often in an unintegrated and ad hoc way, a number of disparate social activities, processes, relations, with a number of architectural, geographical, civic, and public relations. The city brings together economic flows, and power networks, forms of management and political organization, interpersonal, familial, and extra-familial social relations, and the aesthetic/economic organization of space and place to create a semi-permanent but everchanging built environment or milieu.

I will look at two pervasive models of the interrelation of bodies and cities and, in outlining their problems, I hope to be able to suggest alternatives.

In the first model, the body and the city have a de facto or external relation. The city is a reflection, projection, or product of bodies. Bodies are conceived in naturalistic terms, pre-dating the city, the cause and motivation for its design and construction. More recently, we have heard an inversion of this presumed relation: cities have become (or may have always been) alienating environments that do not allow the body a "natural," "healthy," or "conducive" context. Underlying this view in all its variations is a form of humanism: the human subject is conceived as a sovereign and self-given agent who, individually or collectivity, is responsible for all social and historical production. Humans make cities. Cities are reflections, projections, or expressions of human endeavour. On such views, bodies are usually subordinated to and seen as merely a "tool" of subjectivity, self-given consciousness. The city is a product not simply of the muscles and energy of the body, but of the conceptual and reflective possibilities of consciousness itself.

This view has, in my opinion at least, two serious problems: first, it subordinates the body to the mind while retaining their structure as binary opposites. Second, such a view only posits, at best, a one-way relation between the body or the subject and the city, linking them through a causal relation in which body or subjectivity is conceived as the cause, and the city, the effect. In more sophisticated versions of this view, the city may have a negative feedback relation with the bodies that produce it, thereby alienating them. Implicit in this position is the active causal power of the subject in the design and construction of cities.

A second, also popular, view suggests a parallelism or isomorphism between the body and the city, or the body and the state. The two are understood as analogues, congruent counterparts, in which the features, organization and characteristics of one are also reflected in the other. This notion of the parallelism between the body and the social order (usually the state, but clearly there is a conceptual and historical linkage between the state [the domain of politics] and the city [the polis]) finds it clearest formulations in the seventeenth century when the liberal political philosophers justified their various allegiances (the divine right of kings, for Hobbes; parliamentary representation, for Locke; direct representation for Rousseau, etc.) through its use. The state parallels the body; artifice mirrors nature. The correspondence between the body and the body politic is more or less exact and codified: the King usually represents the Head of State; the populace is usually represented as the body. The law has been compared to the body's nerves; the military to its arms, commerce to its legs or stomach, and so on. The exact correspondences vary from text to text. However, if there is a morphological correspondence between the artificial commonwealth (the Leviathan) and the human body in this pervasive metaphor of the body politic, the body is rarely attributed a sex. What, one might ask, takes on the metaphoric function of the genitals in the body politic? What kind of genitals are they? Does the body politic have a sex?

Again, I have serious reservations with such a model. The first regards the implicitly masculine coding of the body politic, which, while claiming it models itself on the human body, uses the male to represent the human, in other words, its deep and unrecognized investment in phallocentrism.

A second problem is that this conception of the body politic relies on a fundamental opposition between nature and culture, in which nature dictates the ideal forms of culture. Culture is a supersession and perfection of nature. The body politic is an artificial construct that replaces the primacy of the natural body. Culture is moulded according to the dictates of nature, but transforms nature's limits. In this sense, nature is a passivity on which culture works as male (cultural) productivity supersedes and overtakes female (natural) reproduction.

A third problem concerns the political function of this analogy: it serves to provide a justification for various forms of "ideal" government and social organization through a process of "naturalization." The human body is a natural form of organization that functions not only for the good of each organ but primarily for the good of the whole. It is given in the functional "perfection" of nature. As a political and hence a social relation, the body politic, whatever form it may take, justifies and naturalizes itself with reference to some form of hierarchical organization modeled on the (presumed and projected) structure of the body.

In such models, which underlie certain conceptions of civic and public architecture, and even more, town planning, there is a slippage from conceptions of the state, which, as a legal entity, raises political questions of sovereignty, to conceptions of the city, a cultural entity whose crucial political questions revolve around commerce. As such, their interests and agendas are separate and at times in conflict: what is good for the nation or state is not necessarily good for the city; conversely, the city may prosper while the state is at war. The state functions to grid and organize, to hierarchize and coordinate the activities of and for the city and its state-produced correlate, the country(side). These are the site(s) for chaotic, deregulated, and unregulatable flows. (The movement of illicit drugs is simply one trail through underground networks of exchange that infiltrate and permeate the city's functioning. The movement of commodities, and of information, are other trails). The city (or town) is formed as a point of transit while the state aims to function as a solidity, a mode of stasis or systematicity:

> The town is the correlate of the road. The town exists only as a function of circulation and of circuits; it is a singular point on the circuits which create it. It is defined by entries and exits; something must enter it and exit from it. It imposes a frequency. It effects a polarisation of matter; inert, living, or human—it is a phenomenon of transconsistency, a network because it is fundamentally in contact with other towns....
>
> The state proceeds otherwise; it is a phenomenon of ultraconsistency. It makes points resonate together, points...of very diverse order—geographic, ethnic, linguistic, moral, economic, technological particulars. The state makes the town resonate with the countryside.
>
> ...the central power of the state is hierarchical and constitutes a civil sector; the center is not in the middle but on top because (it is) the only way it can recombine what it isolates through subordination. (Deleuze and Guattari, 1988: 195–97)

The statist representation of the body politic presumes an organized cohesive, integrated body, regulated by reason, as its ideal model. Such a model seems to problematize this cohesive understanding of the ordered body, and to produce instead a deranged body-image, a body frantic to be linked to and part of the network of flows, a body depleted, abandoned, and derelict insofar as it is cast outside these nets (Lingis, 1994a). The state can let no body outside of its regulations: its demand for identification and documentation relentlessly records and categorizes, though it has no hope of alleviating such dereliction. If the relations between the body and the city are the object of critical focus, the body itself must shake free of this statist investment.

If the relation between bodies and cities is neither causal (the first view) nor representational (the second view), then what kind of rela-

(107)

tion exists between them? These two models are inappropriate insofar as they give precedence to one term or the other in the body/city pair. A more appropriate model combines elements from each. Like the causal view, the body must be considered active in the production and transformation of the city. But bodies and cities are not causally linked. Every cause must be logically distinct from its effect. The body, however, is not distinct from the city for they are mutually defining. Like the representational model, there may be an isomorphism between the body and the city. But it is not a mirroring of nature in artifice; rather, there is a two-way linkage that could be defined as an *interface*. What I am suggesting is a model of the relations between bodies and cities that sees them, not as megalithic total entities, but as assemblages or collections of parts, capable of crossing the thresholds between substances to form linkages, machines, provisional and often temporary sub- or micro-groupings. This model is practical, based on the productivity of bodies and cities in defining and establishing each other. It is not a holistic view, one that would stress the unity and integration of city and body, their "ecological balance." Rather, their interrelations involve a fundamentally disunified series of systems, a series of disparate flows, energies, events, or entities, bringing together or drawing apart their more or less temporary alignments.

The city in its particular geographical, architectural, and municipal arrangements is one particular ingredient in the social constitution of the body. It is by no means the most significant (the structure and particularity of, say, the family is more directly and visibly influential); nonetheless, the form, structure, and norms of the city seep into and affect all the other elements that go into the constitution of corporeality. It affects the way the subject sees others (an effect of, for example, domestic architecture as much as smaller family size), the subject's understanding of and alignment with space, different forms of lived spatiality (the verticality of the city, as opposed to the horizontality of the landscape—at least our own) must have effects on the ways we live space and thus on our corporeal alignments, comportment, and orientations. It also affects the subject's forms of corporeal exertion—the kind of terrain it must negotiate day-by-day, the effect this has on its muscular structure, its nutritional context, providing the most elementary forms of material support and sustenance for the body. Moreover, the city is also by now the site for the body's cultural saturation, its takeover and transformation by images, representational systems, the mass media, and the arts—the place where the body is representationally reexplored, transformed, contested, reinscribed. In turn, the body (as cultural product) transforms, reinscribes the urban landscape according to its changing (demographic) needs, extending the limits of the city ever towards the countryside that borders it. As a hinge between the population and the individual, the body, its distribution, habits, alignments, pleasures, norms, and ideals are the ostensive object of governmental regulation, and the city is both a mode for the regulation and administration of subjects but also an urban space in turn reinscribed by the particularities of its occupation and use.

Now, to draw out some general implications from this schematic survey:

First: there is no natural or ideal environment for the body, no "perfect" city, judged in terms of the body's health and well-being. If bodies are not culturally pregiven, built environments cannot alienate the very bodies they produce. However, what may prove unconducive is the rapid transformation of an environment, such that a body inscribed by one cultural milieu finds itself in another involuntarily. This is not to say that there are not unconducive city environments, but rather there is nothing intrinsic about the city which makes it alienating or unnatural. The question is not simply how to distinguish conducive from unconducive environments, but to examine how different cities, different socio-cultural environments actively produce the bodies of their inhabitants. (109)

Second, there are a number of general effects induced by cityscapes, which can be concretely specified in particular cases. In particular, we can say that the city helps to:

1. orient sensory and perceptual information, insofar as it helps produce specific conceptions of spatiality;

2. orient and organize familial, sexual, and social relations insofar as the city, as much as the state, divides cultural life into public and private domains, geographically dividing and defining the particular social positions individuals and groups occupy. Lateral or contingent connections between individuals and social groups are established, constituting domestic and generational distinctions. These are the roles and means by which bodies are individuated to become subjects;

3. the city structure and layout also provides and organizes the circulation of information and structures social and regional access to goods and services; and

4. the city's form and structure provides the context in which social rules and expectations are internalized or habituated in order to ensure social conformity or, failing this, position social marginality at a safe distance (ghettoization). This means that the city must be seen as the most immediate locus for the production and circulation of power.

And third, if the city is, as I have suggested, an active force in constituting bodies, and always leaves its traces on the subject's corporeality,
corresponding to the dramatic transformation of the city as a result of
the information revolution will have direct effects on the inscription of
bodies. In his paper on "The Overexposed City" (1986), Paul Virilio
makes clear the tendency in cities today towards hyperreality: the
replacement of geographical space with the screen interface, the transformation of distance and depth into pure surface, the reduction of space
to time, of the face-to-face encounter to the terminal screen:

> On the terminal's screen, a span of time becomes both the surface and the
> support of inscription; time literally…surfaces. Due to the cathode-ray tube's
> imperceptible substance, the dimensions of space become inseparable from
> their speed of transmission. Unity of place without the unity of time makes the
> city disappear into the heterogeneity of advanced technology's temporal
> regime. (Virilio: 19)

The implosion of space into time, the transmutation of distance into
speed, the instantaneousness of communication, the collapsing of the
workspace into the home computer system, will clearly have major effects
on the bodies of the city's inhabitants. The subject's body will no longer
be disjointedly connected to random others and objects through the city's
spatiotemporal layout; it will interface with the computer, forming part of
an information machine in which the body's limbs and organs will
become interchangeable parts. Whether this results in the "crossbreed-
ing" of the body and machine—whether the machine will take on the
characteristics attributed to the human body ("artificial intelligence,"
automatons)—or whether the human body will take on the characteristics of the machine (the cyborg, bionics, computer prosthesis) remains
unclear. Yet it is certain that this will fundamentally transform the ways in
which we conceive both cities and bodies, and their interrelations. What
remains uncertain is how.

7

WOMEN, *Chora,* DWELLING

Everywhere you shut me in. Always you assign a place to me. Even outside the frame that I form with you…. You set limits even to events that could happen with others…. You mark out boundaries, draw lines, surround, enclose. Excising, cutting out. What is your fear? That you might lose your property. What remains is an empty frame. You cling to it, dead.

—Luce Irigaray (1992: 24–25.)

A FEMINIST MIGHT TAKE MANY DIFFERENT approaches in exploring the theme of women and architecture. For the purposes of this brief analysis, I will remain silent regarding most of them, leaving undiscussed the sometimes crucial issues of sexism and the often manifest discrimination against women in architectural training, apprenticeship, and practice. Such issues are best discussed and understood by those actively involved in the profession, who have not only first hand experience of the operations of discriminatory practices, but also have insights into the internal exigencies of the system in which they work, and an understanding of the various strategies pragmatically at hand in architectural institutions to transform them into sites of contestation. My concern here is with a series of narrower and more theoretical issues that link the very *concept* of architecture with the phallocentric effacement of women and femininity, the cultural refusal of women's specificity or corporeal and conceptual autonomy and social value.

I wish to make some indirect and tenuous connections between architecture, deconstruction, and feminist theory, forge some rudimentary links, and point out some of the rather awkward points of dis-ease between these various concerns. My goal here will be to present an initial exploration of the cultural origins of notions of spatiality in the writings of the Classical period, most notably in Plato's *Timaeus*, which invokes a mythological bridge between the intelligible and the sensible, mind and body, which he calls *chora*. *Chora* has been the object of considerable philosophical reflection, especially in contemporary French philosophy, having taken on the status of a master term in the writings of Julia Kristeva, in her understanding of the stabilization and destabilization of the speaking subject and, more recently in the writings of Jacques Derrida, particularly in his various theoretical exchanges with architecture, in his commentaries on and contributions to the work of the architects and architectural theorists Bernard Tschumi and Peter Eisenman. *Chora*, which Derrida insists must be understood without any definite article, has an acknowledged role at the very foundations of the concept of spatiality, place and placing: it signifies, at its most literal level, notions of "place," "location," "site," "region," "locale," "country"; but it also contains an irreducible, yet often overlooked connection with the function of femininity, being associated with a series of sexually-coded terms— "mother," "nurse," "receptacle," and "imprint-bearer." Derrida is interested in *chora* in keeping with the larger and more general features of "deconstructive reading," that always seek out terms that disturb the logic, the *logos*, of the text under examination, in order to show that it exceeds and cannot be contained by the logic, explicit framework, and overt intentions of the text. Derrida continually seeks out these terms— impossible to assimilate into the text's logic—which are nonetheless necessary for it to function. They are thus ineliminable from the text's operations and exert a disruptive force, an aporetic effect, on the apparent claims and concerns of the text in question. *Chora* thus follows a long line of deconstructively privileged terms in Derrida's texts, from "writing," "trace," "pharmakon," "dissemination," "supplement," "parergon," in his earlier writings, to "cinders," "ghost," "remainder," "residue" (among others) in his more recent texts. Each term designates and locates a point of indeterminacy or undecidability, a point at which the text's own writings exceeds its explicit goals and logic, where the text turns in on itself and ties itself into a strategically positioned knot.

It will be my argument here, reading Plato and Derrida on *chora*, that the notion of *chora* serves to produce a founding concept of femininity whose connections with women and female corporeality have been severed, producing a disembodied femininity as the ground for the production of a (conceptual and social) universe. In outlining the unacknowledged and unremitting debt that the very notion of space, and the built environment that relies on its formulation, owes to what Plato characterizes as the "femininity" of the *chora* (a characterization he both utilizes and refuses to commit himself to), I will develop some of the insights of Luce Irigaray in her critical analysis of the phallocentric foundations of Western philosophy. Irigaray's reading of the history of philosophy as the erasure or covering over of women's specificity has served to demonstrate that even where women and femininity are not explicitly mentioned or evoked in philosophical and architectural texts, nonetheless they, and concepts associated with them, serve as the unconscious, repressed or unspoken foundations of and guarantee for philosophical value. This essay may be understood as the confrontation of one strand of contemporary architectural theory, represented by Derrida's relatively small and admittedly oblique contributions to architecture, and Irigaray's sweeping analysis of the investment that all modes of knowledge have in perpetuating the secondary and subordinate social positions accorded to women and femininity. Irigaray *contra* Derrida in the domain of the dwelling: where and how to live, as whom, and with whom?

DWELLING: BETWEEN THE INTELLIGIBLE AND THE SENSIBLE

Timaeus represents Plato's attempt to produce a basic explanation of the universe as we know it—a *modest* attempt on the part of a philosopher who believed that only philosophers were fit to rule the well-ordered *polis*—an explanation of the divine creation of the cosmos and the earth. In an age when myth is not yet definitively separated from science or philosophy, Plato presents an account of the genesis of the universe from divine and rational metaphysical principles. He sets up a series of binary oppositions that will mark the character of Western thought: the distinctions between being and becoming, the intelligible and the sensible, the ideal and the material, the divine and the mortal, which may all be regarded as versions of the distinction between the (perfect) world of reason and the (imperfect) material world.

This opposition between what is intelligible and unchanging, being (the world of Forms or Ideas), and what is sensible (which Plato describes as visible) and subject to change, becoming, seems relatively straightforward; but, it is difficult to use as an explanatory model, a ground of ontology, unless there is the possibility of some mediation, some mode of transition or passage from one to the other. Plato complicates and indeed problematizes and undoes this opposition by devising a third or intermediate category, whose function is to explain the passage from the perfect to the imperfect, from the Form to the reality: *chora*. This category, it is claimed, shares little in common with either term in the opposition. Plato does suggest at some points that it shares in the properties of both the Forms and material reality; yet at other points, he claims that it has nothing in common with either. Rather enigmatically and impossibly, he suggests that it has both no attributes of its own, and that it shares some of the attributes of the Forms: "…we shall not be wrong if we describe it as invisible and formless, all-embracing, possessed in a most puzzling way of intelligibility, yet very hard to grasp" (Plato, 1977: 70).

Somehow, in a "puzzling way," it participates in intelligibility yet is distinct from the intelligible; it is also distinct from the material world insofar as it is "invisible and formless," beyond the realm of the senses. It dazzles the logic of non-contradiction, it insinuates itself between the oppositional terms, in the impossible no-man's land of the excluded middle. This is already enough to indicate to Derrida, no less than to Irigaray, that there is something odd at stake here, something that exceeds what Plato is able to legitimately argue using his own criteria.

Plato cannot specify any particular properties or qualities for *chora*: if one could attribute it any specificity it would immediately cease to have its status as intermediary or receptacle and would instead become an object (or quality or property). It is thus by definition impossible to characterize. It is the mother of all qualities without itself having any—except its capacity to take on, to nurture, to bring into existence any other kind of being. Being a kind of pure permeability, infinitely transformable, inherently open to the specificities of whatever concrete it brings into existence, *chora* can have no attributes, no features of its own. Seeped in paradox, its quality is to be quality-less, its defining characteristic that it lacks any defining feature. It functions primarily as the receptacle, the storage point, the locus of nurturance in the transition necessary for the emergence of matter, a kind of womb of material existence, the nurse of becoming, an incubator to ensure the transmission or rather the copying of Forms to produce matter that resembles them. Matter bears a likeness to the Forms. This relation (like the paternal bond between father and son) depends on the minimalized contributions of the receptacle/space/mother in the genesis of becoming. Moreover, it becomes less clear as the text proceeds whether something like *chora* is necessary for the very genesis of the Forms themselves, i.e.. whether *chora* can be conceived as a product or copy of the Forms, or contrarily, whether the Forms are themselves conditioned on *chora*:

> It can always be called the same because it never alters its characteristics. For it continues to receive all things, and never itself takes a permanent impress from any of the things that enter it, making it appear different at different times. And the things which pass in and out of it are copies of the eternal realities, whose form they take in a wonderful way that is hard to describe.... (Plato, 69)

Chora can only be designated by its, by her, function: to hold, nurture, bring into the world. Not clearly an it or a she, *chora* has neither existence nor becoming. *Not* to procreate or produce—this is the function of the father, the creator, god, the Forms—but to nurse, to support, surround, protect, incubate, to sort, or engender the worldly offspring of the Forms. Its function is a neutral, traceless production that leaves no trace of its contributions, and thus allows the product to speak indirectly of its creator without need for acknowledging its incubator. Plato explicitly compares the Forms to the role of the male, and *chora* to the role of the female according to Greek collective fantasies: in procreation, the father contributes all the specific characteristics to the nameless, formless incubation provided by the mother:

> We may indeed use the metaphor of birth and compare the receptacle to the mother, the model to the father, and what they produce between them to their offspring; and we may notice that, if an imprint is to present a very complex appearance, the material on which it is to be stamped will not have been properly prepared unless it is devoid of all the characters which it is to receive. For if it were like any of the things that enter it, it would badly distort any impression of a contrary or entirely different nature when it receives it, as its own features would shine through. (Plato, 1977: 69)

Neither something nor yet nothing, *chora* is the condition for the genesis of the material world, the screen onto which is projected the image of the changeless Forms, the space onto which the Form's duplicate or copy is cast, providing the point of entry, as it were, into material existence. The material object is not simply produced by the Form(s), but also resembles the original, a copy whose powers of verisimilitude depend upon the neutrality, the blandness, the lack of specific attributes of its "nursemaid."

This peculiar receptacle that is *chora* functions to receive, to take in, to possess without in turn leaving any correlative impression. She takes in without holding onto: she is unable to possess for she has no self-possession, no self-identity. She supports all material existence with nothing to support her own. Though she brings being into becoming she has neither being nor the possibilities of becoming; both the mother of all things and yet without ontological status, she designates less a positivity than an abyss, a crease, perhaps a pure difference, between being and becoming, the space which produces their separation and thus enables their co-existence and interchange.

Plato slips into a designation of *chora* as space itself, the condition for the very existence of material objects. (It is no accident that Descartes takes the ability to occupy space as the singular defining characteristic of material objects.) Space is a third kind of "entity" that is neither apprehended by the senses nor by reason alone, being understood only with difficulty, in terms of a "spurious reason," "in a kind of a dream," in a modality that today, following Kant, may be described as apperception. Plato describes a space

> ...which is eternal and indestructible, which provides a position for everything that comes to be, and which is apprehended without the senses by a sort of spurious reasoning and so is hard to believe in—we look at it indeed in a kind of dream and say that everything that exists must be somewhere and occupy some space, and that what is nowhere in heaven or earth is nothing at all. (Plato, 1977: 71–72)

Chora, then, is the space in which place is made possible, the chasm for the passage of spaceless Forms into a spatialized reality, a dimensionless tunnel opening itself to spatialization, obliterating itself to make others possible and actual. It is the space that engenders without possessing, that nurtures without requirements of its own, that receives without giving, and that gives without receiving, a space that evades all characterizations including the disconcerting logic of identity, of hierarchy, of being, the regulation of order. It is no wonder that *chora* resembles the characteristics the Greeks, and all those who follow them, have long attributed to femininity, or rather, have expelled from their own masculine self-representations and accounts of being and knowing (and have thus *de facto* attributed to the feminine). Moreover, this femininity is not itself merely an abstract representation of generic features (softness, nurturance, etc.), but is derived from the attributes culturally bestowed on women themselves, and in this case, particularly the biological function of gestation. While *chora* cannot be directly identified with the womb—to do so would be to naïvely pin it down to something specific, convert it into an object rather than as the condition of existence of objects—nonetheless, it does seem to borrow many of the paradoxical attributes of pregnancy and maternity.

DERRIDA: BETWEEN WRITING AND ARCHITECTURE

Derrida has written a good deal on Greek philosophy and has devoted considerable attention to unravelling the texts of Plato. He has done so not only because Plato's work functions at the cultural horizon of the inauguration of Western philosophy (such an approach would remain tied to the history of ideas), but also because the Platonic tradition has established basic frameworks, assumptions, and methods that have guided philosophy, and Western reason, ever since. It is thus not entirely surprising that for his two contributions written explicitly with an architecturally literate public, Derrida has again chosen to write on, with, or around Plato and the *Timaeus*. As I understand him, Derrida's work is neither architectural in itself (although no doubt it possesses its own "architectonic") nor is it devoid of architectural relevance. He challenges, not architecture itself, but a series of assumptions, categories, and terms *by which architecture is,* as are all *writing* practices—and architecture is clearly a mode of writing in the Derridean sense—implicated in and governed by metaphysics. He challenges architecture with its own irreducibly written traces, its own self-undoing, just as his work in turn is challenged with its own modes of textuality, its obliteration of spatiality and materiality. (117)

Derrida's reading of *chora* is ingenious: he shows how the counter-logic or a-logic of the *chora* as concept-term in Plato's writings, infects the other apparently unrelated claims of the *Timaeus,* its explanation of the origins of the universe, and the ways in which political, physical, and biological factors are rendered explicable. Moreover, it also seeps into Plato's self-conception, that is, the position he accords to Socrates in his texts. The peculiar functioning of *chora* cannot be readily contained in a self-identical place for it seeps into all that it contains, into all the oppositions and metaphysical assumptions that depend on it for their existence: the Forms, the material world, and their interrelations remain inexplicable except in terms of the mediation produced by *chora.* The world of objects, material reality in all its complexity, is in fact infiltrated by the very term whose function is to leave no imprint, no trace. *Chora* is interwoven throughout the fabric of Plato's writing. It effectively intervenes into Plato's accounts of ontology, political rulership, the relations between heavenly bodies (his cosmology), and the organization of the human body—of all that makes up the world. These other relations all exhibit an "abyssal and analogous reflexivity," with what Plato says about *chora*. Moreover and more importantly for the purposes of this argument, it is interwoven into the very *economy* of the architectural project itself.

It is significant that "economy" is derived from the Greek term, *oikos*, meaning home or house, residence or dwelling. An economy is the distribution of material (cultural, social, economic, representational, libidinal) goods in a system of production, circulation, and consumption. An architectural economy consists in the distribution, not only of bricks, stone, steel, and glass, but also in the production and distribution of discourses, writings (including the bodily traces of a building's occupants), and its divisions of space, time and movement, as well as the architectural plans, treatises, and textbooks that surround and infuse building. Derrida's goal seems not to be to destroy, to deconstruct (in a more pedestrian sense), to problematize and render architecture's assumptions unworkable, but rather to see whether it is possible to build/write according to a different economy, to reroute and transform the logic that distinguishes between space and time, form and matter, the intelligible and the sensible, theory and practice, so that it functions in different ways, with unexpected and unpredictable results, innovating different modalities of construction, both conceptual and material. His goal has always been to upset pregiven categories, to demonstrate the textual contortions that they entail, to show their cost and to effect some sort of rupture or transformation in their operations. His contributions to architecture remain of the same order: to open other possibilities for rethinking space, time, dwelling, the built environment, and the operative distinctions with which such concepts function.

Derrida does not intervene *as such* into architectural practice. He reserves a different role for himself: in effect, providing some kind of validation of the writing and building experiments of others (most notably, Eisenman and Tschumi), who themselves challenge the prevailing assumptions of functionalism, form, and measure in their attempts to think and produce what might be considered a "radical architecture," an architecture of transgression. In this sense, *chora*, and the reconceptualization of space that a deconstructive reading of this concept entails, begs rethinking the requirements of those oppositions that have structured architecture to the present: figure and ground, form and function, ornament and structure, theory and practice; and most particularly, both architectural consumerism (whose function is to subordinate materiality to the consumer's will or desire—a fundamentally impossible project, given the inherent open-endedness of desire, its fundamentally volatile and ever-changing nature) and architectural functionalism (whose goal is to subordinate subjects' desires to the exigencies of function, an increasingly impossible project, particularly in an era of rapid transformations in technological and corporate functions). One of his goals remains to contest the intervention into architectural practices of the exigencies of either aestheticism (the demands of beauty) or functionalism (the requirements of dwelling). Not that these requirements can be dispensed with, nor must they be abandoned; rather, they need to be rethought in terms of their role as internal or constitutive factors that function according to a different economy:

> ...you have to *reinscribe* these motifs [the hegemony of the aesthetic and the useful] within the work. You can't (or you shouldn't) simply dismiss those values of dwelling, functionality, beauty and so on. You have to construct, so to speak, a new space and a new form, to shape a new way of building in which those motifs or values are reinscribed, having meanwhile lost their external hegemony. (Derrida and Norris: 73)

This reconceptualization of space and spatiality that Derrida signals without specifying and that he indicates is at the heart of both philosophical and architectural reflection is, I believe, a concern he shares with feminist theory, particularly with feminists involved in architectural theory and practice. It is also one of the major areas of concern in the writings of Irigaray, who, like Derrida, concentrates primarily on philosophical texts, but particularly on those that also have some direct relevance to understanding the built environment.

I do not want to suggest that Derrida's work is directly compatible with the interests of feminist theory, quite the contrary. Whatever relations may exist between Derridean deconstruction and feminist theory have yet to be forged and explored in thorough detail, although it is today clear that a number of feminist theorists, with whatever reservations they may individually have regarding the feminist utility of Derrida's work, nonetheless are interested in and have worked with Derridean texts and concepts for various feminist projects. It seems clear to me that while Derrida's work is neither feminist nor anti-feminist, it retains elements of both. His work is fundamentally ambivalent. Making it relevant to feminist concerns is a matter of considerable negotiation: his writings always contain an unassimilable residue that is not only problematic in feminist terms, but which always tilts his writings into an uneasy and ambiguous alliance with other complex and undecidable interests and issues.

Conceptions of spatiality and temporality have rarely been the explicit object of feminist reflection: they have always appeared somehow above the more mundane concerns of day-by-day politics, too abstract, too neutral and self-evident to take as an object of critical feminist analysis (although this is now increasingly being revised in the work of some feminists working in the area of architecture, for example, Bergren, Bloomer, and Colomina). It has, however, become increasingly clear that the organization and management of space—the project of architecture and regional planning, among others—has very serious political, social, and cultural impact, and in a sense cannot but be of concern to feminists. Among the more interesting writings on (philosophical notions of) space and spatiality are Irigaray's, whose works, while perhaps less well known in the area of architectural theory, have had considerable impact on Anglo-American feminist theory and philosophy and, through them, on the ways in which space, time, subjectivity, and corporeality are currently considered.

While I cannot here outline her claims regarding the opposition between space and time—which she discusses with reference to Kant in *An Ethics of Sexual Difference* (1993)—I would like to use elements of her work to counterpose to the Derridean reading and use of the Platonic *chora* and to show the ways in which a feminist reading of *chora* may be able to reappropriate the maternal dimension implied by the term, and thus to reorient the ways in which spatiality is conceived, lived, and used.

Irigaray's writings on the dwelling are based largely on her readings of a number of philosophical texts, most particularly those of Kant, Heidegger, and Levinas. But more particularly, like Derrida, and a whole history of Western philosophers, she relies heavily on metaphors of dwelling, inhabitation, building, unearthing, tombs, ruins, temples, homes, caves, and prisons. Like Derrida, her work remains indirect in its relation to architectural practice, but her writing, like his, may be readily appropriated by architectural practices in the hope of transforming men's and women's relations to space. Her concerns are directed towards the establishment of a *viable* space and time for women to inhabit as women. The ways in which space has been historically conceived have always functioned to either contain women or to obliterate them. She makes it clear that a reconceptualization of the relations between men and women—as is required for an autonomous and independent self-representation for women and femininity—entails the reconceptualization of the representations of space and time:

In order to make it possible to think through and live [sexual] difference, we must reconsider the whole problematic of *space* and *time*.... The transition to a new age requires a change in our perception and conception of *space-time*, the *inhabiting of places* and of *containers*, or *envelopes of identity*. (Irigaray, 1993: 7)

Irigaray claims that masculine modes of thought have performed a devastating sleight-of-hand: they have obliterated the debt they owe to the most primordial of all spaces, the maternal space from which all subjects emerge, and which they ceaselessly attempt to usurp. Here Irigaray is not talking about specific men, nor even a general tendency in men (although this may in fact be appropriate), but rather, a tendency in phallocentric thought to deny and cover over the debt of life and existence that all subjects, and indeed all theoretical frameworks, owe to the maternal body, their elaborate attempts to foreclose and build over this space with their own (sexually specific) fantasmatic and paranoid projections. The production of a (male) world—the construction of an "artificial" or cultural environment, the production of an intelligible universe, religion, philosophy, the creation of true knowledges and valid practices of and in that universe—is implicated in the systematic and violent erasure of the contributions of women, femininity, and the maternal. This erasure is the foundation or ground on which a thoroughly masculine universe is built:

> He can only touch himself from the outside. In order to recapture that whole sensation of the inside of a body, he will invent a world. But the world's circular horizon always conceals the inner movement of the womb. The imposition of distinctions is the mourning which their bodies always wear. (Irigaray, 1992: 15)

Men produce a universe built upon the erasure of the bodies and contributions of women/mothers and the refusal to acknowledge the debt to the maternal body that they owe. They hollow out their own interiors and project them outward, and then require women as supports for this hollowed space. Women become the guardians of the private and the interpersonal, while men build conceptual and material worlds. This appropriation of the right to a place or space correlates with men's seizure of the right to define and utilize a spatiality that reflects their own self-representations. Men have conceived of themselves as self-made, and in disavowing this maternal debt, have left themselves, and women, in dereliction, homelessness. The question of dwelling, of where, and how, to live, is thus a crucial one in both the production of the male domination of women's bodies and in women's struggles to acquire an autonomous space they can occupy and live as women. In seeking to take up all (social) space themselves, in aspiring to occupy not only the territory of the earth, but also that of the heavens, in seeking a dominion from the earth to the sky, men have contained women in a death-like tomb, which she sometimes refers to as a "sepulchre" (Irigaray, 1985a: 143–44). In a rigid containment or mortification of women's explorations of their own notions of spatiality (and temporality), men place women in the position of being "guardians" of their bodies and their spaces, the conditions of both bodies and space without body or space of their own: they become the living representatives of corporeality, of domesticity, of the natural order that men have had to expel from their own self-representations in order to construct themselves as above-the-mundane, beyond the merely material. To sustain this fantasy of auto-production and pure self-determination in a systematic way, men have had to use women as the delegates of men's materiality. This containment within the (negative) mirror of men's self-reflections strips women of an existence either autonomous from or symmetrical with men's: it relegates women to the position of support or precondition of the masculine—precisely the status of *chora* in the Platonic tradition:

> I was your house. And, when you leave, abandoning this dwelling place, I do not know what to do with these walls of mine. Have I ever had a body other than the one which you constructed according to your idea of it? Have I ever experienced a skin other than the one which you wanted me to dwell within? (Irigaray, 1992: 49)

The containment of women within a dwelling that they did not build, nor was even built *for* them, can only amount to a homelessness within the very home itself: it becomes the space of duty, of endless and infinitely repeatable chores that have no social value or recognition, the space of the affirmation and replenishment of others at the expense and erasure of the self, the space of domestic violence and abuse, the space that harms as much as it isolates women. It is as if men are unable to resist the temptation to colonize, to appropriate, to measure, to control, to instrumentalize all that they survey, reducing the horizon (the horizon of becoming, the measure and reflection of positionality) into the dwelling, as Irigaray claims in the quotation opening this chapter. But this manipulation and containment of women and space always has its costs: in appropriating the body of the other, he must lose access to his own. In succumbing to the inducements of the phallus, and the paternal privilege it entails, he gives up the rest of his body. In exchange for the body he has had to sacrifice (the polymorphous pleasures of the pre-oedipal period) he is granted access to the bodies of women whose bodies replace the place from whence he came (the maternal womb). Women's bodies are the socially guaranteed compensation for men's acquisition of phallic status, the repositories of men's own lost corporeality, and the guardians of men's mortality. It is not surprising, given the massive disavowal necessary to sustain men's vicarious containment of and living from women's energies, that it is seeped in hostility, resentment, and aggression. Dwelling becomes the domain of hatred and murderous control:

> He passes from the formlessness of his relationship with his mother to the measureless excess of his male power.... He enters into paternal power, to keep within him the life he drinks from the other. But enclosed within that form, she dies. (Irigaray, 1992: 53–54)

This enclosure of women in men's physical space is not entirely different from the containment of women in men's conceptual universe either: theory, in the terms in which we know it today, is also the consequence of a refusal to acknowledge that other perspectives, other modes of reason, other modes of construction and constitution are possible. Its singularity and status as true and objective depends on this disavowal.

For women to be able to occupy another space, or to be able somehow to occupy this space in a different way, it is clear for Irigaray that several major transformations need to be effected. Most particularly, a series of upheavals in the organization of personal life (transformations in the way the mother-daughter relation is both conceived and mediated, changes in the ways in which female subjectivity and sexuality are structured according to the privileges of phallic subjectivity and sexuality, changes in the ways in which the two sexes relate to and exchange with each other), in the ways in which women's relations to what is larger than them (the divine, the environment, nature) are conceived, and in the ways in which theory, and cultural production more generally, are regarded. This interconnected cluster of issues cannot be readily untangled or easily resolved: these are more directions to which feminists must now turn rather than issues to be solved and eliminated. One thing remains clear, though: unless men can invent other ways to occupy space; unless space (as territory which is mappable, explorable) gives way to place (occupation, dwelling, being lived in); until space is conceived in terms other than according to the logic of penetration, colonization, and domination; unless they can accord women their own space, and negotiate the occupation of shared spaces; unless they no longer regard space as the provenance of their own self-expression and self-creation; unless they respect spaces and places which are not theirs, entering only when invited, and accepting this as a gift, can they share in the contributions that women may have to offer in reconceiving space and place.

Irigaray's work seems to confirm that its disruptive "logic" is everywhere at work, even today, in the production of phallocentric discourses and patriarchal modes of domination. *Chora* emblematizes a common maneuvre used to maintain this domination: the silencing and endless metaphorization of femininity as the condition for men's self-representation and cultural production. This is no less true of Derrida than it is of Plato: their various philosophical models and frameworks depend on the resources and characteristics of a femininity disinvested of its connections with the female, and especially the maternal, body made to carry the burden of what it is that men cannot explain, cannot articulate or know, that unnameable recalcitrance that men continue to represent as an abyss, as unfathomable, lacking, enigmatic, veiled, seductive, voracious, dangerous, disruptive, but without name or place may well serve as one of the earliest models of this appropriation and disenfranchisement of femininity.

The project ahead, or one of them, is to return women to those places from which they have been dis- or re-placed or expelled, to occupy those positions—especially those which are not acknowledged as positions—partly in order to show men's invasion and occupancy of the whole of space, of space as their own and thus the constriction of spaces available to women, and partly in order to be able to experiment with and produce the possibility of occupying, dwelling or living in new spaces, which in their turn help generate new perspectives, new bodies, new ways of inhabiting.

8

ARCHITECTURE FROM
THE OUTSIDE

[T]hinking is not innate, but must be engendered in thought.... [T]he problem is not to direct or methodologically apply a thought which preexists in principle and in nature, but to bring into being that which does not yet exist (there is no other work, all the rest is arbitrary, mere decoration). To think is to create—there is no other creation....
—Gilles Deleuze, 1994a: 147

[M]odern thought, from its inception and in its very density, is a certain mode of action.... Thought had already 'left' itself in its own being as early as the nineteenth century; it is no longer theoretical. As soon as it functions, it offends or reconciles, attracts or repels, breaks, dissociates, unites or reunites; it cannot help but liberate or enslave.... [A]t the level of its existence, in its very dawning, [thought] is in itself an action—a perilous act.
—Michel Foucault, 1970: 328

THINKING

It would be good to dynamize thinking, to think of a text, whether book, paper, film, painting, or building, as a thief in the night. Furtive, clandestine, and always complex, it steals ideas from all around, from its own milieu and history, and, better still, from its outside, and disseminates them elsewhere. A conduit not only for the circulation of ideas, as knowledges or truths, but also passage or point of transition from one (social) stratum or space to another. A text is not the repository of knowledges or truths, the site for the storage of information (and thus in danger of imminent obsolescence from the "revolution" in storage and retrieval that information technology has provided as its provocation to the late twentieth century) so much as a process of scattering thought, scrambling terms, concepts, and practices, forging linkages, becoming a form of action. A text is not simply a tool or an instrument; this makes it too utilitarian, too amenable to intention, too much designed for a subject. Rather, it is explosive, dangerous, labile, with unpredictable consequences. Like concepts, texts are complex products, effects of history, the intermingling of old and new, a complex of internal coherences or consistencies and external referents, of intension and extension, of thresholds and becomings. Texts, like concepts, do things, make things, perform actions, create connections, bring about new alignments. They are events—situated in social, institutional, and conceptual space.

Thus far, architecture and its related disciplines have happily incorporated or internalized the "postmodern" through the writings of Michel Foucault, and his analysis of the investments and implications of architectural design and the layout of space in the functioning of a disciplinary and observational power. More recently, architectural and urbanist discourses have become enarmored with a Derridean understanding of textuality as trace, inscription, or writing. Non-linguistic texts of all kinds—films, visual images, maps, buildings—become amenable to a deconstructive understanding of textuality, insofar as a text is no longer identified with the book, and writing is no longer reduced to an alphabet. If Foucault could be said to have introduced the notion of power as a mobile, non-personal series of techniques of regulation, supervision, and control of bodies and space, Derrida's contribution could be described more in terms of a textualization of what had previously been regarded as outside or beyond the text, collapsing a text's exterior into its interior. It is only in the last few years that there has been a glimmer of dissatisfaction with the impact of Derrideanism on architecture. It is here that the work of Gilles Deleuze may prove something of an enabling alternative, if not a supplement, to the incursion of Derridean thought on reconceptualizing space.

Instead of a Derridean model of the text as textile, as interweaving— which produces a closed, striated space of intense overcodings, a fully semiotized model of textuality—a model that is gaining considerable force in architectural and urbanist discourses, texts could, more in keeping with Deleuze, be read, used, as modes of effectivity and action which, at their best, scatter thoughts and images into different linkages or new alignments without necessarily destroying their materiality. Ideally, they produce unexpected intensities, peculiar sites of indifference, new connections with other objects, and thus generate affective and conceptual transformations that problematize, challenge, and move beyond existing intellectual and pragmatic frameworks. Instead of the eternal status of truth, or the more provisional status of knowledge, texts have short-term effects, though they may continue to be read for generations. They only remain effective and alive if they have effects, produce realignments, shake things up. In Deleuzian terms, such a text, such thought, could be described as fundamentally moving, "nomadological" or "rhizomatic."[1]

In counterposing architecture and spatiality with Deleuzian rhizomatics, the question becomes: How to *think* architecture differently? How to think *in* architecture, or *of* architecture, without conforming to the standard assumptions, the doxa, the apparent naturalness, or rather, evolutionary fit assumed to hold between being and building: how to move beyond the pervasive presumption that subjectivity and dwelling exist in a relation of complementarity, either of containment (space or dwelling houses or contains subjects) or expression (space or dwelling as the aesthetic or pragmatic expression of subjectivity)? How to see dwelling as something other than the containment or protection of subjects? In short, how to think architecture beyond complementarity and polarization, beyond subjectivity and signification? These are questions which cannot afford easy answers: ready-made answers become a blockage for thought, for architecture, for building and creating. They thus cannot and should not be answered, but need to be continually posed, rigorously raised in such a way as to defy answers, whenever architecture, or for that matter, any disciplinary practice—whether philosophy, science, finance, aesthetics—sinks comfortably into routine, into formulas, accepted terms, a founding father, an accepted history of antecedents, or a pregiven direction.

Deleuze's project, both alone and in collaboration with Guattari, is in part about thinking, about how to think, to think while making, or rather, while doing: to think *as* doing. Does Deleuze's work have something to offer in rethinking spatiality and its constitutive discourses? Conversely, a claim that could be equally plausible: Is architecture antithetical to the Deleuzian endeavor? Can there be such a thing as Deleuzian architecture, perhaps analogous to the apparently (relatively) easy absorption of Derrida into architecture through a not altogether bizarre reading of deconstruction and poststructuralism, terms which have parallel trajectories in architecture and philosophy?[2] Can architecture incorporate/appropriate or cannibalize nomadology or rhizomatics as readily as it has deconstruction? With what effects might such a meeting, ingestion, or conjunction occur?

If Deleuze's work seems to lend itself to a certain understanding of space, spatialization, and movement (his preference for geography over the typical privileging of history by philosophy is well known,[3] as are his metaphorics of territorialization and deterritorialization, and his fascination with Baroque art, philosophy, and architecture[4]), at the same time he seems to disdain the pervasive architectural models that have dominated the history of philosophy—knowledge and its foundations, the edifice of truth, material base and ideological superstructure, even the tree of knowledge—which philosophy has needed in order to develop its own self-conceptions. If Deleuze is the thinker of movement, of difference, the cartographer of force rather than form, if his goal is to produce a certain quaking, or stuttering,[5] then his work may provide a point of mobilization in the ongoing movement to destabilize and rethink space, place, building, and architecture.

To "introduce" Deleuze to architecture is, in any case, a strange proposition, given the peculiarities of a Deleuzian enterprise so resistant to the notion of "application" (theory is not so much to be applied as used), and which, in being transported to other areas so readily spawns jargon-filled replications of the terminology, without the disordering effects of his analysis.[6] Moreover, his work is difficult, wide-ranging, and can only be related obliquely to the work of his peers. His links are with traditions commonly neglected or marginalized in the history of philosophy: the pre-Socratics, medieval semiology, pragmatics, empiricism. It is not true that Deleuze's work is beyond appropriation or application; on the contrary, not only have his writings been happily incorporated into the visual arts,[7] but his concepts have also been wrenched out of context and applied willy-nilly to all manner of objects and relations. (No doubt we will soon face an avalanche of material on "the fold" in the visual arts and architecture.[8]) I am concerned here less with "applying" Deleuzian concepts to the architectural field than with raising some questions inspired by the Deleuzian project of reconceiving thought in order to avoid coming up with recuperable answers, in order to unsettle or make architecture itself, if not stutter, then tremble. Consequently, there is no single Deleuzian text, nor any specific architectural program I want to explore here; instead, I would like to look at how Deleuze's reconceptualization of thought itself may have ramifications for architecture.

For Deleuze, philosophy is a site for the invention of concepts. Concepts can no longer be understood as self-contained nuggets of mental contents, nor as blurred products of continuous streams of consciousness, but are complex assemblages perhaps best understood in terms of *hecceities*, as event or advent. Thought is a consequence of the provocation of an encounter. Thought is what confronts us from the outside, unexpectedly: "Something in the world forces us to think" (Deleuze, 1994a: 139). What confronts us necessarily from outside the concepts we already have, from outside the subjectivities we already are, from outside the material realities we already know is the problem.[9] The problem provokes thought. Thinking involves a wrenching of concepts away from their usual configurations, outside the systems in which they have a home, and outside the structures of recognition that constrain thought to the already-known.[10] Thinking is never easy. Thought-events, like language-bodies, are singularities that mix with and have effects on other materialities, with other political, cultural, cinematic, or architectural events. Deleuze is the great theorist of difference, of thought as difference.

Derrida's work has had a surprisingly powerful effect on the discourses of architecture and urban planning—surprising because his interests *seem* so philosophical, so textually based and hermetically self-contained. The central Derridean concept of *différance* or the trace entails a notion of constitutive inscription: before the word and the thing, before the distinction between space and its "contents," texts and their "ideas," is an originary and impossible trace or difference, which always infects the purity of the container with the impurity of its contents and vice-versa. Up to now, Derrida *seems* to have signalled the limit of tolerance of the "sciences of space" to "postmodern" (that is, French) philosophy. It remains to be seen whether Deleuze will be so happily accommodated.

Unlike a Derridean conception of thought, or representation, as différance—that is, as deferral and detour, the failure to reach a destination—instead of seeing difference as the inherent impossibility of presence (a project that is not without its effects in shaking up the singularity and self-sameness of the logos), Deleuze thinks difference primarily as force, as *affirmation*, as action, as precisely effectivity. Thought is active force, positive desire, thought which *makes* a difference, whether in the image-form in the visual and cinematic arts, in the built-form in architecture, or in concept-form in philosophy. Deleuze's project thus involves the re-energization of thought, the affirmation of life and change, and an attempt to work around those forces of anti-production that aim to restrict innovation and prevent change: to free lines, points, concepts, events from the structures and constraints which bind them to the same, to the one, to the self-identical.[11]

Deleuze's project then is to free thought from that which captures or captivates it, to free thought from the "transcendental illusions of representation," to give it back its capacity to effect transformation or metamorphosis, to make thinking itself scatter and realign:

Thought is primarily trespass and violence, the enemy, and nothing presupposes philosophy: everything begins with misosophy. Do not count upon thought to ensure the relative necessity of what it thinks. Rather, count upon the contingency of an encounter with that which forces thought to raise up and educate the absolute necessity of an act of thought or a passion to think. The conditions of a true critique and a true creation are the same: the destruction of an image of thought which presupposes itself and the genesis of the act of thinking in thought itself. (Deleuze, 1994a: 139)

The four illusions of representation[12] veil the genesis and functioning of thought, for they separate a force from what it can do and thus function as modes of reaction, the conversion of active into reactive force, in the terminology of *Nietzsche and Philosophy* (Deleuze, 1983). This veiling of thought is identified with a refusal of difference. Through these various tactics, pervasive in the history of Western philosophy, thought loses its force of difference, its positive productivity and is subordinated to sameness, becomes reactive. If the goal of the intellectual is not simply the production of knowledge, but more precisely, the production of concepts, of thought, and if the disciplines, including those constituting architecture as well as philosophy, function to thwart thought, to stifle and prevent exploration, to inhibit the production of the new, then the function of the radical intellectual, whether philosopher or architect, is to struggle against what, in discourse and in practice, functions to prevent thought. These, for Deleuze are the regimes of subjectification, signification and representation that continually bind thought to unity or the One. It is as if the forces of knowledge and power cannot tolerate difference, the new, the unthought, the outside, and do all that they can to suppress it, force it to conform to expectation, to fit into a structure, be absorbable, assimilable, and digestible without disturbance or perturbation.

The question remains: How to perturb architecture, given the tendency of some architectural theorists to take in whatever seems outrageous without it seeming to have any effect? How to infect architecture with its outside? In other words, how to force an encounter, to effect a transformation or becoming, in which the series that is architecture can be intercut with an element (or several) from its outside, from that series which is philosophy, in which the two series are thereby transformed through their encounter—the becoming-philosophy of architecture can only be effected through the becoming-architecture of philosophy. Deleuze poses a new understanding of difference, in which thought (thought in concepts, images, building materials) asserts its full force as event, as material modification, as movement beyond. Insofar as architecture is seeking, not so much "innovation," not simply "the latest fad," but to produce differently, to engender the new, to risk creating otherwise, Deleuze's work may be of some help, although it remains unclear precisely how. This lack of clarity is not the risk Deleuze's work poses, but its wager or problem (for thought is provoked by problems): how to keep architecture open to its outside, how to force architecture to *think*?

THE OUTSIDE

In a certain sense, all of Deleuze's works, as Deleuze makes clear in his reading of Foucault,[13] are about the outside, the unthought, the exterior, the surface, the simulacrum, the fold, lines of flight, what resists assimilation, what remains foreign even within a presumed identity, whether this is the incursion of a minor language into a majoritarian one or the pack submerged within an individual. The outside or exterior is what both enables and resists the movements of territorialization and deterritorialization. It is what resists the globalizing sweep of the by now well-worn postmodern catchphrase—"there is no outside" (of discourse, patriarchy, history, power), a formula that encapsulates the lures of signification and subjectification. What plays the role of the excluded or expelled in Derrida's work functions in terms of the outside in Deleuze.

Can the effects of depth, interiority, domesticity, and privacy be generated by the billowing convolutions and contortions of an outside, a skin? What does the notion of outside, exterior, or surface do that displaces the privilege of interiority, architecturally, philosophically, and subjectively? The boundary between the inside and the outside, just as much as between self and other and subject and object, must not be regarded as a limit to be transgressed so much as a boundary to be traversed. As Massumi stresses (1993: 27–31), boundaries are only produced and set in the process of passage. Boundaries do not so much define the routes of passage: it is movement that defines and constitutes boundaries. These boundaries, consequently, are more porous and less fixed and rigid than is commonly understood, for there is already an infection by one side of the border of the other, there is a becoming otherwise of each of the terms thus bounded.

It is significant that Deleuze, like Derrida, does not attempt to abandon binarized thought or to replace it with an alternative: binarized categories, rather, are played off against each other, they are rendered molecular, global, and analyzed in their molar particularities, so that the possibilities of their reconnections, their realignment in different "systems" is established. So it is not as if the outside or the exterior must remain eternally counterposed to an interiority that it contains: rather, the outside is the transmutability of the inside. It is presumably for this reason that Deleuze wants to link the outside, not with the inside, but with the *real*. This is in no way to align the inside with the unreal, the possible, nor the imaginary; it is to see that the outside is a *virtual* condition of the inside, as equally real,[14] as time is the virtual of space. The virtual is immanent in the real.

Thought is a confrontation or encounter with an outside. Deleuze deals with this notion of the outside primarily in two texts, *Foucault* (1988) and *Cinema 2: The Time-Image* (1989b). Following a tradition perhaps initiated by Nietzsche, and following a zigzagging path through Artaud to Blanchot,[15] Deleuze sees in Foucault, as we ourselves may see in Deleuze, the culmination of this confrontation between thought and its outside, between thought and the unthought. This conception of the outside or the unthought is already developed in Foucault's archaeological period, most notably in *The Order of Things* (1970), where Foucault suggests that man and the unthought are born simultaneously, as twin products of the nineteenth century. Where Descartes had brought together consciousness and thought, modern thought dates from the rise of both man and the unthought:

> Man and the unthought are, at the archaeological level, contemporaries. Man has not been able to describe himself as a configuration in the *episteme* without thought at the same time discovering, both in itself and outside itself, at its borders yet also in its very warp and woof, an element of darkness, an apparently inert density in which it is embedded, an unthought (whatever name we give it) is not lodged in man like a shrivelled-up nature or stratified history; it is in relation to man, the Other. (Foucault, 1970: 326)

In the final chapter of his detailed reading of Foucault, Deleuze develops this idea of the necessity of an outside and shows that it remains an ongoing concern in Foucault's writings, from the archaeological period through to his final writings. To briefly contextualize and simplify Deleuze's claims: he suggests that in Foucault's final texts, he does not abandon his commitment either to the materiality of his various objects of analysis nor to the peculiarly "outside" or estranged, to a large extent pragmatic, reading of subjectivity or textuality posed in Foucault's work, no return to anything like a phenomenological or psychological framework. These last works continue, but perhaps inflect, the trajectory of the outside already well-formulated in Foucault's earlier texts. Deleuze relates this to the question of interiority: Does Foucault present an analysis of interiority? What sort of interior might this be? Does Foucault's orientation to the issue of ethical self-formation mean that he is now committed to a notion of (subjective or psychical) interiority?

> Up to now [in Foucault's work] we have encountered three dimensions: the relations which have been formed or formalized along certain strata (Knowledge); the relations between forces to be found at the level of the diagram (Power); and the relation with the outside, that absolute relation with the outside,... which is also a non-relation (Thought). Does this mean there is no inside? Foucault continually submits interiority to a radical critique.... The outside is not a fixed limit but moving matter animated by peristaltic movements, folds and foldings that altogether make up an inside: they are not something other than the outside, but precisely the inside *of* an outside. (1988: 96–97)

Deleuze here describes a relation between two series (which he treats in terms of statements and visibilities in *Foucault*, but in very different terms in other texts). The relations between these series has three characteristics. First, they can only be understood insofar as each series is separate from the other, creating its own "zones of proximity," its own modes of functioning. Second, insofar as both series are located in an outside capable of asserting itself on/affecting an inside (which produces series of statements and of visibilities) that functions as the unsaid or the unseen within discourse or representation. And third, insofar as both series are modified through the encounter of each with the other. With the drawing of linkages between and through them, they are capable of interactions or becomings. More than a description of Foucault's claim, this is a general or abstract articulation of Deleuze's own position (no doubt true of all of Deleuze's writings: they are as much a reflection of his "methodology" as they are rigorous and attuned readings of texts marginalized in the history of philosophy). For Deleuze's Foucault, the inside is an effect of the outside: the inside is a fold or doubling of the outside, a contortion of the exterior surface. "It resembles exactly the invagination of a tissue in embryology, or the act of doubling in sewing: twist, fold, stop, and so on" (1988: 98).

In his understanding of the time-image in cinema (1989b), the outside is what displaces the inside, what burrows from without to effect an interiority. The problem is posed to concepts, to thinking, from/as the outside that can only appear to thought as the unthought, and to sight as the unseen. The outside insinuates itself into thought, drawing knowledge outside of itself, outside of what is expected, producing a hollow it can then inhabit—an outside within or as the inside:

Far from restoring knowledge, or the internal certainty that it lacks, to thought, the problematic deduction puts the unthought into thought, because it takes away all its interiority to excavate an outside in it, an irreducible reverse-side, which consumes its substance. Thought finds itself taken over by the exteriority of a "belief," outside any interiority of a "belief," outside any interiority of a mode of knowledge. (1989: 175)

This outside cannot be equated with Kantian noumena, a prelinguistic Real (as in Lacanian psychoanalysis), or an independently confirmable world (as realists claim). What is truly radical in Deleuze's understanding is his claim that this outside must be thought itself,[16] or perhaps even life itself.[17] The series are themselves the folds of an outside, constituted out of the same stuff. Thought is projected, captured, pinned down insofar as it caught up in the networks of power, knowledge, and subjectification:

The question: "What does thinking signify? What do we call thinking?" is the arrow first fired by Heidegger and then again by Foucault. He writes a history, but a history of thought as such. To think means to experiment and to problematize. Knowledge, power, and self are the triple root of a problematization of thought. In the field of knowledge as problem thinking is first of all seeing and speaking, but thinking is carried out in the space between the two, in the interstice or disjunction between seeing and speaking. (1988: 116)

It is not in the convergence, but in the disjunction of series that the outside is active in the production of an inside. This may be why, for Deleuze, the middle is always the privileged point to begin, why thought is perhaps best captured *in between*. Thought starts in the middle, at the point of intersection of two series, events, or processes that, however temporarily, share a milieu. The interiority of these series is of less interest than the way they are capable of being aligned to connect, creating their plane of consistence or coexistence, which is made possible only through the operations of this outside. Becoming is the way each of the two series can transform: becoming is bodily thought (Massumi, 1992: 99), the ways in which thought, force, and change invest and invent new series, metamorphosing new bodies from the old through their encounter.[18] Becoming is what enables a trait, a line, an orientation, an event to be released from the system, series, organism, or object which may have the effect of transforming the whole, making it no longer function singularly. It is an encounter between bodies, which releases something from each and, in the process, makes real a virtuality, a series of enabling and transforming possibilities. Becoming-animal only makes sense insofar as *both* the subject and the animal are transformed in the encounter.[19]

Thought is what comes between a cause and its habitual effect, between one being and another. It is a fissure between strata that allows something from them to escape, to ramify. It is an unhinging—perhaps a derangment—of expectation, order, organization, not to replace them with disorder, or disorganization, but with reordering. Rather than a pure positivity, the jamming effects of thought need not actively produce (new thoughts and new things or assemblages) but may intervene to insert a stammer, a hesitation or pause within the expected. Thought may actively function passively to interrupt habit and expectation by allowing something already there in the series, in the subject or object, to become.[20] Thought, life, is that space outside the actual which is filled with virtualities, movements, forces that need release. It is what a body is capable of doing, without there being any necessity, and without being captured by what it habitually does, a sea of (possible) desires and machines waiting their chance, their moment of actualization.

BUILDING

This notion of the outside may prove to be of some relevance to the architectural context. Indeed, it is doubly relevant, for it signals both the (135) notion of an outside as the edifice or exterior of a building, and a broader notion of the outside of the architectural discipline itself, a spatial as well as a non-spatial outside. Can architecture, like both subjectivity and signification—two models that have dominated the contemporary forms of its theoretical self-reflections—be rethought in terms of the outside, in terms of surfaces, in terms of a certain flatness, in terms of dynamism and movement rather than stasis or the sedentary? Can architecture inhabit us as much as we see ourselves inhabiting it? Does architecture have to be seen in terms of subjectivization and semiotization, in terms of use and meaning? Can architecture be thought, no longer as a whole, a complex unity, but as a set of and site for becomings of all kinds? What would such an understanding entail?

In short, can architecture be thought, in connection with other series, as assemblage? What would this entail? What are the implications of opening up architectural discourses to Deleuzian desire-as-production? Can architecture work (its or an) *outside*? What is it to open up architecture to thought, to force, to life, to the outside? By outside here, I do not mean the practical, financial, and aesthetic exigencies of building design and construction, nor even the demands on architecture to align with the environment, landscape, interior design, interior or exterior art works, which are in a certain sense, "inside" architecture and its history, part of the necessary structure of compromise that produces a building as a commodity; rather, I refer here to what is alien, other, different from or beyond it. Can it survive such assaults on its autonomy? Can it become something—many things—other than what it is, and how it presently functions? If its present function is an effect of the crystallization of its history within, inside, its present, can its future be something else?

I think that these are also some of the questions that Derrida has helped architecture to pose for itself—the indeterminacy of address, the openness of all systems to the undoings the future proposes. They are formulated in different terms and with different aims and effects through Deleuze's writings as well. But while Deleuze may be seen to share certain of Derrida's political concerns,[21] nevertheless, his work offers something distinctive, and quite different from Derrida's architectural contributions and appropriations. Deleuze remains a philosopher throughout. When he analyzes artworks, explores architecture, interrogates cinema or literature, it is in terms of their concepts, modes of thinking-doing, movements, crossovers, and linkages with philosophical issues, systems, and texts that he draws out or diagrams. This is not to say that he subordinates them to philosophy, makes them simply philosophical illustrations, or merely the objects or occasions of philosophical speculation. Rather, he is interested in the autonomy, the specificity, of these different practices and their modes or manner of interchange with their outside. These are the two series he interrogates together—art, literature, cinema, science, or architecture, and philosophy—seeking their plane of consistency and their modes of becoming.

If Derrida can be described as the philosopher who insists on bringing the outside, the expelled, repressed, or excluded, into the inside by showing the constitutive trace it must leave on that which must expel it (that is, the impossibility of keeping borders and delimitations clear-cut), Deleuze can be understood as the philosopher who evacuates the inside (whether of a subject, an organism, or a text), forcing it to confront its outside, evacuating it and thereby unloosing its systematicity or organization, its usual or habitual functioning, allowing a part, function, or feature to spin off or mutate into a new organization or system, to endlessly deflect, become, make. If we are no longer to explore the textuality of building—its immersion in discourses, its textual implications and investments, its own modes of marking—as Derrideanism entails, but to explore the possibilities of becoming, the virtualities latent in building, the capacity of buildings to link with and make other series deflect and transform while being transformed in the process, Deleuze's work may prove crucial. This is not something I am able to address adequately in specifically architectural terms—it is something for those trained or working in architecture, or perhaps for those just more architecturally-literate than I am: the question of the unthought, the outside *for architecture* itself; but it is a question that I believe needs to be posed in all seriousness whenever the formulaic and the predictable take over from experimentation and innovation, realignment and transformation.

(PART THREE)

PERVERSE
DESIRE

(9)

LESBIAN FETISHISM?

IN PSYCHOANALYTIC DISCOURSE, FETISHISM
is a uniquely male perversion.[1] In the psychoanalytic literature it has been generally
agreed, (with very few exceptions), that
fetishism is a male perversion, and its existence in women is assumed to be impossible.
While in one sense I do not want to disagree
with this claim—in psychoanalytic terms, it
makes no sense for women to be fetishists,
and it is unimaginable that women would get
gratification from the use of inanimate
objects or mere partial objects *alone*[2]—in
another, more strategic and political sense, it
seems plausible to suggest, as Naomi Schor
does in her analysis of George Sand (1985)
that there *can* be a form of female fetishism,
and to claim, further, that lesbianism pro-

vides its most manifest and tangible expression.

Like the fetishist, I too want to have it both ways: along with psycho-analytic orthodoxy, I will agree that female fetishism is psychically inconceivable, while I also want to claim that both "normal" (i.e., heterosexual) femininity and female homosexuality can be seen in socio-political terms in excess of their psychoanalytic descriptions, as modes of fetishism (in the same way that, I would claim, feminism can be seen as a form of mass or collective psychosis, a political disavowal of women's social reality as oppressed). I will not deal specifically with any quasi-fetishistic variations of lesbianism (sado-masochism, transvestism, the use of sexual paraphernalia, implements, or prosthesis). Fascinating as these may be, they cannot be regarded as fetishes until it can first be shown that female fetishism is possible.

In the first part of this essay I will examine orthodox psychoanalytic theorists, outlining Freud's and Lacan's notions; in the second part, I will play with these orthodox views, stretching them beyond the limits of their tolerance. Half-serious, half-playful, this will be not only a reading of psychoanalytic concepts and methods, but also an examination of the ways in which feminist theory may utilize precisely those discourses it wishes—and needs—to subvert in order to ensure its own goals and purposes, using them as strategic tools in its own struggles. This effort is both substantive and methodological, an analysis of the usefulness of psychoanalytic concepts and an illustration of how feminists may read patriarchal texts against the grain, so that they may be actively worked upon and strategically harnessed for purposes for which they were not intended. At the same time, it may be regarded as a highly speculative and preliminary investigation of the possibility of "lesbian theory," theory of and for lesbians. Whether psychoanalysis will prove useful or not for such projects remains one of my key, if underdeveloped, concerns here.

PSYCHOANALYSIS AND FETISHISM

Freud raised the question of fetishism early in his career (in the first edition of *The Three Essays on the Theory of Sexuality* (1905a) and returned to it again in one of the last papers of his life, "Splitting of the Ego in the Process of Defence" (1938). He turned to the topic every few years, in *Jensen's Gradiva* (1907), his case-study of the Rat man (1909), his study of Leonardo (1910), and in the paper "Negation" (1925b), particularly focussing on it in the paper "Fetishism" (1927).

In the first of *The Three Essays*, Freud distinguished two types of sexual aberration, those in which there is a deviation in the sexual *object* (here he mentions homosexuality, pedophilia, and bestiality), and those in which there is a deviation in the sexual *aim* (transvestism, voyeurism, exhibitionism). He included fetishism in the second category, although he claimed that it could equally well be included in the first, because its main characteristic is a sexual overvaluation of a part of the body or an inanimate object. Overvaluation, a characteristic of anaclitic or masculine forms of loving, creates the fetish as such, the fetishistic object's attainment being sufficient in itself to bring about orgasmic gratification.

Freud regarded the perversions as the opposite of neuroses: they are positive and negative sides of the same coin. The perversions avoid the repression that characterizes the neuroses. The pervert expresses precisely what it is that the neurotic represses: the pervert does what the neurotic subject would like to do but is unable to because the expression of a perverse impulse yields more unpleasure than pleasure.[3] Insofar as sexual "normality" has any meaning for Freud, it is defined in social terms as copulative, non-incestuous heterosexuality.[4] Lesbianism, like male homosexuality, is classified as a perversion. (It is quite clear that for Freud the notion of normality is used descriptively rather than normatively, and that he seriously destabilized the term wherever he invoked it .)

There are several ingredients necessary to understand Freud's linkage of fetishism to the paths of development open to the masculine subject. The fetishist, it seems, undergoes the Oedipus complex with one major element that differentiates his position from that of the eventual homosexual or heterosexual. In the latter cases, the boy witnesses the sight of the female genitals and is threatened with castration at two moments separated in time—the order is unimportant. Freud claims that there is a period of time in which the boy is able to disavow one or the other, depending on which occurs first. Little Hans (Freud, 1910a) provides the perfect illustration: with the birth of his sister Hanna, he disavows what he sees when the baby girl's diaper is removed. He exclaims to his mother "but she's got no teeth"(!)— a displacement, Freud suggests, from his perception of her castration. He cannot readily admit to himself that she has no penis (this would imperil the security of his own possession of the organ), so he displaces his perception of what is missing from the genitals to the teeth. At a later time moreover, the boy is directly threatened with castration by his mother for his masturbatory activities. She threatens to call the doctor, who will remove his "widdler." Once again, he disavows the threat and brazenly proclaims: "So what? I'll widdle with my bottom." This kind of disavowal is a "normal" psychical defence mechanism available to children of both sexes, and it operates primarily with respect to the threat of castration (for boys) or its symbolic actuality (for girls). But in the case of fetishism,

> it is different if both factors [i.e., the sight of female genitals and the threat of castration] *occur simultaneously*. In that case the threat revives the memory of the perception which had hitherto been regarded as harmless and finds in that memory a dreaded affirmation. (Freud, 1940: 276, emphasis added)

Here Freud claims that if the boy experiences his observation of the female's castrated condition at the same time as he experiences the threat of castration, he can no longer rely on his ability to disavow his perception; nor, on the other hand, can he accept the implications of the castration threat, which mean the abandonment of his pleasure-seeking sexual impulses and his submission to the Oedipal interdict:

> He replies to the conflict with two contrary reactions, both of which are valid and effective. On the one hand, with the help of certain mechanisms he rejects reality and refuses to accept any prohibition; on the other hand, in the same breath he recognized the danger of reality, takes over the fear of that danger as a pathological symptom and tries subsequently to divest himself of the fear.... The instinct is allowed to retain its satisfaction and proper respect is shown to reality. But everything has to be paid for in one way or another, and this success is achieved at the price of a rift in the ego which never heals but which increases as time goes on. The two contrary reactions to the conflict persist as the centre-point of a splitting of the ego (1940: 275–76).

For the moment, what is crucial is the Oedipal configuration of the fetishist's etiology. The fetishist is the boy/child who, for some reason, whether these two events occur simultaneously or not, is unable to resolve the Oedipal conflict in its various alternatives. He is unable or unwilling to take up the prescribed heterosexual path by abandoning the mother as love-object and accepting the post-Oedipal restraints on his sexual impulses through identification with the authority of the (symbolic) father; nor can he, like the homosexual son, accept symbolic castration in order to take on the "feminine" position and adopt a passive sexual role in relation to his father. Unlike either the heterosexual or the homosexual, the fetishist wants to have his cake and eat it too: he is not prepared to "pay" for his desire by facing the Oedipal prohibition, which gives the boy the ghastly choice—give up the mother or lose the penis—a choice between his most precious object and his most precious organ.

> [The fetish] remains a token of triumph over the threat of castration and a protection against it. It also saves the fetishist from becoming a homosexual,

by endowing women with the characteristic which makes them tolerable as sexual objects.... What other men have to woo and make exertions for can be had by the fetishist with no trouble at all. (Freud, 1927: 154)

Ironically, then, the fetishist is the least likely of analysands to enter a psychoanalytic contract. He remains perfectly happy with his love object (an object unlikely to resist his wishes and fantasies). In all likelihood, if he enters analysis at all, it will be at someone else's request. The fetish is a substitute for, a talisman of, the phallus, but not just any old phallus. For the pre-Oedipal boy, the most valued of phalluses is not his own (for his pre-Oedipal, imaginary penis is not yet elevated to the function of phallus), but his mother's—the phallus, that is, that endows her with power and authority. (Incidentally, it is precisely her role and function as phallic mother that covers over and hides her status as a woman, her sexual difference from the son.) He must disavow maternal castration if he is to protect himself against the possibility of his own castration. The fetish is his homage to the missing maternal phallus, his way of both preserving his belief in it and at the same time accepting her castration and, with it, the possibility of his own:

> Yes, in his mind the woman *has* got a penis, in spite of everything; but this penis is no longer the same as it was before. Something else has taken its place, has been appointed its substitute...and it now inherits the interest which was formerly directed to its predecessor. But this interest suffers an extra-ordinary increase as well, because the horror of castration has set up a memorial to itself in the creation of this substitute. (Freud, 1927: 154)

(145)

The fetish cannot simply be equivalent to the maternal or female penis because it *both* affirms *and* denies women's castration. There is no symbolic equation between the fetish and the penis because, as Lacan so cogently argues, the phallus is not the equivalent of the penis (this is why the mother's phallus is the most significant one in the child's erotic life). The relation between phallus and fetish is already entirely bound up with the order of signifiers. The penis (as real organ) can only take on the role of the phallus because it is *missing*, i.e., because women are castrated. The two terms affirmed and denied as equivalent are both signifiers; at no point does the (Lacanian) Real enter the equation. Lacan suggests that Freud's case of the young man with a fetish for shiny noses (Freud, 1927) can only be explained in terms of a displacement initiated in language, a displacement from one signifier to another, a shift from the English "glance at the nose" to the German *"Glanz auf der Nase."* The penis, insofar as it is conceived as detachable, as something the mother "has" and can "lose"—is as much a representation, a signifier, as the phallus. The fetish is (at the least) the third term in this metonymic chain:

> We are now in a dimension where meaning seems lost, the dimension where is to be found, apparently, the fetishist perversion, the taste for shiny noses. And, if there were no elaboration upon the nose…this would be as impossible to analyse as a true perverse fixation. Indeed, if a slipper were, strictly speaking, the displacement of the female organ and no other elements were present to elaborate primary data, we would consider ourselves faced with a primitive perversion completely beyond the reach of analysis. (Lacan and Granoff, 268–69)[5]

The fetish is heir to all the ambivalences and the indeterminacy of the boy's attitude toward maternal castration. Sandor Lorand's famous case study of the fetishist Little Harry describes Harry caressing the shoes of his mother and of Lorand himself, while also exhibiting impulses to cut them. His whole symptomatology is marked with the same ambivalence that characterizes his relation to the mother's phallus. The boy has ample pre-Oedipal access to the mother's body, having slept in the same bed with her until he was over three (Lorand, 423). He knows that her sexual organ is not the same as his own. Yet he disavows any knowledge of genital differences in order to stave off the castration threat, which he perceives being directed to his own organ. He not only caresses and cuts shoes, he also develops a phobia about pendulum clocks (which remind him of the doctor's surgery when he had an operation for phymosis at the age of two); he obsessively cuts locks of his own hair without knowing why (422); and, most particularly, he develops a mortal dread of amputees: "…a relative came in to visit the family, a man with one leg amputated. Harry could not be induced to enter the room; the moment he had heard the voice of the man outside the door he ran screaming into the bedroom…" (422). Harry both affirms and denies, both acknowledges and refuses to accept, the possibility of his own castration. The fetish (for example, Harry's preoccupation with shoes or Freud's patient's dependence on the shiny nose) only functions as a sign by virtue of its reference to the phallus, not the penis.

The penis must already function as a signifier, an imaginary object, from the moment the boy attributes it to the mother. The fetish is not a representation of the penis any more than a pore of the skin can represent the vagina. The child's perception of the mother's lack, and his symbolic utilization of the last object witnessed before he "sees" the missing phallus—shoes, stockings, underwear, fur, etc.—do not adequately explain fetishism because the fetish is a substitute for the phallus. The penis takes on the function of the phallus only because it is a mark or trace that excludes at least half the population. From being a real organ, the penis is transformed into an imaginary object dividing the sexes according to its presence or absence, possessed by some and desired by others. Only then can it function as a symbolic object (an object of union/exchange) between the sexes. The phallus distributes access to the social categories invested with various power relations: "It is the ultimately significative object which appears when all the veils are lifted. Everything related to it is an object of amputations and interdictions" (Lacan, 1977a: 104). When the veil is lifted there is only the Medusa, women's castrated genitals, lacking, incomplete, horrifying (for men). Salomé's dance, like striptease, can only seduce when at least one veil remains, alluring, yet hiding the *nothing* of women's sex. The fetish thus plays the role of the veil, both outlining and yet covering over women's castration.

DISAVOWAL

Freud attributes the peculiarities of fetishism to its reliance on the psychical defence mechanism of disavowal. Disavowal must be distinguished from three other major forms of psychical defense; repression (the mainspring of neurosis), negation or denial, and repudiation or foreclosure (the major mechanism functioning in the genesis of psychosis). In order to understand what is unique about fetishism and why Freud restricted it to masculine development, it is worth exploring these defense mechanisms in a little more detail.

Negation is a provisional lifting of repression, on the condition that the repressed contents are verbally and affectively negated: "[Negation] is also a lifting of repression, though not of course an acceptance of what is repressed.... The outcome of this is a kind of intellectual acceptance of the repressed, while at the same time what is essential to the repression persists" (Freud, 1925: 236). In negation, there is an affirmation of what is repressed: to negate or deny something one must have previously affirmed it. *Affirmation* is the process of registering or fixing a drive to an ideational content, signifying the former by the latter. Affirmation is both the condition of signification and of repression—something must be signified before it can be relegated to the unconscious—and the return of the repressed. By simply adding a "no" to the affirmation, negation allows a conscious registration of the repressed content and avoids censorship. It is a very economical mode of psychical defense, accepting unconscious contents on the condition that they are denied.

Repudiation involves the rejection of an idea that emanates from external reality rather than from the id. It is a failure to register an impression, involving a rejection of or detachment from a piece of reality:

> The ego creates, autocratically, a new external and internal world.... [T]his
> world is constructed in accordance with the id's wishful impulses, and...the
> motive of this dissociation from the external world is some very serious frus-
> tration by reality of a wish—a frustration which seems intolerable. The close
> affinity of this psychosis to normal dreams is unmistakable. (1924: 151)

The psychotic's hallucination is not the return of the repressed, i.e.,
the return of a signifier, but the return of the Real that has never been
signified—a foreclosed or scotomized perception, something falling on
the subject's psychical blind spot. The subject's perception is not projected outward onto the external world. Rather, what is internally obliterated reappears for the subject as if it emanates from the Real, in hal-
lucinatory rather than projective form. It confronts the subject from an
independent, outside position.

Disavowal exists somewhere mid-way between these psychical
defences. Like repression and negation, it involves the psychical registration of an impulse, most notably the Oedipal impulse; but, like foreclosure or repudiation, it refuses the contents of a perception or a piece
of reality. It does not rely upon or utilize the unconscious. It predates
the establishment of the unconscious, and, like repudiation, involves a
split in the ego. Unlike psychosis, disavowal does not involve a failure of
representation, for it is remarkably prolific in representational means.
Its structure is anchored by the child's acceptance of reality and its simultaneous refusal of reality, which generate the impulse to produce pro-
fuse significatory contexts and fantasy scenarios.

The fetishist maintains two attitudes in *disavowal*: the denial of
women's lack and its recognition and acceptance. The two attitudes "per-
sist side by side throughout their lives without influencing each other.
Here is what may rightly be called a splitting of the ego" (Freud, 1940:
276). Unlike repression, where the ego represses a representative of the id,
in disavowal two parts of the ego utilize contradictory forms of defense.
In this way the fetish, as a substitute for the maternal phallus, affirms
and denies women's castration. The fetishist is midway between neurosis and psychosis: he preserves himself from psychosis by representing
the maternal phallus through fetishistic substitution, yet he is saved from
neurosis by his repression of the castration threat. It is as if one part of
the ego (which accepts castration) is neurotic, and the other part (which
repudiates castration) is psychotic.

What is the major difference between the psychotic and the fetishist
if both share disavowal and rejection of a piece of reality? The difference

seems to lie in the opposition between hallucination and substitution. The fetishist "did not simply contradict his perceptions and hallucinate a penis where there was none to be seen, he effected no more than a displacement of value—he transferred the importance of the penis to another part of the body" (1940: 277). This displacement of value from the penis to another part of the body or onto an inanimate object will become crucial in the following discussion of the possibility of female fetishism, and particularly lesbian fetishism.

FETISHISM AND FEMININITY

Why is female fetishism an oxymoron (Schor, 365)? On Freud's account, female fetishism is not possible because there is no reason or motive for the girl to disavow the mother's castration. Disavowal will not protect her against the acknowledgement of her own castration as it might in the case of the boy. Unlike the boy's threatened or possible castration, the girl has already been castrated and her task is the passive one of accepting her status. Disavowal in girls is by no means uncommon, but it makes no sense for her to disavow the *mother's* castration. Rather, she tends to disavow her own castration. This is indeed the perfectly "normal" first reaction on the girl's part to the idea of her castration.

Freud's position is generally accepted by contemporary psychoanalytic theorists, even where there are reported cases of female fetishism. For example, Juliet Hopkins describes the case of a six-year-old female who develops a foot and shoe fetish. The girl had a particular fetish object, a tobacco tin, that "she used exclusively for sexual purposes... when she masturbated" (Hopkins, 82). Underlying the girl's fetishism, however, (and perhaps explaining it), was a form of psychosis in which "the girl believed herself to be a boy" (83). Hopkins refers to Phyllis Greenacre's claim that the "symptoms of fetishism only develop in females in whom the illusionary phallus has gained such strength as to approach the delusional" (83); that is to say, fetishism is possible in females who believe themselves to be male. Schor also cites four cases of female fetishism, but they all similarly seem to exhibit a strong identification of the girl with the phallic position of masculinity. These girls border on psychosis because they repudiate the psychical reality of castration rather than disavow it. They refuse their castrated condition and continue to believe in their own phallic position. They do not exhibit the ambivalence, the duplicity, of the fetishist's disavowal, for there is no simultaneous affirmation and denial of the kind which saves the fetishist from psychosis.

In order to understand why Freud considered it impossible for women to be fetishists, and yet to understand that lesbianism *could* be seen as a form of female fetishism, we need to explore the operations of disavowal, and its effects on feminine development. There are three distinctive paths which may result from the girl's disavowal of her own castration: heterosexual (secondary) narcissism, hysteria, and the masculinity complex. In "On Narcissism: An Introduction" (1914), Freud outlines a series of object-choices open to the feminine or what he calls the "narcissistic" type. Here the feminine subject (whether male or female) loves an object according to its resemblance, identity, or connection with the self. Indeed, Freud claims that, as a kind of compensation for her recognition of her inferiority, the girl may develop a (secondary) narcissistic investment in her own body, treating it as the corresponding male would an external love-object. She pampers her body, treats it with loving care; it becomes a vital instrument, her means of ensuring that she is loved. It is also her way of developing criteria for measuring her own self-worth. She phallicizes her whole body. If man believes he *has* the phallus (the object of desire), then woman believes she *is* the phallus. The man's penis and the whole of the woman's body are rendered psychically equivalent. In Lacanian terms, he *has* the object of desire while she *is* the object of desire.

In the process of making herself the object of desire, the narcissistic woman displaces the value of the phallus onto her own body, taken as a whole. She *has* the phallus, then, only inasmuch as she *is* the phallus (for someone who loves or desires her). This so-called "normal" path of femininity, the compensation for (and thus acceptance of) her castration, involves the compensatory phallicization of her body. In this sense, "the narcissistic woman" is an effect of the function of the phallus in the constitution of sexual identity. The narcissistic woman, contrary to Kofman's characterization, is far from independent and autonomous. She strives to retain her position as the object of the other's desire only through artifice, appearance, or dissimulation.

Illusion, travesty, makeup, enticement become techniques she relies on to both cover and make visible her "essential assets." They are her means of seducing or enticing the masculine or anaclitic lover, becoming a love-object for him. While thus concealing her "deficiency" by these means, she secures a mode of access to the phallic. Ironically, in this aim of becoming the phallus, the object of the other's desire, she is revealed as the site of rupture, lack, or castration, both idealized and debased, bound up with the masquerade of femininity, the site of both excess and deficiency: "Paradoxical as this formulation may seem, I am saying that it is in order to be the phallus, that is to say, the signifier of the desire of the Other, that a woman will reject an essential part of femininity, namely, all her attributes in the masquerade" (Lacan, 1977a: 289–290).

If the narcissistic woman effects a phallicization of the whole of her body, then in a sense she takes to one extreme the strategies utilized by the hysteric. Hysteria is a specifically feminine neurosis in which, through a somatic compliance of a part of the body, the "hysterogenic zone," the subject's sexuality is able to be displaced. Like the narcissistic woman, the hysteric accepts her castrated position; but unlike the narcissist, her investment is not in a phallic subject who, through his desire, can bestow on her the position of being the phallic object. The hysteric eschews masculine desire, preferring instead the now lost pre-Oedipal attachment to her mother (or mother-substitutes). In rebelling against the passivity usually associated with femininity, she hystericizes—that is to say, phallicizes—not the whole of her body, but a hysterical zone. We can take Dora as an example: She displaces genital pleasure into a form of hysterical choking. Through a series of infantile identifications (about which Freud seems rather confused or over-invested) she phallicizes her throat and uses it to signal her disgust at Herr K's sexual advances. She hystericizes this part of her body as a form of nostalgia, a monument to her maternal pre-history, one she must (but refuses to) abandon in exchange for the father's law. She does not retain the clitoris (as in the masculinity complex), nor does she transfer sexual intensity to the vagina (as occurs in "normal," i.e., heterosexual femininity); her libido is now invested in a non-genital zone.

The difference between the hysteric and the narcissist is the difference between the displacement of the phallus onto a part or onto the whole of the subject's own body (perhaps a difference of degree rather than kind?). Whereas the narcissist's whole body is the phallus (and thus she requires an external love object to bestow on her the status of the object of desire, accounting for her reliance on an anaclitic lover, whether heterosexual or homosexual), the hysteric gains a self-defined status as phallic: a part of her own body takes on the function of the phallus (confirming her object-like status in patriarchy), while her subjectivity remains in an active position (one which takes her own body as its object).

Disavowal, then, is by no means unique to men; it is a defense mechanism open and available to women. Its operations do not necessarily signal psychosis, but may function as a form of protection, though not—as in the case of boys—against potential loss, but rather against the personal debasement and the transformation of her status from subject to object, active to passive, and "phallic" to "castrated"— Freud's "definition" of femininity. It is a strategy of self-protection, even if it implies a certain mode of detachment from socio-symbolic "reality."

The third distinctive effect of the girl's disavowal of her castration is what Freud calls the "masculinity complex." The girl "suffering" from such a complex refuses to accept her secondary and subordinated status; she aspires to be treated like and to act the same as men. Freud suggests that although the masculinity complex may not necessarily imply lesbianism, nevertheless many lesbians can be classified under this label. Where the so-called "normal" path to femininity involves accepting her castration and transferring her libidinal cathexes from the mother to the father (via penis envy), with the accompanying transformation of her leading sexual organ from the clitoris to the vagina (with its associated position of passivity), the woman suffering from the masculinity complex retains the clitoris as her leading sexual organ and the position of activity it implies. She may also retain the maternal figure as the model on which to base her later object attachments, in which case she will continue to love a female mother-substitute: "Thus the girl may refuse to accept the fact of being castrated, may harden herself in the conviction that she *does* possess a penis and may subsequently be compelled to behave as though she were a man" (Freud, 1925a: 253).

Indeed this is how Freud explains female homosexuality in those rare passages and texts when he refers to lesbianism at all. In the case of the unnamed female homosexual (Freud, 1920), he describes her as behaving like a chivalrous male lover, displaying many of the characteristics attributed to the anaclitic or masculine type. She loves "like a man." While we may dispute this description as appropriate to all kinds of lesbian love relationships, it seems clear that it certainly describes the butch-femme relation, which seems to replicate the structural positions of a patriarchal heterosexuality, distinguishing a narcissistic (feminine) lover from an anaclitic (masculine) lover. Here the latter disavows her castration, while the former accepts her castration but refuses to convert her love object from maternal to paternal.

As with male homosexuality, for psychoanalysis female homosexuality generally takes on one of two forms, based on one or the other path of infantile development. In the path that produces the masculinity complex, there is a disavowal of women's castration and a refusal to acknowledge the socially sanctioned meanings of sexual difference. The girl will continue to identify with the phallic mother, and may even see the father as simply another embodiment of the phallic status of the mother (it is significant that this is the fate of the male fetishist, as well). But refusing to acknowledge her difference from the phallic position, she retains the masculinity of her pre-Oedipal position and the mother as love-object. The other path of female homosexuality involves an acceptance of her castrated status and the temporary taking on of the father as a love-object as in "normal" femininity; but, instead of transferring her attachment from the father to a suitable male father-substitute, the girl seeks out a "phallic" woman, a woman precisely, one may suspect, with a masculinity complex. The latter seeks a feminine love-object (as men do) while the former seeks a masculine love-object (whether male or female): this could be described as the homosexual equivalent of the complementary heterosexual association between anaclitic and narcissistic love-objects.

What relation does lesbianism have to female fetishism? In the case of the girl who has accepted her castration complex, there seems to be little or no relation. But in the case of the woman suffering from the masculinity complex, it may be possible to suggest some connection. Like the fetishist, she disavows women's castration, but this castration is her own, not that of the phallic mother. And like the fetishist, she takes on a substitute for the phallus, an object outside her own body. It is this which differentiates her from the narcissist and the hysteric, both of whom phallicize or fetishize their *own* bodies, and not really preserving the fetishistic structure of the displacement of phallic value from the mother's body to an object outside of one's self. By contrast, the masculine woman takes an external love-object—another woman—and through this love-object is able to function as if she *has*, rather than *is*, the phallus. As with the fetishist, this implies a splitting of the ego: it is this which inclines her to feminism itself, insofar as feminism, like any oppositional political movement, involves a disavowal of social reality so that change becomes conceivable and possible.

Where the fetishist remains the most satisfied and contented of all perverts, the masculine woman remains the least content. The more equal—or superior—to men she feels, the less her position is socially acknowledged as such, the less her convictions are validated by others, and presumably the more she is socially ostracized. She displaces phallic value onto an object outside the mother's (or her own) phallus; but, in contrast to the fetishist, her love-object is not an inanimate or partial object, it is another subject. Her "fetish" is not the result of a fear of femininity, but a love of it; it does not protect her from potential danger, for it introduces her to the effects of widespread social homophobia.

What is to be gained by describing this form of female homosexuality as fetishistic? This is not entirely clear to me, and it is for this reason that my answer must remain strategic. Like the fetishist, I want to say both that she is or could be seen in terms of fetishism, and at the same time, that she is not. At stake for me here, in this ambivalence, is the very structure of psychoanalysis itself: Insofar as psychoanalysis may be said to offer real insights about women in general or lesbians in particular in patriarchal society, we need to stretch Freud's terms in order to show that in themselves they do not exclude or discriminate against women— that women are treated with historical accuracy as to their various social positions. Insofar as psychoanalysis can be seen as an active participant in patriarchal social values, we need to show how its terms do not adequately accommodate women's particularities, and differences from men.

The categories that Freud proposed as universally relevant—the function of the phallus, the Oedipus complex, the ubiquity of the castration threat, and women's status as passive—surely need to be contested in order that social relations themselves can be transformed. The choices available to feminist theorists are either to accept psychoanalysis more-or-less wholesale (which implies bracketing off political questions raised by patriarchal power relations); reject it in its entirety (in which case one is left without an account of psychical and fantasy life); or else a little of both (the fetishist's solution), specifically selecting a notion that is deemed impossible or foreclosed by the theory to show how it may not be as implausible as it seems, if the terms themselves are stretched beyond their normal confines. In short, developing paradoxes and contradictions to see how the theory itself copes (or does not cope) with its own unspoken assumptions or unacknowledged implications.

I prefer to have it both ways: psychoanalysis does indeed describe patriarchal power relations and their adoption and internalization by both sexes; yet it is also limited in its historical and socio-geographical specificity. It does not adequately describe cultures not based on the nuclear family, nor does it describe the potential transmutations and revolutionary upheavals feminism seeks to effect. Above all, it does not adequately account for female sexuality even within the confines of Western capitalism, and is thus unable to deal with its most direct expression in lesbian sexual relations. This does not mean women/lesbians must abandon psychoanalytic models and concepts altogether. They still provide among the more useful terms in clarifying our psycho-social interrelations. But a cultivated ambivalence may provide the distance necessary to extract what may be of use in psychoanalysis while using psychoanalytic concepts, such as fetishism, to problematize psychoanalytic assumptions and to move beyond them.

(10)

ANALYZING PERVERSE DESIRE
(AN INTERROGATION OF
TERESA DE LAURETIS'S
The Practice of Love)

BEYOND PHALLIC DESIRE

The recent publication of Teresa de Lauretis's *The Practice of Love: Lesbian Sexuality and Perverse Desire* (1994) provides an ideal occasion to reflect the impact of gay, lesbian, and queer theory on the ways in which psychoanalysis is currently politically utilized, and on the troubled and troubling relations between sexually transgressive practices and the practices of theoretical production. De Lauretis's text can be seen as the culmination and point of intersection of the feminist fascination with psychoanalytic theory, that emerged more than twenty years ago, and the more recent eruption of queer politics. This book allows many crucial questions to be asked with the increasing urgency they deserve: here I will focus primarily on the relationship between psychoanalysis and feminist and lesbian theory. This seems to be the most intense site for feminist theory in its confrontation with the specificities of lesbian (as well as working class, indigenous, and post-colonial) subjects.

The Practice of Love is an attempt—perhaps the most sophisticated, if not the final one—to bring psychoanalysis to account for its strategic and most vulnerable blind-spots, its points of greatest elision or repression, its by now well-recognized failure to account for or even acknowledge the existence of an active and explicitly sexual female desire; that is, the active female sexual desire for other women that defines lesbianism. De Lauretis's book is a call for psychoanalysis to be accountable to a lesbian constituency for both its (hitherto inadequate) characterizations of female and lesbian desire and for its potential to problematize and to surpass itself and thereby to provide the raw materials for a better account. It is also a call to attention for lesbians, and especially those who have disdained or avoided psychoanalytic theory for its presumptions about women: it shows that by ignoring the contributions of psychoanalysis to thinking desire, especially lesbian desire, women have abandoned feminism's preeminent cultural discourse.

A cluster of psychoanalytic terms has proven to be a thorn in the side of all feminists: the Oedipus complex, the castration complex, penis-envy, the status of the phallus, the paternal metaphor, the symbolic order, and so on. Feminists who are still attracted to or fascinated by psychoanalytic theory must ask themselves whether to accept these terms as they stand, and to explain them in political and social terms, thus providing as an acceptable description the (perpetual re-)installation of patriarchal values; or to challenge, problematize, and abandon these terms; or, more recently and with more sophistication, to do both together, bringing out the tension between them and the paradoxes, and points of contradiction that such a tension may generate. At stake here is more than the value of psychoanalytic theory; that is, the question of whether feminists should or should not abandon a discourse that paints so bleak a picture of women's containment within the psychical norms of masculinity. This affects the intellectual and political status of feminist theory itself.

Is feminist theory a reading practice, a practice of interpreting patriarchal texts differently, affirming the capacity of every text (however phallocentric or patriarchal it may be) to be read otherwise? Or is it a practice of the production of alternative or different knowledges, whose goal may be either the production or revelation of "new" objects using given investigative procedures? These key political and ethical questions remain crucially alive and in need of continual assertion if feminist theory is to transform itself through the proliferation of "identities" and "subject-positions," the plethora of "speaking subjects" and "multiple perspectives," through the fragmentation and questioning of its basic gaols raised by the emergence and insistence of its "others"—lesbians, women of color, working class women, neocolonial subjects.

If psychoanalysis has been so useful for feminist theory and its particular concerns, can it remain so for lesbian theory and its distinctive if sometimes overlapping or competing interests? Can theoretical frameworks that have been instrumental in the development of present-day feminist theory be presumed to be similar to those of lesbian theory? At stake here is an assessment of the overlap—or lack of it—between the interests of feminism and those of lesbianism. For too long there has been a presumption that feminist interests incorporate and include those of lesbians, that feminism is a more general category representing the interests of all women, and that lesbian interests are a local subcategory. Such a model assumes a fundamental continuity between feminism and lesbianism, a relation of general to particular that overly homogenizes their relations and is incapable of understanding the dissimilarities, the space of separation and difference, that divide them. Such a model assumes an inclusive and encompassing feminism, a feminism representative of, or at least capable of representing, the interests of all women, a feminism that is strictly speaking impossible. A feminist position that insists on being equally inclusive of all women is a feminism of bland generality, a banalized or vulgar feminism, that includes all but speaks to no one in particular, a muted and depoliticized feminism. If feminism no longer represents itself as the privileged discourse of and for all women but instead openly acknowledges and affirms its particularities, its representation of the values and commitments of some but not all, then the sometimes complex and intricate negotiations between (white, middle-class, heterosexual) feminism and its others, including lesbians, can begin.

(157)

LESBIAN DESIRE IN A PSYCHOANALYTIC FRAME

While the more sexually neutral propositions Freud developed (those regarding the unconscious, the notion of infantile development, the typology of disorders, his understanding of psychical agencies, etc.) seemed to be easily incorporable into a feminist framework without too much political conflict, there remain a number of unpalatable assertions feminists have long questioned: the portrayal of women only in terms of their complementary and supporting role regarding the privileged and (pseudo-)autonomous position accorded to men and masculinity, the presumption of a teleologically copulative and reproductive sexual ideal, and the assertion that women's most gratifying source of sexual satisfaction is the compensatory relation to a child. In short, the problem was, and remains, the structure of containment of women in categories and concepts relevant to men. This structure, which de Lauretis, following and modifying Irigaray, describes as a regime or system of "sexual indifference" is one that views women only insofar as they are commensurable with men: it is this indifference that refuses to grant female sexuality or female genitality any authority or agency, any form or coherence or desire of its own. It reduces female sexuality and genitality to the status of castration, lacking the very organ given presence in men. Woman is man minus the phallus, and its benefits; she lacks the capacity to initiate, to activate.

It is no surprise that on such a model, lesbianism must be either reduced to the terms that govern heterosexuality, with the lesbian lover being assimilated to a masculine norm; or the lesbian relation is regarded in desexualized terms, as a regression to the mother-infant relation, a relation of narcissistic mirroring. Lesbianism has been left largely unexplained by psychoanalytic theory. And it seems as if it is not simply contingently or accidentally obscured through oversight or neglect, for this blind spot is constitutive of the psychoanalytic project. If psychoanalysis has problems in its accounts of (heterosexual) women and ("normal") femininity, these problems are amplified, and consolidate a point of constitutive incoherence and confusion when it addresses lesbianism.

These problems have been well-recognized, even among Freud's most fervent feminist supporters. However, this has not resulted in the abandonment of psychoanalytic theory as irrelevant to theorizing lesbianism, but to renewed attempts to make psychoanalysis more amenable. Psychoanalysis has remained the preferred, though certainly not the exclusive, discourse of sexual pleasure and sexual desire within lesbian theory. It is now time, I believe, that certain epistemological and political questions be asked: Why do we need psychoanalysis to think lesbian desire? What are the limits of its explanatory power regarding subjectivity and desire, the points beyond which it risks incoherence and contradiction? Who are the subjects it is unable to fit into its explanatory schemas? What is at stake in trying to include what was previously excluded, to place at the center what was marginalized, to explain and analyze what was inexplicable and unanalyzable? Is it to try to recuperate a theoretical or epistemophilic commitment in the light of its manifest inadequacies? Is it an attempt to stretch psychoanalysis beyond its limits of toleration? Is it an attempt to legitimize lesbian practices, to ensure that they are amenable to some kind of analysis and explication, even if it is beyond the usual terms provided by psychoanalysis? Does it broaden the notion of desire up to lesbian appropriations such that perversity instead of normalization becomes its explanatory framework? Or is it to shore up and support a discourse whose time has come, an attempt to resurrect a theoretical paradigm facing its limits? Does de Lauretis function to provide a political rationale and credibility for psychoanalysis as it lies dying? Does she, and other lesbian theorists who have tried to appropriate psychoanalysis for lesbian projects, serve to prolong the agonies of this dying discourse, giving it hope for remission when in fact it should be buried?

De Lauretis quite rightly resists the tendency toward romanticism and utopianism in much writing about lesbians and lesbian desire, which leads to a nostalgia for the lost (pre-Oedipal) mother-child relation or the fantasy of an imaginary symbiosis with the mother.[1] In insisting on an oedipalized rather than a preoedipal or imaginary structuring to lesbian desire, de Lauretis affirms the adult, genital, sexual nature of lesbianism against a tendency to see it as a non-sexualized woman-loving. In emphasizing the post-Oedipal or mature nature of lesbianism, in refusing to accord the idea of psychical or libidinal regression to pre-oedipal forms of loving, de Lauretis is not suggesting that the pre-Oedipal or imaginary is unimportant, but merely that it must be symbolically or Oedipally overcoded, that our access to the pre-Oedipal is always mediated—indeed produced—only through the Oedipal. Moreover, in insisting on the sexual nature of lesbian desire, de Lauretis problematizes Adrienne Rich's notion of the "lesbian continuum,"[2] a concept of the fundamental continuity between lesbian relations and the (non-sexual or non-genital) relations between all women, which have been used by some, usually heterosexual, feminists to elide the very real political, social, economic and sexual differences between lesbians and non-lesbians. In insisting on the distinctively erotic and genital relations between women that characterizes the structure of lesbian sexual desire, de Lauretis refuses models of desire proposed by psychoanalytic theory that see female sexual desire as active only according to the notion of the masculinity complex and its correlative conception of penis-envy. Such a model can, at best, though highly problematically, explain masculinized or "butch" lesbian sexuality, but is hard-pressed to account for the non-masculine or "femme" lesbian.[3] In characterizing lesbianism as the active sexual desire of a woman for another woman, she questions the usefulness of any model that explains away women's desire in male terms, or sees lesbianism as a mode of imitation or emulation of heterosexual role models. By refusing to masculinize women's desire for other women, de Lauretis does not lurch into the position that, because psychoanalysis does reduce women to either passivity or masculinity, tries to reject psychoanalysis in its entirety. She represents psychoanalysis as still the most viable discourse of desire, the most potent account of subjectivization.

In order to understand her claims regarding psychoanalysis, two pivotal terms in her elaborate argument need some explanation: the notion of perverse desire and the notion of the lesbian fetish (which in many ways feeds into and elaborates the metaphor of the lesbian phallus put forward in Butler's [1992] analysis).

De Lauretis's explicit goal is the development of a "formal model of perverse desire" (xiii), by which I understand her to mean a general model capable of adequately explaining all the various modalities of lesbian desire (whether "butch" or "femme," "top" of "bottom," sadomasochistic or "vanilla," whether the "real life" experiences of subjects, or the filmic, theatrical, poetic, or literary representations, a model whose particular details need to be filled in and modified according to the subject's particularity). In order to develop such a formal model, de Lauretis needs to specify what she means by the notion of "perverse desire," and how this is related to and differs from the normatively heterosexual model of sexuality and desire that pervades the practice of psychoanalysis. There is already a tension in Freud's writings between an acceptance of the teleology of heterosexual copulation and reproduction, and the perpetual undermining of the naturalness or inevitability of this sexual teleology through his understanding of the constitutive function of the deviations or vicissitudes of sexual aims, objects, and sources of erotic pleasure.[4]

In reading Freud through Lacan, Laplanche, and a number of feminist theorists, de Lauretis proposes a "negative theory of the perversions," a theory of sexuality as inherently perverse, non-normative, impossible to separate from either normality or neurosis. If perversion is, as Freud suggests, a deviation from an instinctual activity, the insinuation of a gap between a drive and its aims and objects, then *all* sexuality is a deviation, all desire perverse, all pleasure an amalgam of heterogenous component drives that refuse any simple subordination to genital and reproductive functions. Heterosexual genital and reproductive sexuality are only the tenuous results of the repression and reordering of the heterogeneity of drive impulses. If one emphasizes the perverse side of Freud's unresolved ambivalences regarding the nature of human sexuality, as de Lauretis, following Laplanche, proposes, then the peculiarities of heterosexual normality are thrown into stark relief; if, instead, one emphasizes Freud's normative understanding, then clearly it is the perversions—and particularly homosexuality—that need explanation:

> Thus perversion, and homosexuality in particular, has a peculiarly paradoxical status in Freud: both central and yet disruptive; necessary and yet objectionable; a "deviation" from the norm and yet more compatible with positive goals; degrading of human relationship and yet more pleasurable than "civilized" sexuality; regressive or involuntary and yet expressive of an originary intensity of being. (25)

What is both intriguing and puzzling about de Lauretis's speculations on the "negative trace of the perversions" (28) is her claim that such a theory will prove as useful an explanatory model for homosexual desire as the positive or normative theory is useful for explaining heterosexual desire.[5] In short, her presumption that the ambivalence surrounding Freud's two contradictory understandings of sexuality can be to some extent resolved by separating the normative, heterosexist model from his theory of desire as perversion so that one account can explain perverse desire and the other "normal" desire. This tends to mute the cutting edge of Laplanche's extrapolation from Freud that the deviation is what both enables and undermines the norm, that the perversions are also capable of characterizing *all* forms of (human) sexuality and *all* forms of desire. Laplanche claims that the sexual drive per se is instituted by way of a (deviant) retracing of psychical and biological processes mapped initially by biological or instinctive processes. Where instincts require a real object for satisfaction and for the material maintenance of life, the drive insinuates a fantasy object in place of the instinct's real object, a fantasy object whose powers of attraction rapidly outstrip, overtake, and incorporate the real. Sexuality is in itself a deviation, a departure from the real, from biology, from necessity into the meandering detours of fantasy. On the other hand, this separation is what is necessary for de Lauretis to accept as relevant the formal structures Freud proposes—the Oedipal scenario, the notion of castration, and the phallus—while transforming the way they operate and how they are commonly understood. This is necessary for her to differentiate her account of lesbian desire from Laplanche's more general understanding of the perversity of all desire. This separation of the normative from the perverse is the condition for de Lauretis's project of rethinking the sexual specificity of lesbian desire; at the same time, it involves unravelling the process of self-undoing Freud's two accounts of sexuality set up for each other. Thus it involves unravelling precisely the productive tension that has so attracted feminists and others to psychoanalytic discourse.

SPLITTING AT THE SEAMS

I cannot hope to cover adequately much of de Lauretis's highly detailed argument regarding the structure of perverse desire. Instead, I will focus on what I believe is the most distinctive and contentious of her claims, her linking of lesbian desire to the structure of fetishism. De Lauretis develops as convincing an analysis of the genesis and structure of lesbian desire using the psychoanalytic framework as has been yet attempted; if she is unable to accommodate lesbian desire within this framework, then it seems unlikely that it can be done. In a sense, her text is a test or limit-case for psychoanalysis. Given that the standard Freudian Oedipus complex and penis-envy are not able to account for lesbian desire, can a modified, transformed, or selectively rewritten version, one, for example, that replaces the privilege of repression as the mechanism of defense which most ably resolves the Oedipus complex fare better as a mode of explanation?

This is de Lauretis's gamble: if psychoanalysis is to remain relevant to understanding lesbian desire, its foundation in male and heterocentric privilege must be overcome, and alternatives, devised from within its frame, put forward. If these or similar transformations are to succeed, then psychoanalysis may be able to retain its political relevance in the face of the political dispersion that "postmodern culture" effects; if, on the other hand, it must be either so drastically modified as to become a different theory, no longer recognizably that psychoanalysis that is based on the privilege of masculinity, the phallus, or heterosexual coupling, or else it is recognized that pushing it to explain social marginality (of which lesbian sexuality is the paradigm example), which may take it beyond its limits of cohesion, then perhaps it is time that the amount of energy and effort feminists, lesbians, and gays have invested in psychoanalysis might be better invested in other theoretical approaches and intellectual endeavours.

De Lauretis develops her analysis of lesbian fetishism from a detailed reading of Radclyffe Hall's *The Well of Loneliness* and Cherríe Moraga's *Giving Up the Ghost*. It is reliant on her revision of the status and nature of the concepts so carefully tied together in an apparently inextricable cluster in Freud's account of oedipalization—the notion of castration, the paternal phallus, the concept of penis-envy, and the masculinity complex. It is clear that these concepts must either be abandoned (and if they are, psychoanalysis as a whole must go with them insofar as the oedipus complex is not only the nucleus of the neuroses, but also the center of a knot which ties together Freud's understanding of sexuality with his understanding of the unconscious), or be stretched and contorted so as to be able to accommodate female, or lesbian, desire. This latter is precisely the task de Lauretis sets herself: to take one of Freud's ambivalent assertions and to leave the other.

It is significant that the notion of castration is composed of two strands: the notion of the (potential or actual) amputation of the child's genital organs as punishment for sexual transgression, and a notion of the prohibition and abandonment of the preoedipal, incestual attachment of the child to the mother. In more orthodox readings of Freud's work, these two claims are intricately linked: the prohibition on desiring the mother has force and effect only because the (boy?) child is threatened with castration, that is, with feminization. De Lauretis tries to extricate these two strands, to think a notion of castration in which the child's desire is disentangled from the desire of the mother (while still remaining linked to it), as Freud suggests, but where amputation does not necessarily entail the privileging of the penis or masculinity. Unlike some lesbian theorists who wish to displace the notion of castration (or to read it in linguistic rather than corporeal terms), de Lauretis maintains that some notion of castration must be retained, and some notion of phallus needs to be developed. But these can no longer be simply linked to the presence or absence of the penis, as Freud suggests, and Lacan, in spite of his denials, also affirms.[6]

Coupled with her disentanglement of the primacy of the penis (and particularly the paternal penis) from the castration complex is de Lauretis's attempt to explain the notion of lesbian desire, not in the terms most suited for discussing neurosis[7]—repression—but in those that may be more appropriate for perverse pleasure: disavowal and fetishism. Following the work of Bersani and Dutoit, she suggests that perhaps the very structure of desire itself—all desire—might be characterized as fetishistic, insofar as it both affirms and denies a founding primal object of desire while creating a substitute for it. This substitute is the series of (endless) objects that are taken, in Lacanian parlance, as the "cause" of desire, its motivation or trigger. Like de Lauretis, Bersani and Dutoit want to distinguish the fetish from the phallus, or rather, from the penis that the mother is assumed to have had, and lost, and that the father is demonstrated as possessing. They claim that the fetishist does not see the fetish as the missing (maternal) penis but as something separate, a sign or talisman or, perhaps better, a metonym related to the penis but in no way resembling it.[8] The fetish is not a replacement penis; rather, it is a "fantasy-phallus" (225), an object/sign invested in fantasy with the status of phallus (= object of desire). It does not replace, resemble, or compensate for the missing penis, which is irrevocably "gone," a function of the castration of women's narcissism and body-image rather than of anatomy. This phallus functions only on the affirmation of castration. It is only if the subject's desire is detached from its first libidinal objects that the perverse freedom of desire to range over all manner of objects with a great variety of sexual aims becomes possible. In this sense, castration is the condition of perversion as much as of neurosis or normality.

De Lauretis needs to disinvest the notion of castration from the amputation of bodily organs, and to see perverse desire in terms of disavowal rather than repression in order to explain how the phallus can be detached from the father and paternity, and to be able to provide an account of lesbian desire beyond the masculinity complex. Where disavowal is also clearly involved in Freud's account of the masculinity complex (in which the girl disavows her castration and clings to the belief that one day the stunted clitoris [or little penis] will grow), it is a question of *what* is disavowed. In the case of the masculinity complex, it seems, the girl disavows her own castrated condition and retains a competitive, "masculine" relation to activity; in case of the lesbian, however, it is not her castration that she disavows (the lesbian accepts that she is a woman who desires a woman, not a woman who desires to be a man). It is the absence or loss of *another woman's* body (in the first instance, the mother's body)—the separation of mother and child that is part of the nexus of terms constituting castration—she must disavow and displace onto a fetishistic substitute (236), a sign that qualifies or modifies a woman's body, which constitutes for her the lure of lesbianism:

> …what the lesbian desires in a woman…is indeed not a penis but a part or perhaps the whole of the female body, or something metonymically related to it, such as physical, intellectual, or emotional attributes, stance, attitudes, appearance, self-presentation—and hence the importance of clothing, costume, performance, etc, in lesbian subcultures. She knows full well she is not a man, she does not have the paternal phallus (nor would her lover want it), but that does not preclude the signification of her desire: the fetish is at once what signifies her desire and what her lover desires in her…. In short, the lesbian fetish is any object, any sign whatsoever, that marks the difference and the desire between the lovers: "the erotic signal of her hair at the nape of her neck, touching the shirt collar" or, as Joan Nestle also suggests, "big-hipped, wide-assed

women's bodies." It could be the masquerade of masculinity and femininity of the North American butch-femme lesbian subculture.... (228–29)

De Lauretis does not deny the notion of castration—to do so, she claims, is to abandon the right to symbolic and signifying efficacy and genital or orgasmic maturity. What is castrated, what is lost and disavowed, covered over and displaced is a lovable or desirable *female body.* Here de Lauretis, as others before her have done, locates the (retrospective?) effect of castration on the earlier narcissistic self-representation that accomplishes an ego and ego-ideal for the subject. Castration does not so much sever the girl from a genital organ of her own as transcribe or rewrite an earlier loss, the loss of a female body (her own, or that of the mother). In the case of Stephen Gordon, for example, it is the mother's incapacity to desire Stephen's body, her failure to find it feminine that performs a wound or castration of Stephen's (imaginary) body-image. In de Lauretis's reading, the narcissistic problem for Stephen is not that her body is phallicly castrated; her body is *too phallic,* too masculine to be desired.[9] What she mourns is the lost female body; what lures and attracts her are the fetish replacements of this lost body (which may, but need not, be understood as the maternal body: the body lost in Stephen's case is her own female body), the irresistible attraction of mannish clothing, and the conventions governing masculine bodily gait and habit within her culture. These are among her particular lesbian fetishes. The fetish is a displacement of the bodily dispossession that constitutes the castration the girl suffers.[10] This fetish cannot be identified with the object of lesbian desire (the woman) but is the subject's means of access to and mode of attraction for the love-object. Ideally, the fetish is what in turn induces an interest from the love-object. No doubt there are a potentially infinite number of signs, traits, gestures, mannerisms that pose the lure Lacan attributed to the *objet petit a.* These "strange attractors" that signal the inducements of the erotic object to a desiring subject, are those special details that attract a woman to a woman.[11]

Significantly, and this is a measure of the improvement de Lauretis's model of lesbian desire has over competing models, she is able to explain both the similarities and the differences between butch and femme sexual positions using her account of lesbian fetishism. In the case of the butch lesbian, paradigmatically represented by the figure of Stephen Gordon, de Lauretis suggests that the lure of mannish clothing and the trappings of masculinity are hardly surprising given that it is the signification of masculinity which, in our culture, most readily and directly represents active sexual desire for the female body:

The reason seems too obvious to belabor: not only is masculinity associated with sexual activity and desire, imaged in the erect penis and its symbolic or ritual representation in the phallus; but…in a cultural tradition pervasively homophobic, masculinity alone carries a strong connotation of sexual desire for the female body. *That* is the lure of the mannish lesbian—a lure for both her and her lover. The fetish of masculinity is what both lures and signifies her desire for the female body, and what in her lures her lover, what her lover desires in her *and with her*. (243)

The butch lesbian does not desire to be a man, or envy what it is that men have (the penis) but rather takes as her own signifiers of desire that have helped characterize men's desire.[12] Her model of lesbian fetishism is also capable of qualifying the position of the femme, for just as the mannish woman is able to take the signs of masculinity as fetish-objects, so too the femme takes the signs of femininity, sometimes in parodied form, as a fetish, as both her mode of attractiveness for another, and as what provides her with satisfaction. De Lauretis sees this as hyper-femininity, a mode of reclamation and restaging of the loss and recovery of the female body:

> The exaggerated display of femininity in the masquerade of the femme per-forms the sexual power and seductivenesss of the female body when offered to the butch for mutual narcissistic empowerment. (264)

The same can be said for all the various scenarios of lesbian desire. In lesbian sado-masochism too, the status, value, and control of the female body that are at stake, as are the implements of sexual desire that serve as fetishes. What lesbians share, de Lauretis suggests, is that "in all these cases perverse desire is sustained on fantasy scenarios that restage the loss and recovery of a fantasmatic female body" (265). The fantasy scenarios within which the fetish functions are always a restaging of the loss or abandonment of the female body. This distinguishes lesbian desire from the structures and desires that mark stereotyped heterosexuality: a kind of primal scene of dispossession by which lesbianism is structured as both compensation and resistance.[13]

LINES OF FLIGHT

There is no doubt that *The Practice of Love* is a significant book. It rep-resents an intriguing last-ditch effort to preserve psychoanalytic theory, to retain the critical and radical edge it achieved when first taken up by feminists as the discourse of subjectivity and desire. I am not convinced that she has succeeded, although I suspect that those perhaps less disillusioned with the political and theoretical implications of too heavy a reliance on psychoanalytic theory would find the project more appealing and quite convincing. My concerns are not about the quality of de Lauretis's work but about the capacity of the framework of psychoanalysis to explain precisely that which it must exclude in order to constitute itself as a system or a discourse.

One of the major strategies of the 1970s and 80s in feminist theory has been the impressive capacity of some feminists to extend one model of power, particularly a masculinist text, so that it covers domains and objects theretofore left out or unthought, which thus constitute a point of blindness or vulnerability for that model (domestic labor for Marxism, lesbian desire for psychoanalysis, feminine modes of discipline or ethical self-regulation for Foucault). While an immense amount of (sometimes productive and rewarding) feminist thought, ingenuity, and labor has gone into this project of stretching or extending the tolerable boundaries of male discourses so they may be useful for or amenable to feminist projects, the long-term benefits of continuing to prop up or support a discourse which has well-recognized problems are not clear. Perhaps the major drawback of such an approach is the claim that the objects or concepts neglected or excluded by these male discourses are *not* simply (passively) forgotten through a kind of oversight. Domestic labor, lesbian desire, female discipline are actively excluded concepts, concepts whose exclusion conditions the field in which they function as blind spots. These concepts that are literally unthinkable in their given frameworks involve either a contradiction in the theoretical model involved, or a space incapable of being theoretically colonized by that framework. Attempts to fit women, or in de Lauretis's case, lesbians, into these frameworks are bound to be intellectually profitable—one learns an immense amount about these frameworks, and their limits in the process—but prove impossible in the long run.

In order to take on and productively utilize Freudian and Lacanian discourses in a context where they not only have manifest shortcomings but also a systematic commitment to these shortcomings for theoretical coherence, de Lauretis must both face and expose what is problematic about psychoanalytic discourses, and then show that these problems are not so overwhelming that they entail the abandonment of its frame. Her critical endeavour of challenging the various uses of psychoanalytic theory by other feminists, lesbian or gay theorists—which I believe is the most powerful part of her book—is necessarily bound up with (an implicitly) recuperative project, that of insulating psychoanalysis from the implications of feminist and lesbian criticisms, keeping it propped up when it is only with major transformations that have unclear and ambiguous effects, for it to maintain its explanatory power in the case of its excluded others.

Her utilization of psychoanalysis has been ingenious, and I believe that her account of "fetishism" (which for me is not really adequately separated from a Lacanian notion of the phallus as mobile, not tied to either the penis or masculinity) provides a complex and quite plausible model for explaining some of the styles and orientations of lesbian desire. But this explanation is built at considerable cost, both to theories of lesbian desire and to psychoanalysis. While I do not have an alternative account of lesbian desire to offer in place of the labor of love she undertook in producing this book and in devising a theory of lesbian desire based on a "rereading" (but actually a reworking) of psychoanalysis, what I can offer are some (sympathetic) criticisms, proffered in the spirit of one committed to a broadly similar project.

My most general concerns are precisely about the status of psychoanalytic discourse (in its various permutations), and de Lauretis's reliance on it as the sole explanatory framework in her account of the structuring of lesbian desire. It is a similar concern I have for other feminist projects that take psychoanalytic explanations as the paradigm or norm for what constitutes an explanation. It seems to me that one must be aware of a certain "ethics" of reading, an ethics of the appropriation and use of discourses. One cannot simply buy into a theoretical system (especially one as complex and as systematically conceived, in spite of its inconsistencies, as psychoanalysis) without at the same time accepting its basic implications and founding assumptions. I am not here suggesting that one must always read Freud from the point of view of accepting it all; but rather, that when one uses a discourse for one's own purposes it is never entirely clear which of its implications or assumptions are incompatible with one's own. Problematic implications cannot be contained and prevented from infiltrating those considered unproblematic. It is not clear, more specifically, that one can utilize a whole range of Freud's concepts (about fantasy, desire, pleasure, sexuality, etc.) without accepting that which underlies and links them—the castration complex, the primacy of the phallus, the relations of presence and absence governing the sexes. This is what de Lauretis's strategy seems to be, and, ironically, it is this wish to both have one's cake and eat it, to both "castrate" and preserve psychoanalysis, which characterizes the fetishist's use of disavowal.

De Lauretis's revisionism is aimed at three target concepts: the notion of castration, the centrality of repression, and the concept of the mas-

culinity complex, a cluster of concepts that deserve rigorous interrogation. It remains unclear to me how one can claim to accept the framework of oedipalization, the notion of the paternal phallus, the concept of
castration and yet locate "castration" as a mirror-stage or imaginary bodily dispossession. This, even in Freud's terms, cannot be a castration,
even if it anticipates and makes castration possible, even if castration
retrospectively inflects its meaning and status. And it remains unclear
how, in claiming that it is the psychical structure of disavowal rather than
repression that characterizes lesbian desire, what implications this has,
for example, with respect to the notion of the unconscious for lesbians.
Or does disavowal exist alongside of repression? Why is the dispossession of a female body the object of disavowal rather than repression, and
why is this one object of disavowal alone significant for lesbians? While
I certainly agree with de Lauretis that the masculinity complex is not an
adequate model for understanding lesbianism, since it subsumes women
under phallic norms, it is unclear that the fetish is any less phallic in its
structure and implications. Her model of the fetish, which she openly
relates to Butler's notion of "lesbian phallus," detaches the phallus from
its metonymic connections with the penis and with paternity and
authority to render it more mobile.[14] But if the fetish is just as fully
implicated in masculinity as the phallus, then a theory that displaces the
masculinity complex with fetishism does not necessarily leave lesbianism
any better explained.

(169)

Perhaps more disconcerting than her revisionist use of psychoanalysis is the potential effect of using psychoanalysis for theorizing lesbian
desire itself. De Lauretis seems to be proposing the possibility of a specific "lesbian psychology," an etiology of lesbianism that distinguishes
the structure of lesbian desire from the structures of heterosexuality, not
simply in terms of a distinction between love-objects, but also in terms
of different body-images and representations, and thus a different symbolic and imaginary. If this is the case, then she is (implicitly) committed
to a concept of a "lesbian psychology." We must ask if there is indeed a
systematic difference of the kind de Lauretis suggests—a common dispossession of a female body and the desire to (re)attain it—that sepa-
rates lesbians from heterosexuals. If there is such a difference, this seems
to problematize the position of those women who "become" lesbians,
which, ironically, is how she characterizes herself (xix). Just as the feminine lesbian constitutes a point of blindness for orthodox psychoanalysis, de Lauretis seems to have difficulty accounting for those who
have *become* lesbians. Do they undergo a change in psychology (a transfer from repression to disavowal)? Or are they simply repressed lesbians

who had to await their chance for sexual pleasure and desire (while suffering under heterocentric ideology)? If one is to grant such women an accepted status as lesbians, then how can de Lauretis account for the apparent mobility of (perverse) desire? How is it that not only can heterosexual women sometimes convert to lesbians, but the converse is also true: some women "become" heterosexual? Do these women, or those who label themselves "bisexual" change their psychologies and the structure of their desire while in lesbian relationships? If there is a systematic difference in the structure of desire of lesbians and heterosexual women, how can such mobility be accounted for? Unless there is a common structure of desire—or at least a very broad continuum on which both lesbian and heterosexual women's desires can be located—the openendedness of desire in its aims, objects, and practices cannot be adequately explained.

Moreover, while I can see the strategic value of focussing on butch-femme relations as those which, when lived out by women's bodies, constitute a transgression of the naturalizing effects of heterosexual "gender roles," and I can see how her analysis of the mannish woman is pivotal to de Lauretis's challenge to the model of the masculinity complex, I remain worried about models of lesbian sexuality and desire that focus primarily on these relations at the expense of others. I have similar reservations about the strategic value of a notion like the "lesbian phallus," "lesbian dildos," and virile display: while they do have the effect of unsettling or disquieting presumptions about the "natural" alignment of the penis with social power and value, they do so only by attempting to appropriate what has been denied to women and to that extent remain tied (as we all are) to heterocentric and masculine privilege. Such modalities remain reactive, compensatory. They still presuppose the normative (heterosexual) complementarity in lesbian couplings. This is more or less the presumption that must be drawn from de Lauretis's ascription of an inadequate mirroring of the female body by the mother. The fetish is compensation for this lost female body, making sexual access to (other) women's bodies possible.

I do not want to suggest that de Lauretis's project is a useless one or a waste of time. On the contrary, it is an immensely important project that needs to be pushed further and further—to its very limits, as de Lauretis has herself pushed psychoanalysis to its limits of tolerance—the limits of *knowing sex* or *knowing desire* that Foucault investigated in terms of its links to power and knowledge and modes of subjectivization. Her work has enabled this question to be placed on the political agenda: what is the (political) value and function of rigorously understanding, theorizing, lesbian desire and lesbian psychology? While clearly it may be, as de Lauretis claims, a mode of rethinking one's own fantasies, of understanding oneself better (xiv), of understanding oneself in terms other than those who confirm the majoritarian heterosexist conception of desire, pleasure, and power; it must also be recognized that by placing lesbian desire under the microscope of intellectual, scientific, or discursive investigation, it is thereby increasingly invested with a will to know that may be part of the very taming and normalization (even if not heterosexualization) of that desire. This depends to a large extent on the status and effects of the discourses one uses. Perhaps now is the time to rethink what discourses these should be.

(171)

LABORS OF LOVE

REFIGURING LESBIAN DESIRE

I knew you'd be a good lover when I noticed you always smelt books before you read them—especially hard-backs...now make love to me.

—Mary Fallon, 1989: 86

EXPERIMENTAL THOUGHT

There has been a great deal of work published in the last decade in the area now known as lesbian and gay studies. Much of this work has been exceptionally powerful in both political and intellectual terms. A whole series of issues vital not just to lesbian and gay studies, but also for understanding the structures of heterosexuality and the notion of identity considered in broader terms, has been engaged with, analyzed, and discussed. Many of these key issues center around questions about the structures of social power, sexuality, and the processes involved in the production of an identity. There are, of course, tensions within the negotiation around a series of polarized positions—essentialism vs. constructionism[1]; coalitionist politics vs. separatism; the alignments of lesbians with feminists vs. their alignments with gay male activists; the entwinement of "alternative" sexual and lifestyle practices with what they attempt to challenge and move beyond (for example the current debates about the political status of lesbian s/m, drag, and issues invested in what is now understood as lesbian or sexual ethics, and whether these are transgressive or recuperative practices) have been fairly thoroughly discussed, if not entirely resolved.[2] I do not plan to make any particular contribution to the richness and complexity of these debates. While I am impressed with the scholarship, knowledge, and political sense made by many working in this area, these issues will not be those that concern me here.

I don't really want to talk about lesbian or gay "identities," whether these are considered as unified, *a priori* totalities (the essentialist position) or as "fractured or dislocated multiplicities" (psychoanalytic and/or so-called postmodern positions). I don't want to talk about lesbian psychologies, about the psychical genesis of lesbian desires, nor about the meaning, signification, or representation of these desires. (This already differentiates this essay from the vast bulk of material now beginning to pour out of the "queer" industry, including my own previous forays into the terrain.[3])

In short, I don't want to discuss lesbian identity or desire in terms of a psychical depth or interiority, in terms of a genesis, development, or processes of constitution, history, or etiology. I am much less interested in where lesbian desire comes from, how it emerges, and the ways in which it develops than in where it is going, its possibilities, its future. I am interested in how to embrace this openness, to welcome unknown readings, new claims, provocative analyses—to make things happen, to shift fixed positions, to transform our everyday expectations and habitual conceptual schemas.

A third trajectory I will not deal with here concerns notions of sexual morality, the desire to produce or enact a "true" sexuality or an "ideologically sound" one.[4] I am not interested in judging the sexual practices, fantasies and desires of others—but I am interested in what kinds of terms may be appropriate for understanding my own. Thus I am not adjudicating what is transgressive or recuperative, nor to what extent drag, sexual role playing, butch-femme relations, for instance, participate in phallocentrism or heterosexism, or serve to undermine them. (*All* sexual practices are made possible and function within the constraints of heterosexism and phallocentrism, but this indeed is the condition of any effective transgression of them: we must no longer understand them as megalithic systems functioning in their immutability and perfection; rather, if they are systems at all, they are contradictory, fraught with complexities, ambiguities, and vulnerabilities that can and should be used to strategically discern significant sites of contestation.) My project is thus not to *analyze* or *explain* lesbian desire, but rather, to experiment with an idea, or a series of them, to see how far they can go, what they enable us see differently—a kind of excessive analysis, one that goes beyond the well-charted terrain, with Nietzschean joy.

I want here to explore two questions that I believe are closely entwined: can feminist theory sustain its ability to think innovatively, experimentally, playing with positions, in order to see how far they take us in rethinking what has been taken as the truth or orthodoxy—even if it is now feminists who, at least in some cases, supply and validate these truths or orthodoxies—in redoing the social and cultural order? And can feminist theory find an adequate, experimental, or hitherto unworked out, way of (re)thinking lesbianism and lesbian desire? Can feminist theory move from beyond the constraints imposed by psychoanalysis, by theories of representation, signification, power relations—all of which implicitly presume the notion of a masculine or sexually neutral subject and the ontology of lack and depth? Can feminist theory eschew the notion of depth? Can we think desire beyond the logic of lack and acquisition, a logic that has rendered women the repositories, the passive receptacles of men's needs, anxieties and desires? Can desire be refigured in terms of surfaces and surface effects?

(175)

THE ONTOLOGY OF LACK

My problem is how to conceive of desire. Particularly, how to think desire as a "proper" province of women. The most acute way in which this question can be formulated is to ask: How to conceive lesbian desire given that it is the preeminent and most unambiguous exemplar of *women's* desire (for other women)? In what terms is desire to be understood such that it can be attributed to women? How can a notion like desire, which has been almost exclusively understood in male (and commonly heterocentric) terms, be transformed so that it is capable of accommodating the very category on whose exclusion it has been made possible? Desire has, up to now, only functioned through the surreptitious exclusion of all women: how can this concept be dramatically stretched to include as subject what it has previously designated only by the position of object, to remake what is attributed passivity into an activity?

There are, in my understanding, three irresolvable problems associated with the notions of desire we have generally inherited in the West.

These signal that desire must be thoroughly overhauled if it is to be capable of accommodating women's desires and those—whatever they might be—that specify and distinguish lesbianism. These I can only briefly indicate, although they clearly warrant a much more thorough investigation.

In the first place, the concept of desire has had an illustrious history, beginning with the writings of Plato (especially in *The Symposium*, where Plato explains that desire is a lack in man's being, an imperfection or flaw in human existence). For him, desire is both a shortcoming and a vindication of human endeavour. Desire is considered a yearning for access to the good and the beautiful that man lacks. It is thus simultaneously the emblem of atrophy and of progress towards the Idea. Born of *Penia* (Poverty) and *Poros* (Wealth), of inadequacy and excess together, this Platonic understanding of desire remains the dominant one within our received history of thought even today. This trajectory for thinking desire reaches a major turning point in Hegel's understanding of desire in *The Phenomenology of Spirit*, where Hegel conceives of desire as a lack, a unique one that, unlike other lacks, can only function if it remains unfilled, a lack, therefore, with a peculiar object all of its own—its object is always another desire. The only object desire can desire is one that will not fill the lack or provide complete satisfaction. To provide desire with its object is to annihilate it. Desire desires to be desired. Thus, for Hegel, the only object that both satisfies desire and perpetuates it is not an object but another desire. The desire of the other is thus the only appropriate object of desire.

Psychoanalytic theory is one of the heirs to this tradition. It is largely through this system, in which, for example, Lacan reads Freud explicitly in terms of Hegel's understanding of desire, that such a conception of desire continues to dominate feminist, lesbian, and gay studies. Freud modifies the Platonic understanding of desire while nonetheless remaining faithful to its terms: the lack constitutive of desire is not an inherent feature of the subject (as Hegel assumed) but is now a function of (social) reality. Desire is the movement of substitution that creates a series of equivalent objects to fill this primordial lack. In seeking to replace an (impossible) plenitude, a lost completion originating (at least in fantasy) in the early mother/child dyad, desire will create a realm of objects substitutable for the primal (lost, forbidden) object. Desire's endless chain is an effect of an oedipalizing process that requires the child's relinquishing its incestual attachments with the creation of an endless network of replacements, substitutes, and representations of the perpetually absent object.

Now this notion of desire as an absence, lack, or hole, an abyss seeking to be engulfed, stuffed to satisfaction, is not only uniquely useful in capitalist models of acquisition, property, and ownership (seeing the object of desire on the model of the consumable commodity), it inherently *sexualizes* desire, coding it in terms of the prevailing characteristics attributed to the masculine/feminine opposition—presence and absence. Desire, like female sexuality itself, is insatiable, boundless, relentless, a gaping hole, which cannot be filled or can be filled only temporarily; it suffers an inherent dependence on its object(s), a fundamental incompletion without them. I would suggest that this model of desire[5] is in fact coded as a sexual polarization. Where desire is attributed a negative status, it is hardly surprising that it becomes coded in similar terms to those attributed to femininity. Moreover, it is precisely such a model, where desire lacks, yearns, seeks, but is never capable of finding itself and its equilibrium, that enables the two sexes to be understood as (biological, sexual, social and psychical) complements of each other—each is presumed to complete, to fill up, the lack of the other. The model of completion provided here is congruent with the logic regulating the goal posited by Aristophanes's hermaphrodite. Such a model, in other words, performs an act of violence: for any consideration of the autonomy of the two sexes, particularly the autonomy of women, is rendered impossible. It feminizes, heterosexualizes, and binarizes desire at an ontological and epistemological level. Its activity is merely a reaction to its perceived shortcomings, its own failure to sustain itself.

If this is the primary model of desire we have inherited in the West, it seems complicit with a second problem, that can be more narrowly circumscribed and directed a single corpus of writing, namely: the notion of desire as it commonly understood can be most readily articulated with reference to a psychoanalytic account of desire (a shorthand version, as a symptom of a broader cultural and intellectual tradition). On such models, the most notable being Freud's, desire is inherently masculine. There is only male or rather masculine libido; there is only desire as an activity ("activity" being, for Freud, correlated with masculinity), in which case, the notion of female or feminine desire is self-contradictory.

Freud gets around this complication in a variety of ingenious ways: for him the so-called normal or heterosexual response on the part of woman is to give up the (masculine, phallic, anaclitic) desire to love and to substitute the passive aim of being loved and desired that constitutes women's adult, secondary version of her primary narcissism;[6] while the woman suffering from the "masculinity complex," by contrast, retains an active relation to desire, but only at the cost of abandoning any self-representation as feminine or castrated. In exchange for the active phallic status she refuses to renounce, and while retaining the structure of virile desire, she abandons femininity. When she loves and desires, she does so not as a woman but *as a man.*

This understanding of female "inversion" (both literally and metaphorically) permeates the two case studies of female homosexuality Freud undertook—his study of Dora (Freud, 1905b) (which he only recognized as a study of *homosexual* desire too late, well after Dora had left analysis with him), and the analysis of the young female homosexual (Freud, 1920), in which he can only represent the young woman's love relations to "her lady" on the model of the chivalrous male lover. In short, insofar as the woman occupies the feminine position, she can only take up the place of the object of desire and never that of the subject of desire; and insofar as she take up the position of the subject of desire, the subject who desires, she must renounce any position as feminine.[7] It is thus rather surprising, given the inherent impossibility of psychoanalysis adequately providing the terms by which an analysis of women, and of female desire, is possible, that it nevertheless provides the basis for a disproportionately large number of texts within the field of lesbian and gay studies.

The third problem with this dominant notion of desire is bound up with the other two: it could be described as the implicit "hommosexuality" of desire.[8] Here the claim is not, as I have just argued, that desire is inherently masculine insofar as it is defined as active; in addition to its phallocentrism is a claim about the circuits of exchange in which desire functions. Irigaray argues that what psychoanalysis articulates as the imposition of oedipalization is in fact the (re)production of a circuit of symbolic exchange in which women function only as objects, commodities, or goods; where women serve as the excuse, the intermediary as it were, the linkage point between one man and another. As evidence, she cites the fascination of many men with prostitution, with the idea of sharing a woman that other men have "had."[9]

Moreover, gay male relations are partly persecuted in our culture, she claims, because they (or many of them) make explicit the fundamentally *hommosexual* nature of exchange itself—including the exchange constituted as desire—they make clear that the stakes do not involve women themselves. If desire is a lack, and if it functions by way of the substitution of one impossible/unsatisfying object for another, then what is significant about desire is not the objects to which it attaches itself; but rather the flows and dynamics of its circulation, the paths, detours, and returns it undergoes. If Irigaray is correct in her readings of psychoanalytic discourse as representative of Western philosophical thought more generally, in terms of its underlying investments in phallocentrism, then it would also follow from her readings that these circuits of exchange, like desire and sexual difference itself in patriarchal cultures, are governed and regulated with respect to the phallus. These circuits are *hommosexual*: for and between men.

It is now clear, I hope, why there may be a problem using theories like psychoanalysis, as many lesbian theorists have,[10] to explain the psychic and sexual economies of lesbians, even supposing that psychoanalysis can provide an explanation/account of male homosexuality (which also seems dubious to me, given Freud's presumption of the primitive, maternally-oriented heterosexuality at the "origin" of male desire). In the terms we have most readily available, it seems impossible to think lesbian desire. To think desire is difficult enough: desire has never been thoroughly reconsidered, instead of a lack, as an intensity, enervation, positivity, or force. Women's desire is inconceivable on models which attribute to desire the status of an activity: women function (for men) as objects of desire. It is for this reason I would propose a temporary abandonment of the attempt to "understand" lesbian desire, and the turning of attention towards the development of very different models by which to experiment with it, to understand desire not in terms of what is missing or absent, nor in terms of a depth, latency, or interiority, but in terms of surfaces and intensities. (179)

REFIGURING DESIRE

If the dominant or received notions of desire from Plato to Freud and Lacan have construed desire as a lack or negativity, there is a subordinated tradition within Western thought that sees desire in quite different terms. In contrast with the model in which desire is doomed to consumption, incorporation, dissatisfaction, destruction of the object, there is a tradition, we can date from Spinoza, in which desire is primarily seen as production rather than as lack. It cannot be identified with an object whose attainment provides satisfaction, but with processes that produce. For Spinoza, unlike Freud, reality does not prohibit desire but is produced by it. Desire is the force of positive production, the action that creates things, makes alliances, and forges interactions. Where Hegelian desire attempts to internalize and obliterate its objects, Spinozist desire figures in terms of capacities and abilities. Thus, in the one case, desire is a pure absence striving for an impossible completion, fated evermore to play out or repeat its primal or founding loss; in the other, desire is a pure positivity, production. If Freud and psychoanalytic theory can act as representatives of the first and dominant understanding of desire as a lack, then Deleuze and Guattari can be seen to represent the second broad trajectory.

At first sight it may appear that I am simply substituting one evil (Deleuze and Guattari's rhizomatics) for another (Freudian and Lacanian psychoanalysis), that I am throwing away what feminists, and many lesbian feminists in particular, have found the most appealing of all theoretical models. I do not do so lightly, having myself invested a great deal of time in psychoanalytic theory. In spite of well-recognized problems that I have tried to discuss elsewhere and that others have also dealt with, I believe that their work does not have to be followed faithfully to be of use in dealing with issues that they do not, or perhaps even cannot, deal with themselves—most specifically the question of lesbian desire. Nevertheless, because they refuse to understand desire in negative terms, because they refuse to structure it with reference to a singular signifier, the phallus, and because they enable desire to be understood not just as feeling or affect, but also as doing and making, I believe that Deleuze and Guattari may have quite a lot to contribute to refiguring lesbian desire.

As production, desire does not provide blueprints, models, ideals, or goals. Rather, it experiments; it makes: it is fundamentally aleatory, inventive. Such a theory cannot but be of interest for feminist thought insofar as women are the traditional repositories of the lack constitutive of desire, and insofar as the oppositions between presence and absence, between reality and fantasy, have conventionally constrained women to occupy the place of man's other. Lack only makes sense to the (male) subject insofar as some (female) other personifies and embodies it for him. Such a model of desire, when explicitly sexualized, reveals how it is impossible to understand lesbian desire. Any model of desire that dispenses with a reliance of lack seems to be a positive step forward, and for that reason alone is worthy of further investigation.

LESBIAN BODIES AND PLEASURE

The terms by which lesbianism and lesbian desire are commonly understood seem to me problematic: it is no longer adequate to think them in terms of psychology, especially given that the dominant psychological models—psychoanalytic ones—are so problematic in thinking femininity. In attempting to go the other way, I want to be able to provide a reading of lesbian sexuality and desire in terms of bodies, pleasures, surfaces, intensities, as suggested by Deleuze and Guattari, Lyotard, and others.

There are a number of features of lesbian theory and characterizations of lesbian desire that, consequently, I would like to avoid. In the first place, I wish to sidestep the sentimentality and romanticism so commonly involved in thinking lesbian relations. While I can understand the political need to validate and valorize lesbian relations in a culture openly hostile to lesbianism, I think it is also politically important to remain open to self-criticism, and thus to change and growth. Lesbian relations are no better, nor any worse, than the complexities involved in all sociosexual interrelations. They are not a solution to patriarchal forms of sexuality, insofar as lesbianism and gay male sexuality are, as much as heterosexuality, products of patriarchy. There is no pure sexuality, no inherently transgressive sexual practice, no sexuality beyond or outside the limits of patriarchal models. This is not, however, to say all forms of human sexuality are equally invested in patriarchal values—for there are clearly many different kinds of subversion and transgression, many types of sexual aberration unassimilable to historically determinate norms and ideals. It is not only utopian but also naïve to take the moral high ground when proclaiming for oneself the right to judge the transgressive or otherwise status of desire and sexuality: the function of moral evaluations of the sexual terrain can only be one of policing and prohibition, which in no way deals with or is capable of explaining the very desire for and energy of transgression.

(181)

In the second place, I would like to avoid seeing lesbian relations on a binary or polarized model: this means abandoning many of the dominant models of sexual relations between women. I want to avoid seeing lesbian sexual partners on either a model of imaginary, mirror-stage duplicates, narcissistic doubles, self-reflections, bound to each other through mutual identification and self-recognition, or in terms of complementarity in which case the lover complements the sexual style and role of the other—butch-femme and bottom-top couplings.

In the third place, I would also like to eschew models that privilege genitality over other forms of sexuality. While it is clear that genitality remains a major site of intensity, and one whose adult, sexual status is obscured without adequate acknowledgement, it is, on a phallic model, the only true sexuality. I would like to use a model or framework in which sexual relations are contiguous with and a part of other relations—the relations of the writer to pen and paper, the body-builder to weights, the bureaucrat to files. The bedroom is no more the privileged site of sexuality than any other space; sexuality and desire are part of the intensity and passion of life itself.

In the fourth place, I want to avoid the kinds of narrow judgementalism that suggest that any kind of sexuality or desire is better, more political, more radical, more transgressive than another; the kinds of feminist and queer analysis that morally and ethically seek to judge the sexual practices of others, adjudicating what is wrong if not what is right.

And fifth, I want to look at lesbian relations and, if possible, all social relations in terms of bodies, energies, movements, inscriptions, rather than in terms of ideologies, the inculcation of ideas, the transmission of systems of representations, modes of socialization or social reproduction, flattening depth, reducing bodies to surface effects.

Sexuality and desire, then, are not fantasies, wishes, hopes, aspirations (although no doubt these are some of its components), but are energies, excitations, impulses, actions, movements, practices, moments, pulses of feeling. The sites most intensely invested in desire always occur at a conjunction, an interruption, a point of machinic connection, always surface effects, between one thing and another—between a hand and a breast, a tongue and a cunt, a mouth and food, a nose and a rose. In order to understand this notion, we have to abandon our habitual understanding of entities as the integrated totality, and instead focus on the elements, the parts, outside of their integration or organization, to look beyond the organism to the organs that comprise it. In looking at the interlocking of two such parts—fingers and velvet, toes and sand—there is not, as psychoanalysis suggests, a predesignated erotogenic zone, a site always ready and able to function as erotic: rather, the coming together of two surfaces produces a tracing that imbues eros or libido to both of them, making bits of bodies, its parts or particular surfaces throb, intensify, for their own sake and not for the benefit of the entity or organism as a whole. They come to have a life of their own, functioning according to their own rhythms, intensities, pulsations, movements. Their value is always provisional and temporary, ephemeral and fleeting: they may fire the organism, infiltrate other zones and surfaces with their intensity but are unsustainable.

These bodily relations are not (even as much of gay male culture presumes) anonymous, quick encounters, but rather are a relation to a singularity or particularity, always specific, never generalizable. Neither anonymous nor yet entirely personal, they are still an intimacy of encounter, a pleasure/unpleasure always of and for themselves. Encounters, interfaces between one part and another of bodies or body-things produce the erotogenic surface, inscribe it as a surface, linger on and around it for their evanescent effects: like diet, clothing, exercise, and torture. Sexual encounters inscribe the body's surface, and in doing

(182)

so produce an intensity that is in no way innate or pregiven. Probably one of the most interesting, and undervalued, theorists of the erotic and of desire is Alphonso Lingis, whose wonderful texts shimmer with the very intensity he describes:

> The libidinal excitations do not invest a pregiven surface; they extend a libidinal surface. This surface is not the surface of a depth, the contour enclosing an interior. The excitations do not function as signals, as sensations. Their free mobility is horizontal and continually annexes whatever is tangent to the libidinal body. On this surface exterior and interior are continuous; its spatiality that of a Moebius strip. The excitations extend a continuity of convexities and concavities, probing fingers, facial contours, and orifices, swelling thighs and mouths, everywhere glands surfacing, and what was protuberance and tumescence on the last contact can now be fold, cavity, squeezed breasts, soles of feet forming still another mouth. Feeling one's way across the outer face of this Moebius strip one finds oneself on the inner face—all surface still and not inwardness. (Lingis, 1985a: 76)

To relate, through someone, to something else; or to relate, through something, to someone; not to relate to some one and only that person, without mediation. To use the machinic connections a body-part forms with another, whether it be organic or inorganic, to form an intensity, an investment of libido is to see desire, sexuality as productive. Productive, though in no way reproductive, for this pleasure can serve no other purpose, have no other function, than its own augmentation and proliferation. A production, then, that makes, but that reproduces nothing. A truly nomad desire unfettered by anything external, for any thing can form part of its circuit, can be absorbed into its operations.

If we are looking at intensities and surfaces rather than latencies and depth, then it is not the relation between an impulse and its absent other—its fantasies, wishes, hoped-for objects—that interests us; rather, it is the spread or distribution, the quantity and quality of intensities relative to each other, their patterns, their contiguities that are most significant. Their effects rather than any intentions occupy our focus, for what they make and do rather than what they mean or represent. They transform themselves, undergo metamorphoses, become something else, never retain an identity or purpose. Others, human subjects, women, are not simply the privileged objects of desire: through women's bodies, to relate to other things, to make connections.

While I cannot give a "real life illustration," I can however refer to one of Australia's few postmodern lesbian writers, Mary Fallon:

...stroking my whole body all night long until your fingers became fine sprays of white flowers until they became fine silver wires electrifying my epidermis until they became delicate instruments of torture and the night wore on for too many hours and I loved you irritably as dawn reprieved us we are two live-wire women wound and sprung together we are neither of us afraid of the metamorphoses transmogrifications the meltings the juices squelching in the body out of the body—a split fruit of a woman we are neither of us afraid to sink our teeth into the peach it's not love or sex it's just that we are collaborating every night on a book called *The Pleasures of the Flesh Made Simple....* (Fallon: 87)

One "thing" transmutes into another, becomes something else through its connections with something or someone outside. Fingers becoming flowers, becoming silver, becoming torture-instruments. This is precisely what the Deleuzian notion of "becoming" entails, entry into an arrangement, an assemblage of other fragments, other things, becoming bound up in some other production, forming part of a machine, a component in a series of flows and breaks, of varying speeds and intensities. To "become-animal" (or more contentiously, to "become-woman") does not involve imitating, reproducing or tracing the animal (woman), becoming like it: rather, it involves entering into relation with a third term, and, with it, to form a machine that enters into relations with an machine composed of "animal" components:[11] becomings then are not a broad general trajectory of development, but always concrete and specific, becoming-something, something momentary, provisional, something inherently unstable and changing. It is not a question of being (-animal, -woman, -lesbian), of attaining a definite status as a thing, a permanent fixture, nor of clinging to, having an identity, but of moving, changing, being swept beyond one singular position into a multiplicity of flows, or what Deleuze and Guattari have described as "a thousand tiny sexes": to liberate the myriad of flows, to proliferate connections, to intensify.

Becoming-lesbian, if I can put it this way, is thus no longer or not simply a question of being-lesbian, of identifying with that being known as a lesbian, of residing in a position or identity; the question is not am I—or are you—a lesbian, but rather, what kinds of lesbian connections, what kinds of lesbian-machine, we invest our time, energy, and bodies in, what kinds of sexuality we invest ourselves in, with what other kinds of bodies, and to what effects? What it is that together, in parts and bits, and interconnections, we can make that is new, exploratory, opens up further spaces, induces further intensities, speeds up, enervates, and proliferates production (production of the body, production of the world)?

While it is a positive view that I offer here, it is not, in my opinion, a utopian one: it is not a prophecy of the future, a vision of things to come, an ideal or goal, but a way of looking at, and doing things here and now, with concepts and ideas in the same ways we do with bodies and pleasures, a way of levelling, of flattening the hierarchical relations between ideas and things, qualities and entities, of eliminating the privilege of the human over the animal, the organic over the inorganic, the male over the female, the straight over the "bent"—of making them level and interactive, rendering them productive and innovative, experimental and provocative. That is the most we can hope from knowledge. Or desire.

(185)

ANIMAL SEX

If there's one thing that animals don't need more information on, it's sex. That's because sex holds no mystery.

—Freedman, 1977: 9

We make love only with worlds.

—Deleuze and Guattari, 1977: 294

Sex continues to fascinate and obsess human subjects, even if, as Freedman suggests, it holds little mystery for animals. That it lacks mystery, that sexual acts and desires are ruled by natural impulses, impelled by instincts, part of a natural cycle of life, reproduction, and death, may not in fact be as clear-cut and uncontentious as Freedman claims, even if one believes in "the natural order." But even if it is true that sex holds no mystery for the animal (what would "mystery" be to an animal?), it is clearly not true that sex, in animal or human form, holds no mystery for man.[1] Animals continue to haunt man's imagination, compel him to seek out their habits, preferences, and cycles, and provide models and formulae by which he comes to represent his own desires, needs, and excitements. The immense popularity of nature programs on television, of books on various animals species, beloved or feared, and the work of naturalists recording data for scientific study, all testify to a pervasive fascination with the question of animal sex: how do animals *do it*? How do elephants make love (the standard old joke: very carefully)? How do snakes copulate? What are the pleasures of the orangutan, the spider, the chimpanzee?

It is ironic that in the rich plethora of animal sex that has been thus far surveyed, two examples taken from the microcosmic insect world continue to haunt the imaginations and projections of men, perhaps more than others taken from entomology/ethology—the black widow spider and the praying mantis. These two species have come to represent an intimate and persistent link between sex and death, between pleasure and punishment, desire and revenge, which may prove significant in understanding certain key details of male sexuality and desire and, consequently, in specifying elements or features of female sexuality and subjectivity.

Any attempt to understand female sexual desire on the models provided by male sexuality and pleasure risks producing a new model that is both fundamentally reliant on (heterosexual) norms of sexual complementarity or opposition, and reducing female sexuality and pleasure to models, goals, and orientations appropriate for men and not women. Such maneuvers shortcircuit any acknowledgement of the range, scope, and implications of erotic pleasure for understanding sexual difference. This is not to say that female and male sexualities must be regarded as two entirely distinct species, sharing nothing in common, each with their own identities and features (the essentialist commitment). This would entail the possibility of attaining a precise and positive understanding of the independent features that characterize each sex (a project that has tempted many women, and perhaps even more men, to outline what they understand to be a universal, characteristic, or essential femininity). Nor do I wish to suggest the contrary claim that the two sexes must be understood only in terms of each other, as mutually defined, reciprocally influential, each conforming to the other's needs and expectations (this is the dominant fantasy that has thus far governed the contemporary West's thinking about relations between the sexes, a fantasy that has left unacknowledged the structural, social, and representational constraints mitigating against any structural possibility of reciprocity).

Originally, I had planned to write on female sexuality, and particularly on female orgasm. After much hope, and considerable anguish that I would be unable to evoke the languid pleasures and intense particularities of female orgasm (hardly a project for which the discipline of philosophy, or for that matter, psychoanalysis, could provide adequate theoretical training!), I abandoned this idea, partly because it seemed to me to be a project involving great disloyalty—speaking the (philosophically) unsayable, spilling the beans on a vast historical "secret," one about which many men and some women have developed prurient interests; and partly because I realized that at the very most, what I write could be read largely as autobiography, as the "true confessions" of my own experience, and have little more than anecdotal value. I could have no guarantees that my descriptions or analyses would have relevance to other women. Instead, in an attempt both to stay obliquely with my self-chosen topic and avoid these dangers and points of uneasiness, I decided to look at what seems entirely other to women's pleasure and desire—at men, at insects—in an attempt, if not to say what female pleasure is, then at the least to say what it is not, to dispel accounts which bind women too closely to representations of men's or animals' sexuality, to clear the air of certain key projections, even if what is left is not a raw truth of women's desire but perhaps another layer in the complex overwriting/exscription of the inscriptive constitution of the body or subjectivity. Thus, instead of focussing on various representations of women's sexual pleasure (in literature, poetry, painting, sculpture, pornography, etc.) or on personal experience, as many feminists and lesbian theorists have tended to, I decided to explore the work of two apparently unrelated male theorists whose candour and intellectual honesty have for some time impressed me, and whose work represents a rare combination of openly expressed personal obsession and scholarly rigor, the rigorous reading and analysis of their driving personal preoccupations:[2] Roger Caillois, the French sociologist and co-founder of the Collège de sociologie,[3] whose life-long preoccupation with insects, with the femme fatale, and with rocks,[4] signals early anticipations of what might be considered a "philosophy" or perhaps even an "anthropology" of the posthuman; and Alphonso Lingis, the distinguished American philosopher and translator of phenomenological theory (most notably, Merleau-Ponty and Levinas), the only professional philosopher I have read who writes openly yet philosophically, and at great length, about orgasm, bodily pleasures, lust, and sexuality in its many permutations and extremes (transvestism, transsexualism, prostitution, pornography, pederasty, and sadomasochism among them). Between them, Caillois and Lingis provide a coverage from among the most primitive and ancient of insects[5] to the most developed and enculturated of human sexual practices—a veritable panorama of sexual pleasures and practices—that may help to specify what is masculine about representations of human, and non-human, sexualities.

HOLY INSECTS: LOVE AND THE PRAYING MANTIS

Caillois's pioneering contributions to ethology have long been recognized. His by now well-known analysis of the function of mimicry in the insect world[6] has proved salutary for any analysis of materiality that reduces it to instrumentality, any attempt to define form in terms of function, being in terms of *telos*. He shows, in this and in his earlier writings, that the particular characteristics defining an insect species—its coloring, camouflage abilities, the organization of its sense organs—are always in excess of their survival value. There is a certain structural, anatomical, or behavioral superabundance, perhaps it is the very superfluity of life over and above the survival needs of the organism:

> It is obvious that the utilitarian rôle of an object never completely justifies its form, or to put it another way, that the object always exceeds its instrumentality. Thus it is possible to discover in each object an irrational residue....
> (Caillois 1990: 6)

This "irrational residue," this going over the mark, this inherently excessive expenditure, an economy of luxury, becomes a locus of intense fascination for him. In his work on mimicry, Caillois makes it clear that an insect's ability to camouflage itself does not have survival value—it does not protect the creature from attack or death, and in fact may leave it open to even more hideous and unimaginable forms of death. He cites cases of the caterpillar cut in half by pruning shears, or the insect devoured by a member of its own species who mistakes it for a leaf. Camouflage is excessive to survival, just as the plumage of the peacock is excessive to sexual reproduction. Instead of demonstrating the finality of instinctual determinations, an existence defined in Darwinian terms, Caillois introduces a wanton dimension to his explanation of such features of animal existence. Camouflage, the capacity to imitate one's habitat or surroundings, far from performing an adaptative function, witnesses the captivation of a creature by its representations of and as space, its displacement from the center, from a "consciousness" of its place (in its body, located in space) to the perspective of another. The mimicking insect lives its camouflaged existence as not quite itself, as another.[7]

Caillois, who described himself as an "insect collector" (1990: 62), seems to have had a life-long fixation with the *Mantis religiosa*, or praying mantis. He claims to have been attracted to this species partly through frustrated curiosity: where he had lived as an adolescent, they were not to be found. His curiosity piqued, he seems determined to possess, to see, to know. His description is couched in the terms of an impassioned epistemophilia: "[T]he difficulty of getting a specimen only increased my desire to possess one. I had to wait two years, and finally during a summer vacation in Royan I was thrilled to capture a fine *Mantis religiosa...*" (1990: 63).

Part of the attraction the praying mantis holds, not only for Caillois, but for many others, and which may help explain the insect's privileged status in the myths of many cultures,[8] is its close and curious association with femininity, with female sexuality—above all, with the fantasy of the *vagina dentata*; with orality, digestion, and incorporation; and with women's (fantasized) jealousy of and power over men. Moreover, its richly evocative power, its ability to be used as a source of fantasy and speculation, must in part be attributed to its uncanny resemblance to the human form, the isomorphism of its limbs with human ones:

> ...of all insects it is the one whose form most reminds one of the human form, mainly because of the resemblance of its rapacious legs to human arms. As for its ordinary pose, it is not that of someone praying, as common consensus would have us believe (one does not pray lying on one's stomach), but that of a man making love [men on top!]. This alone is enough to justify an obscure and constant identification. One can now see why men have always been so interested in the mantis and its habits, and why it is so aptly associated as much with love as with hatred, whose ambivalent unity it condenses so admirably. (1990: 63)

The ambivalence is derived primarily from a narcissistic identification facilitated by the apparent resemblance of the mantis's posture to the human form; the closer this identification, the more horrifying are the consequences, for the more ominous is the fate of the human/male subject identifying with the (male) mantis. What seems to most provoke Caillois's fascination most are its terrifying nuptial habits, the well-known inclination of the female mantis to devour the male in the act of coitus. The female mantis is the most ungrateful of mates, engulfing and ultimately destroying her lover in a frenzy of self-seeking. This scene is rife with possibilities, and Caillois does not hesitate to suggest that the mantis may serve as an apt representation of the predatory and devouring female lover, who ingests and incorporates her mate, castrating or killing him in the process. The *femme fatale* writ small.[9] This small insect is heir to a whole series of fundamentally paranoid projections, whereby it is not the male subject or the phallus that threatens the female lover but rather, the female lover who threatens the phallus. The father's castrating position vis-à-vis the son is transformed into the image of the devouring mother. The mother is no longer the potential object of rape, but rather the perpetrator of a *theft*, castrating the son and keeping his phallus for herself, in a kind of retaliation against the father's authority and law.[10]

Psychoanalysis is clear that this is not what the mother does to the son, but rather what the son fears of the (fantasmatic) mother. She, no less than the mantis, is the projective vehicle for his worst fears. This may help explain the anthropomorphic identification of the female mantis with the female human—a neutralization of the son's investment in the father's image as a threat and a danger, the cost of which is linking castration to the mother, producing the phallus, and sexual pleasure, in connection with mutilation or death. Indeed, for Caillois, this links the mantis to a series of other vampiric and parasitic images—the vampire, the bat, and the mandrake—which, by virtue of their resemblance to the human, particularly the male, form also renders them objects of projection and identification:

> It is by no means coincidental, in my opinion, that the belief in blood-sucking specters uses a bat as a kind of natural point of reference. The anthropomorphism of the bat runs particularly deep and goes well beyond the level of a general structural identity (the presence of true hands with a thumb opposed to the other fingers, pectoral breasts, a periodic menstrual flow, a free hanging penis). (1990: 73 Fn 10)

The female mantis had been "scientifically observed" since at least the sixteenth century in the act of decapitating the male, not only after or during coitus but even before! He would be devoured completely after copulation. For centuries it was believed that such acts of cannibalism could be described in terms of utility: needing protein to make the newly fertilized eggs grow, the female could find great quantities in devouring her mate. However, it seems more likely that the male's decapitation may well serve not only procreative but also specifically sexual functions for the female mantis:

> Dubois's theory…wonders whether the mantis's goal in decapitating the male before mating is not to obtain, through the ablation of the inhibitory centers of the brain, a better and longer execution of the spasmodic movements of coitus. So that in the final analysis it would be for the female the pleasure principle that would dictate the murder of her lover, whose body, moreover, she begins to eat during the very act of making love. (1990: 81–82)

The female decapitates the male to facilitate more vigorous coital movements! Caillois is most interested in the automatic nature of the male's sexual drive: headless, without a brain to take in representations or to undertake voluntary behavior, it nonetheless doggedly persists in its automatic sexual movements, and is even able to utilize various autonomous strategies to evade danger and predators while nonetheless, in a certain sense at least, dead (but still kicking!):

> [T]he fact is that there are hardly any reactions that it is not also able to perform when decapitated.... In this condition, it can walk, regain its balance, move one of its threatened limbs autonomously, assume the spectral position, mate, lay eggs, build an ootheca, and, quite astoundingly, fall down in a false corpse-like immobility when confronted by danger or following a peripheral stimulation. I am deliberately using this indirect means of expressing myself because our language, it seems to me, has so much difficulty expressing, and our reason understanding, the fact that when dead, the mantis can simulate death. (1990: 82)

The automatism of this whole procedure strikes Caillois as one of the significant features of the mantis; not only can the mantis "play dead" while decapitated, its sexual behaviour is induced reflexively, like a wind-up (sex) toy. It can perform its functions without the organizational structure of consciousness (whatever that might mean in the case of the mantis), the structurings provided by a even a loosely linked nervous system or an intact perceptual apparatus.

Caillois quotes Binet's claim with approval: "The insect seems to us very much like a machine with a perfect mechanism, capable of functioning automatically" (cited in Caillois, 1990: 82). The mantis as perfect machine: not a machine for survival (the shark is commonly referred to as the perfect feeding or killing machine), but a fucking machine, whose reaction, under threat of imminent death, is coital. Caillois takes Binet's point even further: if the mantis is a human-like machine, an android, it is distinctively coded as female:

> Indeed, the assimilation of the mantis to an automaton—that is, in view of its anthropomorphism, to a female android—seems to me to be a consequence of the same affective theme: the conception of an artificial, mechanical, inanimate, and unconscious machine-woman incommensurable with man and other living creatures derives from a particular way of envisioning the relation between love and death, and, more precisely, from an ambivalent premonition of finding the one within the other, which is something I have every reason to believe. (Caillois 1990:82)

Caillois posits a network of associations, an implicit linkage between the praying mantis, religiosity, food and orality, blood-sucking vampires, the mother who feeds the child, cannibalism, the *vagina dentata*, the devouring female, the *femme fatale*, the mechanisms of automatism, and the female android. He has the insight to suggest, not that this is somehow a natural or innate set of connections, but that it is largely a function of a constellation of concepts that are overdetermined in their mutual relations: by linking sexual pleasure to the concept of death and dying, by making sex something to die for, something that is a kind of anticipation of death (the "little death"), woman is thereby cast into the category of the non-human, the non-living, or a living threat of death.

Caillois's intuition about the formative character of the link between sexual pleasure, death, and dying, finds clear confirmation in abundant examples in everyday life: the production of weapons on the model of the phallus, the functioning of the phallus as a weapon of war and retaliation, the dependence of the phallus on the castration complex, the operations of psychical impotence, the link between male orgasm and detumescence, the depletion of psychical energies after orgasm, the fantasmatic projection onto woman of phallic power during the act of intercourse,[11] the "evolutionary" linkage of the death of the individual to the (sexual) reproduction of the species (the perceived link between sexuality and immortality) prefigure or attest to the tenacity of the link between desire and death.

LIBIDINAL INTENSITIES: THE DISARRAYS OF LOVE

In turning away from Caillois's musings about the praying mantis, I will now look in more detail at the work of Lingis on erotic sensibility, libido, or lust to see if we can glean a better understanding of the connections between sexual pleasure and death, and, more challenging and difficult, to see if these two terms might be extricated so that their relations of influence, their particular specificities and details, and thus their possibilities of transformation and change may be explored.

Lingis distinguishes between bodily needs and satisfactions, and lust or erotic desire. Corporeal gratification, functioning in the register of need, takes what it can get, lives in a world of means and ends, obtaining satisfaction from what is at hand. Lingis relates the operations of need and gratification to the functioning of the body-image or corporeal schema, which maps inner physiological and psychological functions onto exterior or "objective" comportment and movements, thereby establishing the body's posture and positioning in the world through a mediating representational schema. Lingis makes it clear that the body image provides the subject with an experience, not only of its own body, but also of the ways in which its body is perceived by others. The subject's experience of the body is irreducibly bound up with the body's social status.

By contrast, libido or erotic desire involves a certain dis-quieting or troubling of the body-image, even while functioning in conformity with it. Rather than resolving itself, gratifying its urges as quickly and simply as possible, erotic craving seeks to prolong and extend itself beyond physiological need, to intensify and protract itself, to revel in "pleasurable torment" (Lingis 1985: 55). It no longer functions according to an "intentional arc," according to the structures of signification, meaning, pattern, or purpose;[12] voluptuous desire fragments and dissolves the unity and utility of the organic body and the stabilized body-image. The limbs, erogenous zones, orifices of the other, provoke and entice, lure and beckon, breaking up the teleological, future-directed actions and plans of a task to perform.[13] If, for Merleau-Ponty, eroticism is the structuring and reorientation of the body-subject according to the lure that the other's body poses, a re-signifying of one's body-parts in a new light, Lingis will nevertheless argue that sensuous desire and voluptuous experience do not involve the affirmation of a bodily totality, nor the passage from formless non-sense to a body offering sense and meaning. Quite the contrary. The voluptuous sense of disquiet engendered by and as lust disarrays and segments the resolve of a certain purposiveness, unhinging any determination of means and ends or goals. (195)

Carnal experience is uncertain, non-teleological, undirected. While not entirely involuntary, it lacks the capacity to succumb wilfully to conscious intentions or abstract decisions. It upsets plans, resolutions; it defies a logic of expediency and the regimes of signification (one often cannot say or know what it is that entices and allures, a gesture, a movement, a posture or look, which becomes loaded with more affect and impetus than is required to explain it). It is like an ever-increasing hunger that supplements itself, feeds itself, on hunger, and can never be content with what it ingests, that defers gratification to perpetuate itself as craving, languishing in its erotic torments rather than hastening to quench them. Its temporality is neither that of development (one experience building on the last in order to create a direction or movement) nor that of investment (a relation between means and specific or pregiven ends). Nor is it a system of recording or memory (erotic pleasures are evanescent; they are forgotten almost as they occur); the memory of "what happened," or movements, setting, gestures, behavior may be open to reminiscence, but the intensity of pleasure, the sensations of voluptuousness, the ache of desire have to be revivified in order to be recalled. In this case, there is not recollection but recreation, or rather, creation, production:

Carnal intimacy is not a practical space; it does not open a field for action. The erotic movements are agitation that handles and fondles without keeping anything in its place, without extending its force outward and without going anywhere. Here nothing will be accomplished; one will waste time, unprofitably. Voluptuousness has no tasks and no objectives and leaves no heritage; after all the caresses and embraces, the carnal is left intact, virgin territory.... It is not the locus from which would emerge the meaning of one's history. (Lingis 1985: 67)

Erotic desire cannot be recorded or stored, cannot be the site for the production of information or knowledge. Masters and Johnson's empirical research on human sexuality can only measure and record physiological transformations, reactions, responses, bodily changes. It comes nowhere near to mapping desire. Desire's turbulent restlessness defies coding into signs, significations, meanings; it remains visceral, affective, which is not to say that it is in any way reducible to physiology.

Libido is not irrational, illogical, or even non-rational; rather it exhibits a logic of its own governed by modes of intensification. It does not provide information or knowledge, although it probes (this may be part of the problem of the metaphor of knowledge-production as sexual conquest: conquest can only make sense where lust does not operate but something else—the struggle for prestige, control). It breaches the innermost regions, secret parts, of the body, but does not learn anything except that it cannot hold onto, cannot keep itself in its state of excitation. Lust cannot know itself, it does not know what it is or what it seeks. It does not discover, but immerses itself, insisting on a certain formlessness, indeterminacy, the very excess of materiality that makes any creature resist reduction to its functions alone. It insists on an open responsiveness that can be viewed as a passivity or susceptibility to the appeals and resistances of the other. Lust throws one into the vagaries of the other's libidinal intensities.

If the sexual drive is object-directed, and takes for itself a specific series of objects, it is significant that eros, desire, has no objectives, no privileged objects, only a series of intensities. Having outlined the elements of a phenomenology of carnal experience relying on the various writings of Sartre, Merleau-Ponty, and Levinas, Lingis shifts his focus in *Libido* (1985) away from the structures of consciousness, intentionality and givenness to focus more sharply on what might be understood as a materialist analysis of sexual desire, using the work of Lyotard and Deleuze and Guattari. He moves away from a framework, or series of them, which privilege the psyche and systems of representation, and which understand carnality in terms of concepts, reasons, motives, causes, intentions, fantasies, projects—that is, in terms of interiority, however conceived—to one, or several, that privilege the erotogenic surface, the body's "outside," its locus as a site for both the perception of the erotic (as phenomenology recognized) but also for the inscription and intensification of the sensitivity of bodily regions.

The orgasmic body cannot be identified with the organic body, but is more an interference in and displacement of the body of "nature."[14] This is not the intervention of a supervising consciousness, but the reorganization or the rebinding of bodily energies, passing along the body's surface. Relying on a model established by Lyotard in *Libidinal Economy* (1993), where the subject is viewed in terms of the twisting, contortions, and self-rotations of the Moebius strip,[15] Lingis refigures carnal desire in terms of the lateral ("horizontal") contamination of one erotogenic zone or bodily surface by another, rather than in terms of a "vertical relation" between (bodily) surface and (psychical) depth. The intensification of one bodily region or zone induces an increase in the excitation of those contiguous with it. Significantly, the two or more interacting zones or regions need not be part of the one body but may come from different bodies and different substances. Their relations cannot be understood in terms of complementarity, the one completing the other (a pervasive model of the heterosexual relation since Aristophanes), for there can be no constitution of a totality, union, or merger of the two. Each remains in its site, functioning in its own ways.

The relationship between these regions or zones cannot be understood in terms of domination, penetration, control, or mastery, but in terms of *jealousy*, as one organ jealous of another, as the desire of organs and zones for the intensity and excitations, the agitations and tumultuousness of others. In order that one bodily part (whether an orifice, a hollow, a protuberance, a swollen region, a smooth surface) intensify its energetic expenditure, it must drain intensity from surrounding regions. It is impossible to conceive of a situation in which there is an even intensity throughout the whole body, a situation of pure equilibrium or stasis: any activity at all "prefers" or privileges some bodily regions over others, and even sedentary inactivity focuses on some parts of the body at the expense of others. This creates a gridding or marking of the body in terms of sites of uneven intensity, patterns or configurations of feeling, labyrinthine maps of voluptuous pleasures and intensities. Each organ envies the intensity of its surrounding bodily context, craves enervation, seeks incandescence, wants itself to be charged with excitations.

Lingis seeks to evoke, to replay in words, the intensities that charge all

(197)

erotic encounters, whether the amorous relations of the carpenter to wood and tools, the attachment of the sadist to the whip, the liaison of breast and mouth, lips and tongue. There must be some coming together of disparate surfaces; the point of conjunction of two or more surfaces produces an intensification of both.

Modes of greatest intensification of bodily zones occur, not through the operations of habitual activities, but through the unexpected, through the connection, conjunction and construction of unusual interfaces which re-mark orifices, glands, sinews, muscles differently, giving organs and bodily organization up to the intensities that threaten to overtake them, seeking the alien, otherness, the disparate in its extremes, to bring into play these intensities. The interruption and interaction of a surface with another, its disengagement from the circuit of organic functioning (where it operates within an hierarchical and systematic whole) so that it realigns itself in different networks and linkages performs the intensification of libidinal circulation that Lingis seeks. In this way, the subject's body ceases to be *a* body, to become the site of provocations and reactions, the site of intensive disruptions. The subject ceases to be a subject, giving way to pulsations, gyrations, flux, secretions, swellings, processes over which it can exert no control and to which it only wants to succumb. Its borders blur, seep, so that, for a while at least, it is no longer clear where one organ, body, or subject stops and another begins.

It is the lateral alignment of intensities that makes a hand, the fingers, an elbow, a sexual organ, a site, not just for the production of pleasure in another, but for their own orgasmic intensities, though they cannot be classified as a orifice or genital organ on a psychoanalytic or physiological model. The hand, while in a sense "jealous" of the pleasure it induces in the body it caresses, also participates in the intensities it ignites in a vagina or around a penis: it does not simply induce pleasure in another, for another, but also always for itself. The contiguity of hand and region instils in both a yearning for intensity, a craving for more intensity that both enlivens them, rouses their "jealousy" of each other, and propels them into a path of unpredictable and restless movement.

These sites of intensity—potentially any region of the body including various internal organs—are intensified and excited, not simply by pleasure, through caresses, but also through the force and energy of pain. Pain, as Nietzsche well recognized, is as capable, perhaps more so, of inscribing bodily surfaces, as pleasure. This may help to explain some of the appeal of sadism and masochism, even if we accept, following Deleuze (1989a), that they do not compose a single complex and reversible relation, as Freud suggests. These are modes of intensification of the body's sensations.[16] Sadism and masochism intensify particular bodily regions—the buttocks being whipped, the hand that whips, bound regions of the body in domination practices—not using pain as a displacement of or disguise for the pleasure principle, but where pain serves as a mode of corporeal intensification. We cannot readily differentiate the processes by which pleasurable intensities are engendered from those by which painful intensity is produced. One craves repetition of these practices because the intensity is ephemeral, has no life span—it exists only in the moments of its occurrence, in the present (the evanescence of pure difference, the momentary shimmering and dazzling of a zone or orifice: it is the trace, the marking of a pathway, *frayage*). This repetition (or rather, the inherent openness of these practices to repetition) produces the intensity of affect, pleasure or pain, but can never repeat its initial occurrence. Each repetition engenders a version of the same without any presumption of identity. Strictly speaking, exact repetition remains impossible.

Erotogenic zones do not desegment the fully functional organic body, for this body is itself a product of the organization and hierarchization of localized and particular libidinal zones: the organic, unified body is the provisional end-result of the alignments and coagulations of libidinal zones. These regions, moreover, continually intervene in the functioning of the organic body and its attendant body image(s). Instead of adopting the psychoanalytic position, which takes erotogenic zones as nostalgic reminiscences of a preoedipal, infantile bodily organization—that is, instead of seeing the multiplicity of libidinal sites in terms of regression—these libidinal zones are continually in the process of being produced, renewed, transformed, through experimentation, practices, innovations, the accidents or contingencies of life itself, the coming together of surfaces, incisive practices, inscriptions. There is nothing particularly infantile about these regions, insofar as to be effective, to function as the sites of orgasmic intensity, they must continually be invested through activity.

Moreover, if libidinal impulses are fundamentally decomposing, de-solidifying, liquefying the coherent organization of the body as its performs functional tasks, unhinging a certain intentionality, they are more dependent on the sphere of influence of otherness, on an other which, incidentally, need not be human or even animate, but which cannot simply be classified as a passive object awaiting the impressions of an active desiring subject. The other solicits, beckons, implores, provokes, and demands. The other lures, oscillates, presenting everything it has to offer, disclosing the whole body without in fact giving up anything, without providing "information" as such.

Resisting redeployment in pragmatic projects, it functions in its own ways, seeking to endlessly extend itself, to fill itself with intensity. But it is incapable of being filled up, completed, for it contains ineliminable traces of alterity: it is an otherness in the subject, something that overtakes one, induces one to abandon what one has planned, and even what one understands, in exchange for its dazzling agitations and stirring sensations. The other erupts into the subject, and interrupts all the subject's aims and goals: "the approach of the other is dismemberment of the natural body, fragmentation of the phenomenal field, derangement of the physical order, breakdown in the universal industry" (1985: 72).

Libidinal desire, the carnal caress, desire as corporeal intensification, then, is being thrown into an interchange with an other whose surface intersects one's own. One is opened up, in spite of oneself, to the other, not as passive respondent but as co-animated, for the other's convulsions, spasms, joyous or painful encounters engender, or contaminate, bodily regions that are apparently unsusceptible. It is in this sense that we make love to worlds: the universe of an other is that which opens us up to and produces our own intensities. We are placed in a force field of intensities that we can only abandon with libidinal loss and in which we are enervated to become active and willing agents (or better, agen*cies*). The other need not be human or even animal: the fetishist enters a universe of the animated, intensified object as rich and complex as any sexual relation (perhaps more so than). The point is that both a world and a body are opened up for redistribution, dis-organization, transformation; each is metamorphosed in the encounter, both become something other, something incapable of being determined in advanced, and perhaps even in retrospect, but which nonetheless have perceptibly shifted and realigned. The sexual encounter cannot be regarded as an expedition, an adventure, a goal, or an investment, for it is a directionless mobilization of excitations with no guaranteed outcomes or "results" (not even orgasm).

THE MURDEROUS LOVER; OR KISS ME DEADLY

In *Beyond the Pleasure Principle* (1919b) Freud raises the question of the necessary binding or linkage of the pleasure principle with the death drive. He links the accumulation of unbounded intensities or affects with unpleasure, and the relief or satisfaction of libidinal impulses with pleasure. He uses Fechner's constancy principle to suggest that the organism attempts to keep the quantity of energy or excitation as low as possible—not so low as to "wind down," to approach death, but low enough not to "overstimulate" the organism, causing it to seek all sorts of inappropriate outlets to vent the excessive energy that would otherwise accumulate. There is an entropic principle internally directing the organism towards simplicity and quiescence, impelling it gradually towards death. Life can be seen, on this Freudian scenario, as the limited deferment or delay of the death drive, a detour of death through the pleasure principle. These two principles, Eros and Thanatos—life/pleasure and death/unpleasure—are both complementary and opposed: they function together, each operates through the other; and, as it were, against the interests of the other. The pleasure principle provides a way in which the death drive can express itself through the processes of gratification, in this "unwinding" or diminution of psychical energies; and the death drive provides, as it were, the medium, the material—the accumulation of tension—through which the pleasure principle gains its satisfaction.

Paradoxically, the death drive and libido do not cancel out but reinforce each other. Libido or the life-drives produce self-preservative and pleasurable (respectively, instinctual and drive) processes that aim to protect the organism from dangers coming from without and from the unpleasant accumulation of energies within the organism. In this sense, they allow the death drive to take its own course and its own time: they protect the organism from outside dangers, so that it can be carried towards death by its own immanent processes.

Particularly in Freud's phylogenetic perspective, sex or pleasure and death are internally linked. The pleasurable sexual activities of individuals are closely linked to the reproduction of the species, and the reproduction of the species is contingently dependent on the life, reproduction and death of individuals. Such an assumption has proved very strong in ethology: it is significant that the simplest of living organisms, amoeba and other single-celled organisms, those which do not reproduce sexually through interchange with "the opposite sex" but reproduce through the division of cells, are considered immortal. Sexuality introduces death into the world; or, perhaps the converse: death is inevitable, and sexuality may function as a compensation for and supplement to death. Not only is the sexual act *grosso modo* linked to death and through it, to the reproduction of the species, but more significantly, the eroticism of orgasm—at least of male orgasm (the case of female orgasm is considerably more complicated, and it is not clear to what degree it conforms to this model, if it does so at all)—is modelled by Freud on the build-up of excitation, the swelling of the sexual organ, the accumulation of energies and fluids, their release, and then the organ's detumescence and state of contentment.

The immediacy and the directness of this link between death and sex is perhaps the intriguing thing about the praying mantis: it provides a tangible example of the worst fears surrounding the ways in which sexuality and relations between the sexes are conceived, the most horrific consequences of amorous passion (even though it is not clear that the mantis is either amorous or passionate outside of any anthropomorphic projection). Severing this link between death and sexual desire is particularly crucial at this historical conjuncture, not only because of the constricting effects it has on female (not to mention male) sexuality, but also because of its potentially lethal effects within gay men's and other communities.[17]

Lingis has recognized the link between horror and lust: the transformative, transubstantiating effects of erotic attachments are echoed in the seeping out beyond boundaries and the dissolution of lines of bodily organization prompted by orgasmic dissolution. There is something about the compulsive incitements of sexuality that may bring one to the brink of disgust and to the abject, not only accepting but seeking out activities, objects, and bodily regions that one might in other contexts disdain. The melting of corporeal boundaries, the merging of body parts, the dripping apart of all the categories and forms that bind a subject to its body and provide it with a bodily integrity—so fascinating for the surrealists, not to mention with the current android and cyborg fantasies that sell movies and feminist science fiction—imperil one in a way that alarms and horrifies, and at the same time, entices to the highest possible degree. It is this lust has in common with the appeal of illicit drugs: their intensity melts a certain subjective cohesion, the "high" more or less obliterates key boundaries between the body and its others, more or less pleasurably and more or less temporarily.

Although his perspective admits a connection between horror and desire, Lingis resists the temptation to make the link between desire and death intrinsic, as psychoanalytic theory has tended to. This may prove particularly instructive insofar as, in the last ten years, Lingis has primarily published material either directly related to sexuality (in its broadest sense) (Lingis, 1983; 1985; 1991a; 1992; 1994b; 1994c) or on the question of death (Lingis, 1989) but has not attempted to link these two projects. This may be because he is attempting, among other things, to disconnect the two, to sever the bond between sexual pleasure and the death drive, to think libido in terms other than the hydraulics of the Freudian model of sexual discharge or cathexis. All of Freud's works can be understood as a generalization of and abstraction from the model of male orgasm to the fundamental principle of life itself: the constancy principle, and indeed the pleasure principle, the notion of psychical investment or cathexis, the movements of repression that sever an ideational representative from its energetic intensity, all accord with this hydraulics of tumescence and detumescence. The death drive is not simply a "new discovery" made by Freud in his later writings, for it is already inscribed in his understanding of the pleasure principle even in his earliest psychoanalytic texts.

The fantasy of the *vagina dentata*, of the non-human status of woman as android, vampire, or animal, the identification of female sexuality as voracious, insatiable, enigmatic, invisible, and unknowable, cold, calculating, instrumental, castrator/decapitator of the male, dissimulatress or fake, predatory, engulfing mother, are all consequences of the ways in which male orgasm has functioned as the measure and representative of all sexualities and all modes of erotic encounter. Lingis's project is of relevance to the disentangling of masculinist and Freudian conceptions of sexuality, pleasure, and desire insofar it provides an understanding of (male) subjectivity and desire beyond and in breach of the opposition between pleasure and death.[18] He demonstrates that sexual passion is not reducible to the goal of sexual satiation, but lives and thrives on its own restless impetus. Orgasm need not be understood as the end of the sexual encounter, its final culmination and moment of conversion towards death or dissipation; instead, it can be displaced to any and every region of the body, and in addition, seen as a mode of transubstantiation, a conversion from solid to liquid:

(203)

> The supreme pleasure we can know, Freud said, and the model for all pleasure, orgasmic pleasure, comes when an excess tension built up, confined, compacted is abruptly released; the pleasure consists in a passage into the contentment and quiescence of death. Is not orgasm instead the passage into the uncontainment and unrest of liquidity and vapor—pleasure in exudations, secretions, exhalations? ...Lust surges through a body in transubstantiation. (1991a: 15)

Caillois also recognizes the binding of the death drive to the pleasure principle in the masculine projection of woman as cold, mechanical, inanimate, machine-like: if we recall, such conceptions "derive from a particular way of envisioning the relation between love and death, and, more precisely, from an ambivalent premonition of finding the one within the other" (Caillois 1990: 82), a particular, presumably not a universal or inevitable, relation between love and death, which in principle can be disentangled. Desire can be reconsidered in terms that do not see it entwined with death.

The fantasy that binds sex to death so intimately is the fantasy of a hydraulic sexuality, a biologically regulated need or instinct, a compulsion, urge, or mode of physical release (the sneeze provides an analogue). The apparently urgent and compulsive nature of sexual drives is implicit in the claim made by many men who rape, those who frequent prostitutes, and those prostitutes who describe themselves as "health workers," insofar as they justify their roles in terms of maintaining the "health" of their clients. It is a model of sexuality based upon the equation of sexual desire with orgasmic release, with instrumental or functional relief of the body. It is a model that men commonly transfer from their own lived experiences onto the experiences of women, and it reappears in another guise in the current reclamation of female ejaculation by some feminists.[19] When eroticism is considered a program, a means to an end ("foreplay"), a mode of conquest, a proof of virility or femininity, an inner drive that periodically erupts, or an impelling attraction to an object that exerts a "magnetic" force (i.e., as actively compelling, or as passively seduced), it is reduced to versions of this hydraulic model.

The provocations and allure of the other can have no effect on the erotic receptivity of the subject without resonances with the intensities and surfaces of the subject's body. Indeed nothing seems sillier and less erotic than someone else's unreciprocated ardor or passion. The other cannot excite without the subject already being excited or excitable. The other cannot induce erotic impulses and caresses from the outside alone. I am not suggesting a necessary reciprocity here, but rather a co-implication. There is always equivocation and ambiguity in passion: on the one hand, the erotic is self-contained and self-absorbed—lovers are closed off to the world, wrapped up in each other, disinterested in what is outside; on the other hand, in a contrary movement, eroticism and sensuality tend to spread out over many things, infecting all sorts of other relations.[20] Erotic desire is not simply a desire for recognition, the constitution of a message, an act of communication or exchange between subjects, a set of techniques for the transmission of intimacy; it is a mode of surface contact with things and substances, with a world, that engenders and induces transformations, intensifications, a becoming something other. Not simply a rise and fall, a waxing and waning, but movement, processes, transmutations. That is what constitutes the appeal and power of desire, its capacity to shake up, rearrange, reorganize the body's forms and sensations, to make the subject and body as such dissolve into something else, something other than what they are

(204)

habitually. Sexual relations need not presume desire—habitual orgasmic (or non-orgasmic) practices are not the most conducive milieu for the ignition and exploration of desire. Desire need not culminate in sexual intercourse, but may end in production. Not the production of a child or a relationship, but the production of sensations never felt, alignments never thought, energies never tapped, regions never known.

(205)

EXPERIMENTAL DESIRE

To me, queer transcends any gender, any sexual persuasion and philosophy. Queerness is a state of being. It is also a lifestyle. Its something that's eternally the alternative. To both the gay and lesbian mainstream. What's queer now may not be queer in five years' time. If transgender queer was accepted by both communities, then there would be no queer. It's a reflection of the times you live in.

—Jasper Laybutt, "male lesbian," female-to-male transsexual who edits the Australian edition of *Wicked Women* in *Capital Q,* October 9, 1992: 9

I WANT TO LOOK AT A SET OF RATHER OLD-fashioned concepts and issues that I believe remain useful and can be revitalized if they are reconsidered in terms of the politics and theory of lesbian and gay sexualities: *oppression,* and i*dentity.* I do not want to replay the usual anti-humanist critiques of identity which seek to displace, decenter or even destroy the notion of subjective/sexual "identity," but to work, using their presumptions and insights, on the terrain taken up by notions of oppression, sex, and sexual identity, to rewrite them, to reclaim them in different terms, and, in the process, to clarify some issues that I believe are crucial to the area now known as "queer theory."[1] It is not simply the political history and former power of these terms that I wish to resuscitate: I am not really interested in nostalgic replayings, but in refusing to give up terms, ideas, strategies that still work, whose potentialities have still not been explored, and which are not quite ready to be junked just yet.

SYSTEMATIC STRUCTURES OF POWER

For notions like oppression, discrimination, or social positioning to have any meaning, they must be articulated and explained outside any particular form (whether racist, imperialist, sexual, class, or religious). In other words, there must a common strand shared by all the different forms of oppression, something (or many things) that enables them to be described by the same term, even if there is a strong recognition that oppressions may take on massive historical and cultural variations. This core or even "essence," and the range and variability of the term, need to be addressed if one is to come to a clearer understanding of the relations and interactions between different forms of social domination. In short, it requires a very careful and precise understanding if it is not only to be appropriately used to cover a wide variety of different types of oppression; but also, perhaps more politically relevantly, if it is to be able to articulate the interlockings and transformations effected by the convergences, points of reinforcement and/or tension between different forms of oppression. My goal, though, in attempting to render more precise these interlocking systems of oppression is not to set up a kind of hierarchy of oppressed subjects, an index of degrees of oppression,[2] nor to provide a typology which is inclusive of all types of oppression (this seems to be the current trend in much contemporary theorizing about oppressions[3]), but to understand the inflections any particular category must undergo when it is coupled with or related to other categories.

If there is a broad core of meaning to the term, oppression, it must be minimally understood as:

1. The production of systematically differentiated positions for social subjects, which function as modes of specification, constitution, and valuation, within a general structure which distributes to those positions and thus the subjects occupying them, various benefits, power, authority, and value. This implies that whatever skills, capacities, and attributes members of the subordinated groups have, their ability to take up the privileged positions remains extremely limited, if not impossible;

2. These differential positions distribute benefits to those in privileged positions only at the expense of other, subordinated positions. This privilege is possible only because its cost is borne by subordination. This explains why structures of power and authority remain tenaciously

difficult to transform: it is not in the interests of the dominant groups, who have benefits without actual paying for them, to readily give up those benefits without struggle. Certainly the impetus and motive for change cannot come from this group, which stands to lose much of its privilege in any realignment of relative positions;

3. Not only are specific groups positioned in differential locations within the social structure (positions that may be interlocked or inter-dependent, but which serve only the interests of the dominant group), these positions are directly or indirectly linked to values, attributes, benefits, mobility, that are not specifically inscribed in but are pre-conditioned by these positions. Being born male, white, middle class, Christian, etc. gives one access to wealth, decision-making, and naming capacities that, while not entirely out of the reach of other groups, is made extremely difficult for them, except perhaps at the cost of renouncing or overcoming their definitional linkage to a subordinated group;

4. Relations of domination and subordination are characterized not simply in terms of tangible material benefits, although these could be easily documented, but also in terms of the ease and ability of dominant groups to produce meanings, representations—which present their interests—perspectives, values, and frameworks in positive, self-evident terms, and define their others (non-reciprocally) in terms of these inter-ests. This ease is denied to members of subordinate groups. Here, I do not want to suggest that the capacity to change meaning, to develop new meanings and frameworks, is impossible for dominated groups, but it is nonetheless made considerably more difficult and is a matter of bitter struggle and contestation; and

5. The relations of domination and subordination constituting oppres-sion are more complicated than the occupation of fixed, stable positions of power and powerlessness or centrality and marginality. While they clearly accrue privileges and benefits at the expense of subordinated posi-tions, positions of domination also have their long-term complications, insofar as those who occupy these positions lose access to certain skills of self-determination, skills acquired through struggle, resistance, and the necessary ingenuity of those in subordinated positions. The position of subordination, while it requires the loss or absence of many of the rights and privileges of the dominant position, also produces certain skills and modes of resourcefulness, the capacity precisely for self-sustenance and creativity that are lost for the dominator. They become complaisant and self-satisfied, while the subordinated must sharpen their wits and continuously develop themselves or succumb to their oppressed positions. It is only through the engagement, the encounter between the

dominators and the dominated, through the resistances posed by the dominated to the dominators that social change follows a certain direction (even if that direction and the rates of progress to any pre-given goal cannot be guaranteed by members of either or both groups).

The notion of oppression is clearly linked to power, to the relations, forms, and goals that power may take. But since Foucault's genealogies of power, notions of power and oppression have undergone relatively major transformations. The relations between power, domination, and subordination are no longer quite so clear-cut and unambiguous in their status. The subordinated are implicated in power relations even if they are not directly complicit in them: They are implicated in the sense that, as a mobile set of force relations, power requires the structural positions of subordination, not as the outside or limit of its effectivity, but as its internal condition, the "hinge" on which it pivots. Foucault's work, in spite of the by-now well documented problems in feminist terms,[4] has at least one (but no doubt also many more) insight to offer feminist and lesbian theorists: He has rendered the notion of oppression considerably more sophisticated, he has alerted us to the idea that the attribution of social value is not simply a matter of being rendered passive and compliant, being made into victims, who, occupying certain social positions, cannot be stripped of all capacities and all modes of resistance. The positions of subordination cannot be placed within a singular schema, framework, representation, or universally enforced operation; rather, resistance engenders its own kinds of strategies and counterstrategies, it exerts its own kind of forces (which are not simply the opposite or inverse of domination), its own practices, and knowledges, which, depending on their socio-cultural placement and the contingencies of the power game that we have no choice but to continue playing, may be propelled into positions of power and domination. Foucault, in short, and by no means on his own, has provided a sense of hope, a signal of the possibility, indeed necessity, of a certain agency and efficacy for those classified as oppressed. Admittedly, Foucault's work has the effect of problematizing megalithic understandings of capitalism, patriarchy, racism, and imperialism as systematic, coherent global programs, which makes it more difficult to assert hard and fast allegiances and interlockings between these great systems. He has rendered their interconnections more expedient, less programmed and cohesive, and thus more amenable to realignment and transformation, even if they are now murkier, less clear-cut, less easy to read than any simple assertion of good (politically correct) or bad.

Given this more diffused and less structurally precise understanding of relations of power and domination, notions of oppression and social valuation can be wrenched from humanist history and made to do the work of specifying, rendering visible, the issue of difference, which seems to me to be the fundamental terrain of contestation of our political era. Difference, alterity, otherness are difficult concepts to incorporate into the humanist and phenomenological paradigm of oppression, which seeks to recognize all subjects (or, more commonly, *most* subjects) on the model of a bare or general humanity. Such a conception of humanity has no choice but to cast those different enough from the definition of humanity into the arena of the pre, proto- or non-human. Otherness can enter, at best, as a secondary modification of this basic human nature, a minor detail, but not a fundamental dimension or defining characteristic which alters all the other general capacities attributed to "human" existence. Feminism, along with anti-humanism, is probably the most direct line of assault on that humanism, which took as its standard of the human, the presumptions, perspectives, frameworks, and interests of men.

SEX AND SEXUALITY

Are the characteristics I have outlined adequate to outline "sexual oppression," the disqualification, devaluation and misrepresentation of subjects and practices on the basis of either (or both) their sex and/or their sexuality? Do they encompass the specific modalities of oppression experienced by women in general, by lesbians and gay men, by various perverts, transsexuals, transvestites, drag queens, butches, cross-dressers, and all the other variations of sexual transgression? This is the anti-humanist question: do the apparently universal characteristics common to all modes of oppression include all types of oppression? If they do, then in what ways do they help to explain misogyny and homophobia in their specificity? If they only serve to characterize oppression but not to specify its homophobic dimension, then what needs to be added to them or modified in them to make them appropriate? These questions give rise to a series of further anxieties: is there is such a thing as homophobia, and a common oppression for *both* lesbian and gays? Do lesbians experience the same forms of homophobia as gay men? Can we presume that it takes on universal forms? Does the fact that they are women and men (however one chooses to define these terms) alter the forms of homophobia each experiences? Moreover, does the very category of sex/sexuality differ sexually, that is, according to the sex of the subject under question?

Here I want to use these terms, "sex" and "sexuality" in the light of but in variance from Foucault's understanding. For Foucault, and this is one of his major innovations, sex can no longer be understood as the ground, the real, the (biological/natural) foundation of later superstructural ramifications: it is not a base onto which the superstructure of "gender" and of "sexuality" can be securely added. There is no biological substratum onto which to hang a discursive and cultural overlay. For him, the very notion of sex as origin, as given, as fundamental, to subjectivity, identity and/or cultural harmony, is itself the product or effect of a socio-discursive regime of sexuality. A well-known quote makes this clear:

> We must not make the mistake of thinking that sex is an autonomous agency which secondarily produces manifold effects over the entire length of its surface of contact with power. On the contrary, sex is the most speculative, most ideal, and most internal element in a deployment of sexuality organized by power in its grip on bodies and their materiality, their forces, energies, sensations and pleasures. (Foucault, 1980: 155)

In *Gender Trouble: Feminism and the Subversion of Identity* (1990) and *Bodies That Matter* (1993), Judith Butler largely affirms Foucault's understanding of sex as an artificial, conventional, or cultural alignment of disparate elements linked together, not through nature, reason, or biology, but historical expedience, alignments produced by and required for the deployment of discourses, knowledges, and forms of power. However, Butler adds a third term to the Foucauldian pair sex/sexuality, the notion of gender, a concept I see as more antithetical to Foucault's account than she admits, insofar as gender must be understood as a kind of overlay on a preestablished foundation of sex, a cultural variation of a more or less fixed and universal substratum, an overlay that, moreover, can be identified too readily with the notion of performance, insofar as the body that performs, however much Butler insists it is produced by the performance itself, must nevertheless abide between performances, existing over and above the sum total of its performances. For Butler, performance is the mediating term between sex and gender: gender is the performance of sex. This notion of gender now seems largely irrelevant or redundant, a term unnecessary for describing the vast social arrangements, contexts, and variations in the ways in which we live, give meaning to, and enact sex. While not wishing to deny this range of variations in the cross-cultural and historical scope of sex, nor the performative and self-productive notion of "identity" Butler develops, I am reluctant to see gender regarded even as the expression of sex, as Butler suggests, insofar as sex is itself always already expression, which in itself does not require (or forbid) a second order expression:

The notion that there might be a "truth" of sex, as Foucault ironically terms it, is produced precisely through the regulatory practices that generate coherent identities through the matrix of coherent gender norms. The heterosexualization of desire requires and institutes the production of discrete and asymmetrical oppositions between "feminine" and "masculine," where these are understood as expressive attributes of "male" and "female." The cultural matrix through which gender identity has become intelligible requires that certain kinds of "identities" cannot "exist"—that is, those in which gender does not "follow" from either sex or gender. (Butler, 1990: 17)

In my understanding, the term "sex" refers, not to sexual impulses, desires, wishes, hopes, bodies, pleasures, behaviors, and practices: this I reserve for the term "sexuality." "Sex" refers to the domain of sexual difference, to the question of the *morphologies of bodies.*[5] I do not want to suggest that sex is in any sense more primordial than or exists independent of "sexuality." With Foucault, I agree that sex is a product, an end effect, of regimes of sexuality (which is another way of saying that the inscription, functioning, and practices of a body constitute what that body is). With Butler, and against Foucault, I want to argue that both sex and sexuality are marked, lived, and function according to whether it is a male or female body that is being discussed. Sex is no longer the label of both sexes in their difference, as in Foucault's writings, a generic term indicating sexed, as opposed to inanimate, existence; it is now the label and terrain of the production and enactment of sexual difference. Gender, it seems, is a redundant category: all its effects, the field that it designates, are covered by the integration of and sometimes the discord between sexuality and sex.

Butler enjoins us to "Consider gender, for instance, as a *corporeal style,* 'act' as it were, which is both intentional and performative, where 'performative' suggests a dramatic and contingent construction of meaning" (1990: 139). She needs the category of gender to mark the discontinuity, the alarming and threatening disjunction of gender from sex, the possibility of masculine behaviour in a female subject and feminine behavior in a male subject, the point of tension and uneasiness separating heterocentric demands from the subversive transgressions of the queer subject, the subject in drag, the subject performatively repeating but also subverting heterosexual norms and imperatives, the site of radical disconnection. But all the force and effect of her powerful arguments could, I believe, be strengthened, not through the play generated by a term somehow beyond the dimension of sex, in the order of gender, but within the very instabilities of the category of sex itself, of bodies themselves. Isn't it even more threatening to show, not that gender can be at variance with sex (which implies the possibility or even social desirability or necessity of the Stollerian solution of realigning the one, usually sex, to conform to the other, gender, forcing their readjustment through psychical or surgical means), but that there is an instability at the very heart of sex and bodies, the fact that the body is what it is capable of doing, and what any body is capable of doing is well beyond the tolerance of any given culture?

AFFECTIVE BODIES

Rather than invoke Foucault's *History of Sexuality* to provide an account of the production of sex through the regimes of sexuality, I am more interested at this moment in exploring the relevance of the work of Deleuze, and Deleuze and Guattari, on affectivity, in their understanding the difference between what a body is and what a body can do, between an ontology and a pragmatics, even though Deleuze and Guattari are less vocal and explicit about questions of sexuality, sex, and sexual identity than Foucault. Deleuze's work unsettles the presumptions of what it is to be a stable subject and thus also problematizes any assumption that sex is in some way the center, the secret, or truth of the subject. This unsettling may or may not have positive effects for feminist and queer theory. This will depend on what it enables us to do, to change. If a body is what a body does, then lesbian and gay sexualities, and above all, lifestyles, produce lesbian and gay bodies, bodies not just distinguished by sex, race, and class characteristics, but also by sexual desires and practices.

The second chapter of Deleuze's reading of Nietzsche (Deleuze, 1983) stresses Nietzsche's privileging of affect, force, energy, and impulse over depth, psychology, interiority, or intention. Nietzsche not only corporealizes knowledge, he also reconceptualizes the ways in which these are now judged: philosophy, theory, knowledge are now understood in terms of movement, action, production. Philosophy is best undertaken dancing, with joyous bodily affirmation, with revelry and delight. Knowledge is the unrecognized effect of bodies that, through habits, errors of grammar and cultural imperative, have been somehow misconstrued as conceptual or purely mental. Knowledge is the consequence of bodies, and in turn enables bodies to act or prevents bodies from acting, expanding themselves, overcoming-themselves, becoming.

To be very brief: where Nietzsche distinguishes between noble and base impulses, between the moralities of the aristocrat and the slave, Deleuze reads Nietzsche in terms of the distinction between active and reactive forces. In systematizing Nietzsche's openly chaotic and unsystematized writings, Deleuze links the will to power to the functioning of differential forces (in individual and social bodies). These differential forces can be described as either (or variously both) active or reactive depending on their quality. Their qualities, in turn, are a function and effect of the differing quantities of excitation carried by impulses. Not only active forces exhibit the will to power, as if reactive forces have somehow succumbed to them or given them up; rather, both active and reactive are equally effects or products of the will to power. Where active and reactive are terms that express force, corresponding to them, at the level of the will to power (the level of interpretation rather than affect) are affirming and negating: "Affirming and denying, appreciating and depreciating, express the will to power just as acting and reacting express force" (1983: 54). Affirmation clearly functions in some alignment with action, just as negation is reactive, but these alignments are much more tenuous. They do not define entities but processes: "Affirmation is not action but the power of becoming active, *becoming active* personified. Negation is not simply reaction but a *becoming reactive*" (1983: 54).

Reactive forces do not steal the activity from active forces; rather, they convert active forces into the forces of reaction, they separate a force from its effects, through the creation of myth, symbolism, fantasy, and falsification. Reactive forces can be regarded as seductive, enticing: they ensnare active force for their own purposes and procedures, for their own falsifications and rationalizations.

In short, active force is that which stretches itself, takes itself as far as it can go (a limit that cannot be known in advance), moves in its directions without regard for anything other than its own free expansion, mindless of others. It is guileless, open, perhaps even naive in its openness to what befalls it. Reactive forces, on the contrary, are cunning, clandestine, restricting, intervening, secondary, mindless, diligent, and obedient. They function ingenuously, living in modes of sensibility and sentiment (nostalgia, self-justification, and hatred of the other are its primary features). Where active forces affirm, produce, and stretch, reactive forces judge, pontificate, produce ideologies and modes of explanation, devise ingenious theories, compromise. They can be identified with the production of religion, morality, and law, with the systems constrained to endless reproduction of the same, without affirming the infinite nature of chance, change, and transformation. Although it is common to describe affirmative judgements and active force as aristocratic or noble, and negative forces as servile and base—that is, to see affirmation as the domain of the powerful, those *in* power, and negation and *ressentiment* as attributes of the oppressed and the powerless—this is to oversimplify Nietzsche's more sophisticated understanding of these as microforces, alignments, and interactions *within* individuals as much as *between* them. It can just as readily be claimed, as I will, that homophobia, heterosexism, racism, and so on are reactive forces, which function in part to *prevent* alternatives, to negate them and ruminate on how to destroy them; and that gay and lesbian sexualities and lifestyles can be seen as innovative, inventive, productive, and thus active insofar as they aim at their own pleasures, their own distributions, their own free expansion. Heterosexism and homophobia are to be countered insofar as they prevent this and react to it.

Although neither Nietzsche nor Deleuze directly discuss the question of sexual orientations and lifestyles, it is plausible to suggest that those forces, activities, and impulses governed by the regime of compulsory heterosexuality (in all of us—for none of us can remain free of this imperative even as we may choose to defy or transform it) *could* be understood on the model of slavish or reactive forces, forces that separate a body from what it can do, that reduce a body to what it is rather than what it can become; while gay and lesbian sexual practices and lifestyles, insofar as they risk a certain stability, a certain social security and ease, insofar as they refuse these imperatives, can and should be seen as a triumph of active and productive forces. We are prevented however, from too-ready a generalization, too black and white a characterization of straights as the emotionally crippled slaves, and gays, lesbians and other queers as the transgressive sexual radicals if we simply assume there are singular impulses directed solely to conformity or subversion. In each of us there are elements and impulses that strive for conformity and elements which seek instability and change: this is as true for heterosexuals as it is for queers of whatever type, although it may well be less enacted, there may be less external impetus for expansion and change for those who reap its benefits (heterosexual men, primarily). Indeed, one of the avowed reasons why many claim to have adopted the term "queer" was to set themselves outside both the heterosexual as well as the gay communities, which, many claim, function as coercively, and as judgementally as each other (this sentiment is expressed in the opening quotation of this essay). It is a question of degree or more or less, rather than of type, a matter of varying investments that all of us have, one way or another, in certain types of complicity with stability and social imperative.[6]

This is not, however, to say that all of us, from the 2.2 child suburban family to the queerest of queers, are the same;[7] of course not. Simply that it is a matter of degree, of location, and of will. The heterosexual can,

I believe, remain a heterosexual but still undertake subversive or transgressive sexual relations outside the copulative, penetrative, active/passive, stereotyped norm (but does so only rarely); and lesbians and gays can of course produce sexual relations that duplicate as closely as they can the structures, habits, and patterns of the straightest and most suburban heterosexuals (but succeed only rarely). So simply *being straight* or *being queer*, in itself, provides no guarantee of one's position as sexually radical: it depends on how one lives one's queerness, or renders one's straightness, one's heterosexuality as queer.

REGIMES OF SEXUALITY

If we return to Foucault and his distinction between sex and sexuality, his claim that the discursive regimes of sexuality produce as their historical effect the phenomenon called sex, we see that, although he is at great pains to deny it elsewhere, Foucault does in fact distinguish between the functioning of power (the deployment of sexuality) and a somehow pre-power real, a real he describes in terms of a set of timeless "bodies and pleasures." There is a notorious passage in *The History of Sexuality*, one which Butler has also taken as a significant site of tension in and between his works, where he discusses the game called "curdled milk" (which today we would have to regard as a case of child sexual abuse), between the simple-minded farm hand and a young girl:

> At the border of a field, he had obtained a few caresses from a little girl, *just as he had done before* and seen done by the village urchins round him.... What is the significant thing about this story? The pettiness of it all; the fact that this *everyday occurrence* in the life of village sexuality, these *inconsequential bucolic pleasures*, could become, from a certain time, the object not only of a collective intolerance but of a judicial action, a medical intervention, a careful clinical examination, and an entire theoretical elaboration. (Foucault, 1980a: 31, emphasis added)[8]

Foucault seems to imply here that there are certain activities, "inconsequential pleasures," the interchange of bodies and pleasures, which are somehow below the threshold of power's reach: these pleasures are relatively innocent, disinvested, and pedestrian. They are everyday occurrences, which only after a certain period become the object of power's ever-intensifying scrutiny. But before this time they exist somehow outside of power's scope. He makes a similar claim, though perhaps with less sinister effects, in one of his more inciting and direct statements.

It is the agency of sex that we must break away from, if we aim—through a tactical reversal of the various mechanisms of sexuality—to counter the grips of power with the claims of bodies, pleasures, and knowledges, in their multiplicity and their possibilities of resistance. The rallying point of the counter-attack against the deployment of sexuality ought not to be sex-desire, but bodies and pleasures.(1980a: 157)

To remain within the domain of sexuality (as he implies much of sexual liberationist politics does), is to not only remain complicit in the functioning of power—for there is a constitutive complicity between power and resistance, he insists—but also to extend power's operations. He implies that there is a lever there, as it were, readily at hand, in the multiplicity of possibilities for bodies and pleasures, as if these were no longer somehow bound up with the functioning of the regime of sexuality, as if they were somehow outside. This means that even if sexual liberationists submit themselves uncritically to the domination of the repressive hypothesis and tie liberation to an affirmation of sex, nonetheless gay and lesbian (though he certainly does not mention the latter) bodies, pleasures, practices, and lifestyles may provide precisely the kind of rallying point that he seeks.

This cannot simply be asserted without some explanation of the status and political position of bodies and pleasures. Bodies and pleasures cannot be understood as fixed or biologically given constants, somehow outside of or beyond the constraints of power—no matter how much Foucault himself may have yearned for a disinvested ground, a pure datum, onto which the operations of power can be directed, no matter how much he believed, in spite of himself, in harmless, timeless pleasures and bodies as yet unmarked by power. What Foucault means, on the most generous reading, is that bodies and pleasures are themselves produced and regulated as distinct phenomena, through, if not forms of power as such, at least various interlocking "economies," libidinal, political, economic, significatory, which may congeal and solidify into a sexuality in "our" modern sense of the word, but which also lend themselves to other economies and modes of production and regulation. A different economy of bodies and pleasures may find the organization of sexuality, the implantation of our sex as the secret of our being, curious and intriguing instead of self-evident.[9] The reorganization of this libidinal structure—which Foucault nowhere discusses—is precisely what I believe that psychoanalysis has not been able to adequately address;[10] this may be why Deleuze's distinction between active and reactive forces, and between affirmative and negative judgements or interpretations, may prove useful in rethinking the issue of a different libidinal organization, a mode of living and utilizing bodies and pleasures beyond the regimes of sexuality that establish heterocentrism (and its mode of ideological validation, homophobia) as regulative norms of subjectivity, as well as beyond the regimes of signification and discursivity, the alignments of power/knowledge that Foucault sees as the necessary conditions for the codification, reorganization, and production of bodies into and as a series of sexualities.

PLEASURES

Neither Foucault nor Deleuze devote any time to the question of sexual difference, although both appropriate some of the energy generated by this question for their own reconceptualizations of power and desire. Devising a theory of queer pleasures and their relations to the straight (complicity, support, transgression, or subversion), cannot in fact rely on their works even if they have helped mark out the present limits of theorizing sexual politics.

Because we are now dealing with sexual specificities, differences between the sexes, and those differences that constitute each sex, I can no longer afford to generalize about "queerness": this term covers a vast range of sexual practices, partners, aims, and objects (heterosexual as well as homosexual). The term "queer" as it is currently used is basically a reactive category that sees itself in opposition to a straight norm: it is only this norm that defines the others that it cannot tolerate. These others—deviant sexual practices of whatever kind—may find that they share very little in common with each other (indeed they may be the site of profound tension and contradiction). I find it less useful to talk about queerness, or even gayness when theorizing sexed bodies and their sexual relations than specifying at least broadly the kinds of bodies and desires in question.

I must, then, concentrate on lesbian desire and sexual relations between women, the area which still remains the great domain of the untheorized and the inarticulate—something I believe may function to lesbians' advantage rather than to their detriment. It is clear, especially in the era of the AIDS crisis, that there is an ever more detailed analysis, observation, and theorization, not only with the work of sexologists of the 1950s and 1960s on heterosexual couples, but now with the ever-increasing medical and legal investment in gay and bisexual men's sexual practices. Lesbianism still remains untheorized and largely unspecified. It is significant too that while gay men's sexual practices have been under the scrutiny of the law for over a century, in Australia at least, there have never been laws specifically prohibiting lesbianism.

Legally, it remained unrecognized until recent equal opportunity and anti-discrimination legislation. I don't want to suggest that lesbians are either more or less oppressed than gay men, that it is better or worse to be recognized or not recognized in the eyes of the law (arguments could be made both ways): my point here is simply that there is no representation of lesbians as lesbians in certain key discourses deeply invested in power relations. This is in the process of change, and of course varies from one state and country to another, but as a generalization, there is a distinct underinvestment in theorizing and extracting knowledge about lesbian sexual practices. This is partly illustrated not only by the status of lesbianism in the eyes of the law, but also in the discourses of medicine, especially those now developing around the AIDS crisis, where the rate of transmission of the virus in lesbian practices is relatively low and the modes of transmission remain unknown.

This same underrepresentation, or failure of representation, occurs in discourses of the erotic, particularly visual pornography, where clearly lesbianism (or a certain male fantasy of lesbianism) is construed and representable only under sanitized, safe, male-oriented terms. There is a manifest inadequacy of erotic language to represent women's sexual organs, sexual pleasures, and sexual practices in terms other than those provided either for male sexuality or by men in their heterosexual (mis)understanding of the sexualities of their female partners. All the terms for orgasm, for corporeal encounters, for sexual exchanges of whatever kind are not only derived and modified from heterosexual models, but, more alarmingly, from the perspective of the men, and not the women involved in these relations. The very terms for sex, for pleasure, for desire—"fucking," "screwing," "coming," "orgasm," etc.—are most appropriate for and are derived from men's experiences of sexuality (both their own and that of women).

But perhaps the solution to this problem is not simply the addition of a set of new words to the vocabulary, new labels to describe "things" that, while they exist as such, are not signified or referred to, are not explicitly named: for such an understanding presumes female sexuality, and especially lesbian sexuality, is readily enumerable and can be described and referred to as distinct entities, objects, and organs. To wish to create a new set of terms implies that one knows in advance what one wants to designate by these terms, that the sexual pleasures, desires, organs, and activities of women together are a known or knowable quantity and that, like the new discoveries of science, now that they have been "discovered," need appropriate names.

This does not seem possible, or entirely desirable: to "know" female sexuality, to "know" what lesbian desire is, is to reduce it to models of subjectivity, sexuality, and corporeality, to notions of self-identity, ontology, and epistemology that are still logically dependent on the ways these terms are defined and have been understood in a male-dominated culture. I don't want to suggest that new terms can't be coined and new labels cannot be created—the regimes of knowledge/power are certainly capable of providing such resources. Perhaps a more interesting question is, given the enormous investment of knowledges in the codification and control of sexuality, why has lesbianism been so decidedly ignored where heterosexuality and male homosexuality are increasingly thoroughly investigated, particularly in medical discourses? Has lesbianism been underestimated, or has it been too threatening (or perhaps too trivial) to be taken seriously? Is this a lapse in the regime of sexuality, a sign of its imperfections and its capacity to create sites of resistance? Or is it a mode of further delegitimizing lesbianism, a ruse of power itself? This is not an idle question, for whether one reads it as a shortfall of power, or as one of its strategies, will dictate whether one seeks to retain the inarticulateness, the indeterminacy of lesbianism, and of female sexuality—my present inclination—or whether one seeks to articulate lesbianism as loudly and as thoroughly as possible, which Marilyn Frye seems to advocate.   (221)

Frye seems to believe that the silence on the details of lesbian sexual relations is an effect of the obliteration or subsumption of women under heterosexist sexual norms. In her largely phenomenological reflections on lesbian "sex," Frye seems to yearn for a language and a mode of representation for lesbian sexual practices. She implies that without an adequate language, without appropriate terms, women's experiences themselves are less rich, less rewarding, less determinate than they could be.

> I once perused a large and extensively illustrated book on sexual activity by and for homosexual men. It was astounding for me for one thing in particular, namely, that its pages constituted a huge lexicon of *words*: words for acts and activities, their sub-acts, preludes and denouements, their stylistic variation, their sequences. Gay male sex, I realized then, is *articulate*. It is articulate to a degree that, in my world, lesbian "sex" does not remotely approach. Lesbian "sex" as I have known it, most of the time I have known is, is utterly *in*articulate. Most of my lifetime, most of my experience in the realms commonly designated as "sexual" has been pre-linguistic, non-cognitive. I have, in effect, no linguistic community, no language, and therefore in one important sense, no knowledge.... The meaning one's life and experience might generate cannot come fully into operation if they are not woven into

language: they are fleeting, or they hover, vague, not fully coalesced, not connected, and hence, not *useful* for explaining or grounding interpretations, desires, complaints, theories. (Frye, 1990: 311)

While I have sympathy for this claim, and recognize that certain delegitimated social and sexual practices may require modes of representation to affirm and render these practices viable and valuable, it is not clear to me that articulateness and representation are in themselves a virtue: the most intense moments of pleasure, the force of their materiality, while certainly broadly evocable in discourse, cannot be reduced to adequate terms, terms which capture their force and intensity. A distinction must be drawn between discourse and experience even with the understanding that language or systems of representation are the prior condition for the intelligibility of experience. Moreover, it is ironic that the very features Frye attributes to the failure of representation for lesbian desire: that these relations and experiences are rendered "fleeting," that they "hover," are "vague," not "coalesced," "connected," or "useful," accord precisely with the more positive characterization accorded to these concepts and to female sexuality itself in the writings of Luce Irigaray,[11] for whom female sexuality is itself non-self-identical, non-enumerable, not made of distinct and separate parts, not one (but indeterminately more than one).

Here we must be careful not to erect a new ontology based on what woman *is*, in and of herself. Irigaray, and other theorists of female sexuality have not provided an account of female sexuality in its essence or in its fixed form, but rather have worked on the paradoxes and consequences generated for female sexuality by a culture, a value system, forms of knowledge and systems of representation that can only ever take female sexuality as object, as external, and as alien to the only set of perspectives presenting themselves as true—men's.[12] Female sexuality, lesbian desire, is that which eludes and escapes, that which functions as an excess, a remainder uncontained by and unrepresentable within the terms provided by a sexuality that takes itself as straightforwardly being what it is.

Part of the reason that there is such an explosion of sexual terminology, details, distinctions, nuances, phases, modalities, styles, organs, practices in gay male literature, and especially in pornography and in personal columns in newspapers is that male sexuality, straight and gay, continues to see itself in terms of readily enumerable locations defined around a central core or organizing principle. When sexuality takes on its status as phallic, entities, organs, pleasures, and fantasies associated with it become definitive, distinguishable from their environment or context, separable, nameable, and capable of being reflected on, fantasized and experienced in isolation from one another. Distinct organs, separable bodily regions, with distinct states, definitive and readily measurable goals, are possible only because of the capacity to have a reflective and analytic relation to one's own body and experiences, to distance oneself as a knowing subject from oneself as the object known. Any experience, any organs, any desire is capable of categorization and organization, but only at the expense of its continuity with the rest of the body and experience, and only at the cost of separating oneself from immersion in its complexity and intensity. To submit one's pleasures and desires to enumeration and definitive articulation is to submit processes and becomings, to entities, locations, and boundaries, to become welded to an organizing nucleus of fantasy and desire whose goal is not simply pleasure and expansion, but control, and the tying of the new to models of what is already known, the production of endless repetition, endless variations of the same.

I think that this is borne out most clearly in the fascination sexology has shown with various (long-term) debates surrounding female sexuality (debates that, in a certain sense, logically precede discussions of lesbianism, insofar as lesbianism in its broadest sense must be understood as female sexual desire directed to other women): a clitoral versus vaginal location for female orgasm, the existence or non-existence of the legendary "G-spot," the homology or lack of it of female stages of sexual arousal and orgasm with the male and so on. I continue to find it astounding that these debates exist at all, that there is such confusion not only among male researchers, but also among the female objects of investigation, that there continues to be such mystery and controversy surrounding the most apparently elementary features of female sexuality. Male sexuality by comparison, *seems* to be completely straightforward, completely uncontentious, knowable, measurable, understandable. This manifest asymmetry cannot be readily explained without the assumption that one already knows what female sexuality is; nonetheless it must clearly be a consequence, in part, of the imposition of models of knowing, of identity, distinctness, and measurability that are in some sense alien to or incapable of adequately explaining female sexuality. Instead of assuming an inherent mystery, an undecipherable enigma, female sexuality must be assumed to be knowable, even if it must wait for other forms of knowledge, different modes of discourse, to provide a framework and the broad parameters of its understanding. There is no object of reference, no concept or term so inherently opaque that it cannot be known.

After all, it is language that makes such concepts possible. It cannot be that they are somehow inherently resistant to representation. The question is not, then, simply, *how* to know woman (what theories, concepts, and language are necessary for illuminating this term); but rather, the *cost* and *effects* of such knowledge, what the various processes of knowing *do* to the objects they thereby produce.

One thing remains clear though: whenever the same models are used to discuss female and male sexuality, when sexuality is conceived in generic or human terms, it will remain inadequate for assessing the particularities, the differences that mark female sexuality as other than male sexuality. Lesbianism remains the site of the most threatening challenge to this phallocentrism, which subsumes the female under the generic produced by the male insofar as it evidences the existence of a female sexuality and sexual pleasure outside of male pleasure and control.

PLEASURE AND SUBVERSION

I asked a series of questions at the beginning of this essay that have thus far remained unanswered: Is oppression still a politically and theoretically useful term in the light of postmodern and anti-humanist assaults on the category of identity? Can heterosexism or homophobia be understood as a regional variant of a generic oppression, an oppression also characteristic of racial, ethnic, religious, and ability discrimination? Does homophobia have any distinctive features? Does the term "homophobia" cover different kinds of oppression experienced by gay men and lesbians? Utilizing the work of Foucault, Deleuze, Butler, de Lauretis, and others, at least the broad outlines of some possible answers may be sketched.

The general characteristics of oppression I outlined in the first section of this paper, if they are valid at all, are also appropriate for describing the oppression of lesbians and gay men. But these broad criteria do not seem particularly appropriate for distinguishing the oppression faced under homophobia from other oppressions. What then is it that *distinguishes* the oppression of lesbians and gays from other oppressed groups, bearing in mind that of course many lesbians and gay also suffer from these other modalities in such ways that it may not be possible to always and readily distinguish the features of their homosexual oppression from their oppression as people of color, or from their class, religious or ethnic oppression. Given an acknowledgement that both homosexuality and homophobia are always invested in other forms of oppression—whether in complicity with them, or as their objects—it also has its own, however precarious, "identity."[13]

I would argue that the oppression of lesbians and gay men has a form quite different from that taken by other oppressions (such a claim can no doubt be made of each particular modality of oppression, for each must have its own distinguishing features). Forms of oppression, to my knowledge, are generally based primarily on what a person *is* quite independent of what they do. Or rather, what they do is inflected and read through who they are. Peoples of color, women, Jews, are discriminated against at least in part because of the fact that whatever they do, it is as people of color, as women, or as Jews, that they do it. Prejudice and oppression dictate that the qualities and achievements of members of most of oppressed groups are read, interpreted, to mean something different from that of the privileged group, even if the behavior seems ostensibly identical with that of white, Christian men. Their racial, religious, sexual, and cultural characteristics, characteristics, which are in some sense undeniable (although their meanings and significances are the objects of considerable contestation) are used against them, an excuse or rationalization for their being treated inequitably, and for their own phenomenological realities being discounted or unvalued. Sartre argues that such oppression is a fundamental gesture of bad faith, the very opposite, in his understanding, of a scientific attitude (Sartre, 1961). The oppressor refuses to allow anything to count as evidence against his prejudices.

(225)

In the case of homosexuals, I believe that it is less a matter of who they *are* than what they do that is considered offensive.[14] This explains the quite common "liberal" attitude of many straights who claims something like: "I don't care what they do, I just wish they would do it only in the privacy of their own homes!" or "What you do in your bedroom is your own business," which more or less means that as long as you don't do queer things, as long as your sexuality is not somehow enacted in public, they don't mind who you are—that is, they can assume you are the same as they. It is this split between what one is and what one does that produces the very possibility of a notion like "the closet," a distinction between private and public that refuses integration. Moreover, it also accounts for the very possibility of coming out—after all, a quite ridiculous concept in most other forms of oppression. This is what enables homosexuals to "pass" as straight with an ease that is extraordinarily rare for other oppressed groups. Homopobia is an oppression based on the *activities* of members of a group, and not on any definitive group attributes.

This is precisely why the forces of cultural reaction are so intent, in the case of homophobia more than in other forms of oppression, on separating a body from what it can (sexually) do. Such an assumption on the one hand affirms that lesbian and gay sexual practices and lifestyles are active and affirmative, that they progress and develop according to their own economies and not simply in reaction to the constraints provided by heterosexism; yet on the other hand, it shows that the forces of reaction have themselves made this choice both immensely difficult and yet also enticingly attractive. The constraints of heterosexism are not simply being reacted to but are obstacles whose overcoming may be self-expanding and positive. Homophobia is an attempt to separate being from doing, existence from action. And if what constitutes homosexuality is not simply a being who *is* homosexual, who has a homosexual personality, a "natural inclination" towards homosexual love objects, (the "persona of the homosexual," Foucault claims, is an invention of the nineteenth century), but is a matter of practice, of what one does, how one does it, with whom and with what risks and benefits attached, then it is clear that forces of reaction function by trying to solidify or congeal a personage, a being through and through laden with deviancy. This reduces homosexuality to a legible category in the same way as women (of whatever color) and peoples of color (of either sex) are presumed to be, and in a certain way minimises the threat that the idea of a labile, indeterminable sexuality, a sexuality based on the contingency of undertaking certain activities and subscribing to certain ideas, has on the very self-constitution of the heterosexual norm.

Lesbianism, for example, attests to the fundamental plasticity of women's (and also presumably men's) desire, its inherent openness not only to changes in its sexual object (male to female or vice-versa), but also its malleability in the forms and types of practices and pleasures available to it. In other words, to the more or less infinite possibilities of becoming. It attests to the rigidity, the fearfulness, the boring, indeed endless repetition, of form in stable male/female Western sex roles, the roles to which stable relationships become accustomed, and to the possibilities of change inherent in them, possibilities that need to be ignored or blotted out in order for them to continue these roles. The threat homosexuality poses to heterosexuality is its own contingency, and open-endedness, its own tenuous hold over the multiplicity of sexual impulses and possibilities characterizing all human sexuality. Its own un-naturalness, its compromise and reactive status. Queer pleasures show that one does not have to settle for the predictable, the formulaic, the respected, although these too are not without their cost.

This is both the power and the danger posed by lesbian and gay sexual relations: that what one does, how one does it, with whom and with what effects are ontologically open questions, that sexuality in and for all of us is fundamentally provisional, tenuous, mobile, igniting in unpredictable contexts with often unsettling effects: its power, attraction, and danger, the fundamental fluidity and transformability of sexuality and its enactment in sexed bodies. In separating what a body is from what a body can do, an essence of sorts is produced, a consolidated nucleus of habits and expectations take over from experiments and innovations. Bodies are sedimented into fixed and repetitive relations, and it is only beyond modes of repetition that any subversion is considered possible.

I am interested instead in the ways in which homosexual relations and lifestyles, expelled from and often ignored by the norms of heterosexuality, nonetheless, seep into, infiltrate the very self-conceptions of what it is to be heterosexual, or at least straight. The rigid alignments of sexual stimuli and responses, the apparently natural coupling of male and female lovers, are unstuck by the existence of lesbians and gays; further, the very existence of a mode of lesbianism not dependent on the phallus or even on a mediated relations with a male sexual subject demonstrates that sexuality as such does not require the phallus, as function or as organ. But more than this flow-on effect—which does effect a certain loosening or contagion of the sphere of sexual "normality," rather than endlessly theorize, explain, analyze, reflect on, reconstruct, reassess, provide new words and concepts for sexuality—we need to experiment with it, to enjoy its various modalities, to seek its moments of heightened intensity, its moments of self-loss where reflection no longer has a place. This is not, I hope and believe, either an anti-intellectualism or a naïve return to a 1960s style polysexualism, which sought pleasure with no responsibility, and which moreover, lived out only men's fantasies of sexual freedom while subsuming women's under their imperatives. Rather, it is a refusal to link sexual pleasure with the struggle for freedom, the refusal to validate sexuality in terms of a greater cause or a higher purpose (whether political, spiritual, or reproductive), the desire to enjoy, to experience, to make pleasure for its own sake, for where it takes us, for how it changes and makes us, to see it as one but not the only trajectory or direction in the lives of sexed bodies.

NOTES

INTRODUCTION

1 Here I am inclined to quote Bennington's introductory remarks to his own recent collection of essays, *Legislations* (1994). How he describes his relation to his own older writing pretty well sums up my own feelings:

> [This] implies that there are not just 'theoretical' essays about a variety of problems in philosophy, literary studies or even politics, but that they are themselves inscribed in a political situation. This means among other things, that all these texts are essentially dated; but this datedness...no text can escape (no text can be exclusively mastered by reference to any one or any finite set of dates, [and] is readable only to the extent that it is perpetually escaping from its dates). (1994: 3)

2 I wrote all the papers during the long gesta-

tion of another book, a book focused on rethinking the mind/body relation (Grosz, 1994), and consequently, all bear some relation to a reconsidered corporeality based on a notion of sexual difference.

CH 1

1 I am reminded here of a recent (1994) incident in which I had initially agreed to co-edit a collection of papers on women's studies in Australia. A serious disagreement soon emerged between the three co-editors concerning whether to solicit the work of a newly graduated feminist scholar, of undisputed brilliance, who had written very difficult and complex work on postmodern theory. Was she really a feminist? my co-editors asked. How could they think she was not? I replied. What evidence would have counted for her to be seen as a feminist by my colleagues, and for her to be seen as not a feminist by me? Surely at stake here was not the issue of whether she is a feminist or not, but what of feminist concerns her work addresses, that is, whether she is the *right kind* of feminist, *our* (this presumption eventually broke down—we as co-editors could not form a "we") kind of feminist. What is at stake is the immense power of inclusion and exclusion, of more or less exactly the same kind that feminists have fought against academic traditionalists. Only now, the battle is being waged within feminist and women's studies circles, between its different factions, without the open acknowledgement that these are in fact the terms of dispute. Needless to say, the brilliant young scholar was not asked to be part of the project, and eventually my co-editing difficulties forced me to leave. The question of what constitutes a feminist text is thus crucial in both the ongoing negotiations between feminist scholars and the mainstream academy, and, more urgently, in the ongoing negotiations between hostile and at times vicious forms of exclusion within feminism itself.

2 Although the problematic of the signature haunts all of Derrida's writings, see in particular *Glas* (1986a), *Signsponge* (1984a), and *Limited Inc* (1988a), and on Benveniste's understanding of the relations between subjectivity and language, see *Problems in General Linguistics*.

3 Among them, Barthes, Foucault, Benveniste, Jakobson, and Derrida, as well as Irigaray, Le Doeuff, and Kofman.

4 See, for example, Nancy K. Miller's argument that it makes a difference to one's interpretation of a text if one knows that the author is a male or a female:

> …I like to know that the Brontean writing of female anger, desire and selfhood issue from a female pen. This preference…is not without its vulnerabilities. It could, I suppose, one day be definitively that the heroines of [*Portuguese*] *Letters* and *The Story of O* were female creations after all. I would then have to start all over again. But it would be a different story, since the story of the woman who writes is *always* another story. (Miller, 1990: 115)

In a different vein, but on a related point, Rosi Braidotti also affirms the separation of the discursive subject from the "real" subject, resurrecting a nominalist feminism:

> In order to make sexual difference operative within feminist theory I want to argue that one should start politically with the assertion of the need for the presence of real-life women in positions of discursive subjecthood.... (Braidotti, 1989b: 90)

5   What matter who is speaking? I would answer it matters, for example, to women who have lost and still routinely lose their proper name in marriage, and whose signature—not merely their voice—has not been worth the paper it was written on; women for whom the signature—by virtue of its power in the world of circulation—is *not* immaterial. (Miller, 1990: 118)

6   For example, the not uncommon patriarchal claim that "there are no great women writers/ philosophers/ artists/ scientists/ composers." Here it makes perfect sense to stress the contributions of "real women," artists, writers, scientists, etc. But this is a limited strategy, not very useful in other more complex contexts.

7   It is moreover, as Gayatri Spivak has convincingly argued, catachrestical, taking a name to be a referent. Spivak is making precisely this point in her reexamination of the relations between feminism and deconstruction, in Brennan (1989):

> Incanting to ourselves all the perils of transforming a 'name' to a referent— making a catechism, in other words, of catachresis—let us none the less name (as) 'woman' that disenfranchised woman whom we strictly, historically, geopolitically *cannot imagine* as literal referent. Let us divide the name of woman so that we see ourselves in naming, not merely named. (220)

8   In *Signsponge* (1984a) as well as in *Glas* (1986a).

9   Ironically, it is through this notion of the addressee or counter-signature that Derrida introduces, and problematizes, an oblique and ironically indeterminate notion of sexual difference:

> ...one finds that the question of the ear of the addressee returns. It concerns the other to whom, at bottom, I entrust my signature. The question is whether the difference constituting the other as other has, a priori, to be marked sexually.... When I say "I don't know" I mean that in order to ask the question as I have posed it, one must presuppose that the addresser himself or herself is determined before the other's signature, that the sex of the addresser is itself determined before the other assumes responsibility for the signature. The sex of the addresser awaits its determination by or from the other. It is the other who will perhaps decide who I am—man or woman. Nor is this decided once and for all. It may go one way one time and another way another time. What is more, if there is a multitude of sexes (because there are perhaps more than two) which sign differently, then I will have to assume this polysexuality. (Derrida, 1988b: 52)

1 Dromio the slave to Antipholus his master in William Shakespeare, *The Comedy of Errors*, ed. Harry Levin (New York: New American Library, 1965), Ill. v. 13–14.

2 This is precisely Foucault's claim in "The Discourse on Language" (1972): that the division of knowledge into disciplines is one of the internal modes of regulation and supervision that power exerts over discourses.

3 Here I do not want to affirm an interdisciplinary approach, considered in terms of prevailing models of inter- or cross-disciplinary research, which broadens the bases of knowledges without necessarily questioning their founding theoretical commitments. My point is rather that the ways that disciplines classify propositions either as "their own" or as "outside" their disciplinary boundaries is a political and not simply an intellectual matter.

4 See Lacan (1977b).

5 This is not to advocate its inverse—a romantic subjectivism or relativism, whereby all things are judged according to what individuals think or feel about them. Objectivism and subjectivism are equally problematic; neither provides a solution to the status of the knower in the production of knowledge.

6 In the second volume of his history of sexuality, *The Uses of Pleasure* (1985), Foucault seems to recognize more sharply than in his earlier works that the regimentation and self-understanding of sexual pleasures is sexually specific, such that generalizing from one sex to the other is not clearly possible. Although he acknowledges this sexual specificity, nevertheless he leaves unexplained what women's "use of pleasure" must have been in the classical period. His rationale is rather feeble; it relies on a claim that the regulation of female sexuality was only elaborated at a much later date:

> Later, in European culture, girls or married women…were to become themes of special concern; a new art of courting them, a literature that was basically romantic in form, an exacting morality that was attentive to the integrity of their bodies and the solidity of their matrimonial commitment—all this would draw curiosity and desire around them…. It seems clear, on the other hand, that in classical Greece the problematization was more active in regard to boys…. (1985: 213)

7 See Alphonso Lingis, "Savages" (in Lingis, 1984).

8 The inscription of the body's insides and outsides is an effect of historically and politically specific inscriptions and exscriptions that penetrate it using a "social tattooing" system. Codes mark bodies and trace them in particular ways, constituting the body as a living, acting, and producing subject. In turn, bodies leave their trace in laws and codes. A history of bodies is yet to be written, but it would involve looking at the mutual relations between bodily inscription and lived experience.

9 There has of course been considerable feminist literature on the Foucauldian metaphorics of body writing. See, in particular, Probyn (1991)

and McNay (1991); and Diamond and Quinby (1988).

10 Cf Irigaray, "Is the Subject of Science Sexed?" (1985c).

11 "The problem is that of a possible alterity in masculine discourse..." (Irigaray 1985a, 140).

CH 3

1 For an account of the challenges feminist theory has posed to male conceptions of objectivity, particularly in the sciences, see Grosz and de Lepervanche (1988).

2 See Julia Kristeva, 1981: 18–19.

3 Kristeva makes this point forcefully in her analysis of the "two generations of feminists" in her 1981 paper. She refers specifically to Beauvoir's anti-maternal position.

4 This is Kristeva's understanding of the effects of a fundamental egalitarianism that produces, among other things, the oppressive structure of anti-semitism: assimilationism entails the repression of the specific history of oppression directed towards the Jew. This is why Sartre's position in *Anti-Semite and Jew*, in spite of his intentions, is anti-semitic. As Kristeva suggests:

> the specific character of women could only appear as nonessential or even nonexistent to the totalizing and even totalitarian spirit of this ideology. We begin to see that this same egalitarian and in fact censuring treatment has been imposed, from Enlightenment Humanism through socialism, on religious specificities, and, in particular, on Jews. (Kristeva, 1981: 21)

5 This difference between difference and distinction is suggested by Derrida's conception of *différance*, which in turn is in part based on his reading of Saussure's notion of pure difference.

CH 4

My thanks to Pheng Cheah for his helpful comments and suggestions on my reading of Derrida.

1 This general label of postmodernism has always seemed to me to be a shorthand formula of dismissal for the various—highly disparate—positions thus categorized. It is not at all clear that writers like Lacan, Derrida, Deleuze, Foucault, Baudrillard, and Lyotard, not to mention Kristeva and Irigaray, share a common denominator that could be called postmodern. This label designates the giving up of certain features that characterize the project of modernity, including the opposition between structuralism and humanism, but beyond this negative concern, the names thus lumped together seem to me to share little in common. The label of postmodernism has helped serve as a justification for treating these figures together without paying any particular attention to their specific contributions, to their major differences and inconsistencies, to the various debates and disagreements that have marked their complex and often uneasy relations. And perhaps

more alarmingly, postmodernism has functioned as a marketing label to designate what is new, difficult, and hip, to mark the contemporaneity of the various academic or intellectual "products" or "commodities" thus being marketed—a book, a conference, a seminar, a program.

2 As Derrida himself affirms, the issue of the yes, what yes is, what it means, what it designates has preoccupied all of his writings: "For a very long time, the question of the *yes* has mobilized or traversed everything I have been trying to think, write, teach, or read." ("Ulysses Gramophone," 1992: 287) The yes is for him the condition of all language, representation, and thus intimately tied to the trace, writing, pharmakon, etc.; it functions in the modality of the promise or the signature (and hence also requires countersignature, doubling); in itself it always calls forth its repetition, a double affirmation; and finally (though not exhaustively), it is linked to, and echoed by the figure of "a certain kind of woman" (in Joyce, in Nietzsche, in Blanchot):

> ...the relationship of a *yes* to the Other, of a *yes* to the other and of one *yes* to the other *yes*, must be such that the contamination of the two *yeses* remains inevitable. And not only as a threat: but also an opportunity. With or without a word, a *yes* demands *a priori* its own repetition, its own memorizing, demands that a *yes* to the *yes* inhabit the arrival of the 'first' yes, which is never therefore simply originary. We cannot say *yes* without promising to confirm it and to remember it, to keep it safe, countersigned in another yes, without promise and memory, without the promise of memory, Molly remembers (and recalls herself), the memory of a promise initiates the circle or appropriation, with all the risks of technical repetition, of automatized archives, of gramophony, of simulacrum, of wandering deprived of an address and destination. A *yes* must entrust itself to memory. Having come already from the other, in the dissymmetry of the request, and from the other of whom it is requested to request a *yes*, the *yes* entrusts itself to the memory of the other, of the *yes* of the other and of the other yes. All the risks already crowd around from the first breath of *yes*. (1992a: 305)

3 I am thinking here of the attempt on the part of a few women philosophers (I hesitate to call them feminists) to correct the bad arguments and inconsistencies of feminist theory with a good dose of philosophical thinking, rewriting feminist propositions in more rigorous and accurate form, of course at the expense of major feminist political commitments. Janet Radcliffe Richards, for example, rewrites feminist notions of women's oppression in terms of a broader, human concern with issues of social justice.

4 As Derrida himself explicitly states, his goal has never been to eliminate or decenter the subject:

> I have never said that the subject should be dispensed with. Only that it should be deconstructed. To deconstruct the subject does not mean to deny its existence. There are subjects, operations or effects of subjectivity. This is an incontrovertible fact. To acknowledge this does not mean, however, that the subject

is what it says it is. The subject is not some meta-linguistic presence; it is always inscribed in language. My work does not, therefore destroy the subject; it simply tries to resituate it." (1984b: 125)

5 Indeed this is the ground of a quite different objection to Derrida's work articulated by Braidotti—that he is ignorant of feminist writings, and that consequently his conclusions regarding feminism remain intellectually sloppy:

> [Derrida's] disconcerting conclusions [that feminism wants the castration of women] emanate from a misunderstanding and downright ignorance of feminist texts, of the history of women's struggles, and from a carelessness as regards the theoretical aspects of feminism, coupled with a determination to denigrate them. (Braidotti, 1991: 105)

6 Possibly the starkest example of this is Brodrib (1992), who takes it upon herself to criticize wholesale the general field of postmodern. For a more detailed criticism of various feminist critiques of Derrideanism, see Elam, 1994.

7 Derrida himself distinguishes his project's fascination with the question of femininity from a feminist impulse towards "liberation" for women, while acknowledging their interimplications:

> The philosophical and literary discoveries of the feminine—and even the political and legal recognition of the status of women—are all symptoms of a deeper mutation in our search for meaning which deconstruction attempts to register.... One could describe the transformation effected as good without positing it as an a priori goal or telos. I hesitate to speak of liberation in this context because I don't believe that women are liberated any more than men are. They are of course no longer enslaved in many of the old socio-political respects and even in the new situation woman will not be ultimately freer than man. One needs another language besides that of political liberation to characterize the deconstructive import of the feminine as an uprooting of our phallologocentric culture. (1984b: 121–22)

8 See Derrida's response in Creech, Kamuf, and Todd, 1985 : 13–19.

9 This is one of the central concerns I attempt to address in Grosz, 1994.

10 See Derrida, 1979, 1983a, 1985, 1989a, and 1991a; and Derrida and McDonald, in Derrida, 1988b.

11 Christie McDonald provides a detailed and convincing explanation of this point of resistance or inconsistency in Levinas's work; see "Choreographies" in Derrida, 1988b.

12 See Simon Critchley's analysis of this text:

> One might say that sexual difference is Levinas's "blind spot." But what economy governs this blind-spot?... two enclosures can be detected in Levinas's work: 1) By making sexual difference secondary and by seeking to master the un-said alterity of the feminine, the 'il' of the wholly other would risk enclosing itself within the economy of the same. 2) By seeking the enclose sexual difference within ethical difference, the feminine is enclosed within the economy of the same.

> ...Levinas's work encloses the trace of illeity within the economy of the same and encloses the feminine within a crypt.... Levinas's work can only go unto the wholly other on the condition that feminine alterity is circumscribed and inhumed. The strange consequence of the latter is that Levinas's work is itself engaged in a denial of (feminine) alterity and thus remains enclosed within the economy of the same which it has constantly striven to exceed. (Critchley, 1991: 183)

13 While there is much with which I agree in Cornell's general defence of deconstruction from largely misconstrued feminist objections, I do have one major point of disagreement with her analysis. It is her ongoing commitment to the basic terms in which the sex/ gender distinction is framed by feminists. The sex/ gender opposition must be read as a retranscription of the opposition between nature and culture or mind and body that Derrida has elsewhere been at great pains to challenge. One cannot understand the structures of sexual privilege simply in terms of a gender hierarchy that somehow hangs, unanchored to any sexual terms, as if the opposition between masculine and feminine makes any sense without its implicit or explicit reliance on the opposition between men and women.

14 I believe that an exception to this generalization is probably Lyotard, who has also addressed the question of sexual difference and the struggles of women in what I believe is a sensitive and productive way. See Lyotard, 1978.

15 Here I do not want to simply deny that there are individuals whose sexual status is ambiguously neither clearly male nor female but who have characteristics of both or neither. Such individuals, medically classified as "intersexed," cannot be understood as *indeterminate*, except in the sense that they do not conform to the binary division of the sexes into two clear-cut categories. Nonetheless, such individuals remain concrete, determinate, specific in their morphologies.

16 This rift need not, indeed should not, be understood simply in anatomical or biological terms, for these themselves are in constant social transformation, as Derrida acknowledges:

> ..."hymen" and "invagination," at least in the context into which these words have been swept, no longer simply designate figures for the feminine body. They no longer do so, that is, assuming that one knows for certain what a feminine or masculine body is, and assuming that anatomy is in this instance the final recourse. (1988b: 181)

17 See also Geoffrey Bennington's similar justification of what might be understood as Derrida's politics:

> That there is political concern among Derrida's readers does not worry us, on the contrary: but it could easily be shown that this 'worry' claims in fact to resolve politics in such a way that one should no longer have to worry about it, so that nothing should happen in it, so there should be no more politics...it is precisely where one protests most against a supposed lack of political reflection that such reflection is most sorely lacking. (Bennington and Derrida, 1993: 197)

1 I use the generic "he" advisedly; the relevance of the question of sexual difference to Caillois's account needs careful consideration if it is to be taken as relevant for women as well.

2 Newton's three Laws are:
1. A body continues in a state of rest or uniform motion along a straight line, unless it is subject to a force (the law of inertia);
2. If a force acts on a body, then the body has an acceleration in the direction of that force, and the magnitude of the acceleration is directly proportional to the force and inversely proportional to the mass of the body; and
3. The forces exerted by two bodies on each other are equal in magnitude and opposite in direction, along the line joining their positions. (Van Fraassen, 1970: 53)

3 Euclidean geometry is frequently reduced to five fundamental axioms that, between them, generate his propositions regarding geometrical figures. They are: (1) if x and y are distinct points, there is a straight line incident with both; (2) any finite straight line is part of a unique, infinite straight line; (3) if x is a point and r is a finite distance, there is a unique circle with x at its centre and r defining the length of its radius; (4) any two right angles are equal; and (5) if a straight line falling on two straight lines makes the interior angles on the same side less than two right-angles, if they are indefinitely extended, the two straight lines meet on the side where the angles are less than two right angles. Cf van Fraassen, 1970: 117. Incidentally, non-Euclidean geometry denies the 5th postulate, and some forms also deny the 2nd and 3rd axioms.

4 If one is referring to two points on a sphere or any curved surface, then there are n-lines linking them, not just one. Parallelism is impossible in curved spaces.

1 Brian Massumi, in his rewarding *A User's Guide to Capitalism and Schizophrenia*, characterizes nomad thought in the following terms:

> "Nomad thought" does not lodge itself in the edifice of an ordered interiority; it moves freely in an element of exteriority. It does not repose on identity; it rides difference. It does not respect the artificial division between the three domains of representation, subject, concept and being; it replaces restrictive analogy with a conductivity that knows no bounds.... Rather than reflecting the world [the concepts it creates] are immersed in a changing state of things. A concept is a brick. It can be used to build the courthouse of reason. Or it can be thrown through the window. (1992: 5)

2 The bizarre reading is based on the use and inherent ambiguity of the building metaphor in the philosophical tradition. De*construction*, post-*structuralism* lend themselves to an architectural appropriation insofar as they are already appropriated from architecture. The architectonic remains a

guiding philosophical ideal. For further examples of the power and impact of Derrida on recent architectural theory and practice, see Peter Brunette and David Wills, eds, 1994, especially, Peter Brunette and David Wills "The Spatial Arts: An Interview with Jacques Derrida", 9–32; see also Marco Diani and Catherine Ingraham, 1989; and Mark Wigley, 1993.

3 He frequently compares geography to history, and privileges the former for its amenability to concepts of movement, direction, and change:

> We think too much in terms of history, whether personal or universal. Becomings belong to geography, they are orientations, directions, entries and exits. (Deleuze and Parnet, 3)

He links history to the sedentary and the functioning of the State, while geography is nomadic:

> History is always written from the sedentary point of view and in the name of a unitary State apparatus, at least a possible one, even when the topic is nomads. What is lacking is a Nomadology, the opposite of a history. (Deleuze and Guattari, 1987: 23)

4 As developed in Deleuze, 1993.

5 This is one of many notions Deleuze uses as a scattergun in rethinking transgression: not how to stutter in language, but how to make language itself stutter:

> It is when the language system overstrains itself that it begins to stutter, to murmur, or to mumble, then the entire language reaches the limit that sketches the outside and confronts silence. When the language system is so much strained, language suffers a pressure that delivers it to silence. (Deleuze, 1994b: 28.)

6 For two non-jargon filled architecturally oriented projects that utilize Deleuze's work without thereby applying it, see Meaghan Morris, 1992; and John Rajchman, 1994a and 1994b.

7 See, for example, the "Dossier on Gilles Deleuze" in *Agenda. Contemporary Art Magazine* No. 33, Sept 1993, 16–36.

8 This process is already under way with talk now of the building as envelope—a metaphor that in fact should acknowledge a debt to Irigaray even more than to Deleuze, whose project is only peripherally related to enveloping and envelopement. See Eisenman, 1993.

9 Deleuze distinguishes the problem from the theorem insofar as the latter contains within itself its own consequences while the problem is inherently open:

> The problematic is distinguished from the theorematic (or constructivism from the axiomatic) in that the theorem develops internal relationships from principle to consequences, while the problem introduces an event from the outside—the removal, addition, cutting—which constitutes its own conditions and determines the 'case' or cases.... This outside of the problem is not reducible to the exteriority of the physical world any more than to the psychological interiority of a thinking ego. (Deleuze, 1989b, 174–75.)

10 Artaud says that the problem (for him) was not to orientate his thought, or to

perfect the expression of what he thought, or to acquire application and method or to perfect his poems, but simply to manage to think something. For him, this is the only conceivable 'work': it presupposes an impulse, a compulsion to think which passes though all sorts of bifurcations, spreading from the nerves and being communicated to the soul in order to arrive at thought. Henceforth, thought is also forced to think its central collapse, its fracture, its own natural 'powerlessness' which is indistinguishable from the greatest power—in other words, from those unformulated forces, the *cogitanda*, as though from so many thefts or trespasses in thought. (Deleuze, 1994a: 147)

11 As Rajchman puts it, in a related point raised in a different context:

A concept…has an open-ended relation to design. It tries to free a new complex, which serves, as it were, as a 'strange attractor' to certain features or strategies, assembling them in new ways. To do this, it must itself become complex, inventing a space of free connection to other concepts. "A concept is never simple," Jean Nouvel says, taking up in architecture a phrase from Gilles Deleuze. It is connected to others in a kind of force field that serves to displace the current doxa, stimulating thinking to go off in other directions, or inviting one to think in other ways. (1994a: 5)

12   The first illusion consists in thinking difference in terms of the identity of the concept or the subject, the illusion of identity; the second illusion is the subordination of difference to resemblance (which is linked by Deleuze to various strategies of equalisation and assimilation); the third is the strategy of tying difference to negation (which has the effect of reducing difference to disparateness); and fourth, the subordination of difference to the analogy of judgement (which disseminates difference according to rules of distribution). (see Deleuze, 1994a: 265–70)

13 See Deleuze, 1988.

14 The virtual is the *unsaid* of the statement, the unthought of thought. It is real and

subsists in them, but must be forgotten at least momentarily for a clear statement to be produced as evaporative surface effect…. The task of philosophy is explore that inevitable forgetting, to reattach statements to their conditions of emergence. (Massumi, 1992: 46)

15   Between Heidegger and Artaud, Maurice Blanchot was able to give the fundamental question of what makes us think, what forces us to think, back to Artaud; what forces us to think is "the inpower [*impouvoir*] of thought," the figure of nothingness, the inexistence of the whole which could be thought. What Blanchot diagnoses everywhere in literature is particularly clear in cinema: on the one hand the presence of an unthinkable in thought, which would be both its source and barrier; on the other hand the presence to infinity of another thinker, who shatters every monologue of a thinking self. (Deleuze, 1989: 167–68)

16 Significantly, elsewhere in the same text, Deleuze instead wants to equate the outside with force: "Forces always come from the outside, from an outside

that is farther away than any form of exteriority" (1989: 122). Does this mean that thought and force can be equated? There is some plausibility to this claim, given Deleuze's "activist" understanding of thought; moreover, such a reading would enable the Nietzschean distinction between the forces of action and reaction Deleuze develops in *Nietzsche and Philosophy* to apply directly to thought itself. It is clear that Deleuze is advocating an active thought, thinking that is productive and self-expanding.

17 When he posits the outside of thought as life itself, as the impetus, and resistance, of life to categories, and its push beyond them. In *Cinema 2. The Time-Image* (1989b), Deleuze wants to link the unthought to the body, which can no longer be conceived in terms of being a medium of thought or a blockage to it (as in the Platonic and Cartesian traditions): rather, the body is the *motive* of thought, its source or well:

> The body is no longer the obstacle that separates thought from itself, that which it has to overcome to reach thinking. It is on the contrary that which it plunges into or must plunge into, in order to reach the unthought, that is life. Not that the body thinks, but, obstinate and stubborn, it forces us to think, and forces us to think what is concealed from thought, life. Life will no longer be made to appear before the categories of thought; thought will be thrown into the categories of life. The categories of life are precisely the attitudes of the body, its postures. 'We do not even know what a body can do': in its sleep, in its drunkenness, in its efforts and resistances. To think is to learn what a non-thinking body is capable of, its capacity, its postures. (Deleuze, 1989b: 189)

18 Cf.

> What counts is…the interstices between images [in cinema], between two images: a spacing which means that each image is plucked from the void and falls back into it. (Deleuze, 1989: 179)

19 Deleuze's own explanation of the movements and speeds of becoming continually emphasizes the ways becoming-other refuses imitation or analogy, refuses to represent itself as like something else: rather, becoming is the activation or freeing of lines, forces, intensities from the boundaries and constraints of an identity or fixed purpose to the transformation and problematization of identity:

> …an Eskimo-becoming…does not consist in playing the Eskimo, in imitating or identifying yourself with him [sic] or taking the Eskimo upon yourself, but in assembling something between you and him, for you can only become Eskimo if the Eskimo himself becomes something else. The same goes for lunatics, drug addicts, alcoholics…. We are trying to extract from madness the life which it contain, while hating the lunatics who constantly kill life, turn it against itself. We are trying to extract from alcohol the life which it contains, without drinking. (Deleuze and Parnet: 53)

20 Massumi says it much better than I am able to:

> A crack has opened in habit, a 'zone of indeterminacy' is glimpsed in the hyphen between the stimulus and the response. Thought consists in widening

that gap, filling it fuller and fuller with potential responses, to the point that, confronted with a particular stimulus, the body's reaction cannot be predicted.

Thought-in-becoming is less a willful act than an undoing: the nonaction of suspending established stimulus-response circuits to create a zone where chance and change may intervene. (Massumi, 1992: 99)

21 Boundas, in his introduction to Deleuze (Boundas, ed., 1993), suggests a close convergence between Derrida's notion of supplementarity and Deleuze's understanding of the outside, which does seem to me to capture the spirit in which there may be a political allegiance between them in spite of the question of the (possible) incommensurability of their theoretical concerns:

The outside is not another site, but rather an out-of-site that erodes and dissolves all the other sites. Its logic, therefore, is like the logic of difference, provided that the latter is understood in its transcendental and not in its empirical dimension; instead of difference between x and y, we must now conceive the difference of x from itself. Like the structure of supplementarity whose logic it follows, the outside is never exhausted; every attempt to capture it generates an excess or supplement that in turn feeds anew the flows of deterritorialization, and releases new lines of flight…the outside is Deleuze-Leibniz's virtual that is always more than the actual; it is the virtual that haunts the actual and, as it haunts it, makes it flow and change. (Boundas, 1993: 15)

CH 9

1 Fetishism shares this characteristic with exhibitionism, where kleptomania is considered the equivalent feminine perversion.

2 This is analogous to the claim that pornography, like fetishism, is a male preserve; in themselves, they remain inadequate as forms of sexual satisfaction for they reduce women to the position of (voyeuristic/fetishistic) objects, not subjects.

3 Incidentally, Freud quite dramatically changed his mind about the negative and positive roles of the perversions and neuroses in his paper "A Child Is Being Beaten" (1919a), where he claims that even perversions are the result of repression.

4 Interestingly, Lacan claims that fetishism is the only perversion for which there is no corresponding neurosis (Lacan and Granoff, 265).

5 This quote is worth reproducing in full: "The word is a gift of language and language is not immaterial. It is subtle matter but matter nonetheless. It can fecundate the hysterical woman, it can stand for the flow of urine or for excrement withheld. Words can also suffer symbolic wounds. We recall the 'Wespe' with a castrated W, when the wolf man realized the symbolic punishment which was inflicted upon him by Grouscha…. The imaginary is decipherable only if it is rendered into symbols" (Lacan and Granoff, 286–89). In short, the fetish is interpretable, not because of any analogy or correspondence between the penis or vagina and the fetish, just as dreams are

not interpretable based on visual resemblances. Psychoanalysis is the talking cure and as such it relies on the verbal elaboration of the symptom and its linguistic context, provided by the web of free associations. Fetishism emerges at the moment when the imaginary tilts into the symbolic, the pre-Oedipal is transformed into the Oedipal, or anxiety is transformed into guilt.

CH 10

1 Such a fantasy of wholeness, harmony, and completion in the imaginary mother-child dyad rewrites the major sources of tension and bodily upheaval in the infant's earliest relations. In describing this as a period of corporeal fragmentation and incapacity, and in linking the structure of the imaginary order to frustration and aggressivity, Lacan provides a necessarily sobering counterbalance to this retrospective idealization.

2 Adrienne Rich, 1986, 23–75.

3 With regard to lesbianism, the masculinity complex has little or no explanatory power, for it fails to account for the non-masculine lesbian, that particular figure that since the nineteenth century has baffled sexologists and psychoanalysts, and that Havelock Ellis named "the womanly woman," the female invert (de Lauretis, xiii).

4 Freud's equivocation with regard to this issue—whether a normal sexual instinct, phylogenetically inherited, preexists its possible deviations (in psychoneurotic individuals) or whether instinctual life is but a set of transformations, some of which are then defined as normal, i.e., non-pathogenic and socially desirable or admissible—is a source of insoluble debate. (10)

5 What if one set out to pursue a theory of sexuality along the negative trace of the of the perversions—let us say, fetishism? Such theory might not, perhaps, account for the majority of people, but then the positive theory of sexuality does not either, and then again, the notion of "the majority of people" is as troubled as the notion of "the normal"... (28).

6 Her question is posed under the rubric of the "negative theory of the perversions":

What if, then, one were to reframe the question of the phallus and the fantasy of castration in this other perspective provided by Freud's negative theory, so to speak, of the perversions? ...the two lesbian texts under discussion [Hall's and Moraga's] speak fantasies of castration; but they also, and very effectively, speak desire; and thus they are fully in the symbolic, in signification. Yet the desire they speak is not masculine, nor *simply* phallic. But again, if the phallus is both the mark of castration and the signifier of desire, then the question is, What acts as the phallus in these lesbian fantasies? (222)

7 De Lauretis rather mysteriously distinguishes this from hysteria, although hysteria can only be understood as a particular form or type of neurosis.

8 De Lauretis quotes a crucial passage from Bersani and Dutoit's analysis:

The crucial point—which makes the fetishistic object different from the phallic symbol—is that the success of the fetish depends on its being seen as authentically different from the missing penis. With a phallic symbol, we may not be consciously aware of what it stands for, but it attracts us because, consciously or unconsciously, we perceive it *as* the phallus. In fetishism, however, the refusal to see the fetish as a penis-substitute may not be simply an effect of repression. The fetishist has displaced the missing penis from the woman's genitals to, say, her underclothing, but we suggest that if he doesn't care about the under-clothing resembling a penis it is because: (1) he knows that it is not a penis; (2) he doesn't want it to be only a penis; and (3) he also knows that nothing can replace the lack to which in fact he has resigned himself. (Bersani and Dutoit, 68–69, quoted in de Lauretis, 224)

9 De Lauretis claims that Stephen's revulsion of her own body image, cap-tured in a kind of "primal scene" in viewing her own body in a mirror, is too phallic rather than, as classical psychoanalysis would represent her, a woman under the sway of the masculinity complex, a woman envious of the penis:

> What Stephen sees in the mirror (the image that establishes the ego) is the image of a phallic body [de Lauretis claims]…a body Stephen's mother found repulsive. Thus, since 'the other person' who serves as model of bodily desir-ability is Stephen's mother, the image of herself that Stephen sees in the mirror does not accomplish 'the amorous captivation of the subject' or offer her a 'fundamentally narcissistic experience', but on the contrary inflicts a narcissis-tic wound: that phallic body-image, and thus the ego, cannot be loved, cannot be narcissistically invested *because* it is *phallic*. (240–41)

One with a more orthodox psychoanalytic bent might perhaps respond by claiming that the problem for Stephen's representation is that, while her body may be imaged or signified as *virile*, nonetheless, what it lacks, what prevents it from attaining the status of the phallic body is the absence of the very signifier (the imaginary, detachable penis) that signals her female status. Her personal misery comes, in her own eyes, from her being neither properly feminine nor properly masculine, from her lacking the signifiers of femininity (as de Lauretis affirms) *and* the signifiers of masculinity (the phallus).

10 In her characterisation of bodily dispossession, de Lauretis lurches per-ilously close to implying that it is the mother who is responsible for the daughter's sense of bodily dispossession. This is clear in her discussion of the genesis of Stephen Gordon's body-image, and in her more general char-acterization of what it is that the girl disavows. Such an implication is dis-turbing insofar as it leaves the father out of the account of the "origin" of lesbian desire, when it seems clear that the father's position must have some effect on the psychology of the daughter. Any model which "blames" the mother (although her position is not as crude as attributing straightfor-ward blame) must itself explain the mother's position as well, and how it is that she is unable to narcissistically validate the daughter's embodiment:

> Failing the mother's narcissistic validation of the subject's body-image, which

constitutes the imaginary matrix or first outline of the ego, the subject is threatened with a loss of body-ego, a lack of being. (262)

11 It remains unclear why this highly suggestive model, not so much of lesbian *desire* as de Lauretis claims, but more of lesbian *attraction*, is not as appropriate for men and heterosexual women as it is for lesbians. That strange elusive "thing" that attracts one person to another (whether the attraction culminates in a sexual relation or not) could be thought in terms of this very specific notion of fetish that de Lauretis develops.

12 Cf.

> If the lesbian fetishes are often, though certainly not exclusively objects or signs with connotations of masculinity, it is not because they stand in for the missing penis but because such signs are most strongly precoded to convey, both to the subject and to others, the cultural meaning of sexual (genital) activity and yearning toward women. Such signs can also most effectively deny the female body (in the subject) and at the same time resignify (her desire for) it through the very signification of its prohibition. (263)

13 De Lauretis claims an inherent political status to lesbian sexualities, and particularly for the fetish of masculinity, which seems to me rather disturbing and problematic:

> ...the signs of masculinity are the most visually explicit and strongly coded by dominant discourses to signify sexual desire toward women, and hence their greater visibility in cultural representations of lesbianism, which correlates to their greater effectivity in a political use of reverse discourse. (264)

While I do not want to deny that in specific contexts lesbianism, and particularly the adoption of the signs of masculinity, may perform a transgressive function, there seems to be nothing inherently transgressive about any particular sexualities or desires. It is not clear whether de Lauretis wants to claim that greater visibility constitutes greater political effectivity (which seems a rather dubious principle) or whether she wants to suggest that women's adoption of precisely *those* sexual positions is transgressive here and now. This again seems to me conditional on the context: where the butch lesbian may certainly transgress the expectations of a straight community, in the context of lesbian social life, it is clearly a mode of conformity to a set of shared images or fetishes.

14 We need not just to refuse to anchor ourselves *firmly* on one or the other side of the paternal phallus, but to loosen ourselves from it altogether, and to really follow through the idea of a mobility of fetishistic or perverse desire by giving up the convenience of notions such as oscillation and undecidability. (269)

CH 11

1 In my understanding, a mistaken bifurcation or division is created between so-called essentialists and constructionists insofar as constructionism is inherently bound up with notions of essence. Constructionism, in order

to be consistent, must explain what the "raw materials" of the construction consist in; these raw materials must, by definition, be essential insofar as they precondition and make possible the processes of social construction.

2 The work of a number of feminists in this area is clearly laudable and provides a model or ideal for politically engaged knowledges. In this context, see the work of Butler, de Lauretis, and Fuss.

3 See, for example, my paper "Lesbian Fetishism?" republished here.

4 Along these lines, the work of Sheila Jeffreys, Janice Raymond, Andrea Dworkin, and Catherine MacKinnon comes to mind.

5 Such models are of course not the only ones spawned by Western thought; alternative models, which see desire as a positivity, a production or making, while considerably rarer in our received history, nonetheless still develop and have exerted their influence in the writings of, amongst others, Spinoza, Nietzsche, Deleuze, and Lyotard, as I will discuss in more detail below.

6 I have tried to elaborate in considerable detail the differences between masculine, anaclitic forms of love/desire and feminine/narcissistic forms in Grosz, 1990: chapter 5.

7 This idea has been effectively explored in Jacqueline Rose's penetrating analysis of Freud's treatment of Dora (1985).

8 See Irigaray, 1985b; and Whitford, 1991.

9 See Irigaray, "Commodities Among Themselves" and "Women on the Market" (in 1985b).

> Explicitly condemned by the social order [the prostitute] is implicitly tolerated…. In her case, the qualities of woman's body are "useful." However, these qualities have "value" only because they have already been appropriated by a man, and because they serve as the locus of relations—hidden ones—between men. Prostitution amounts to the *usage that is exchanged*. Usage that is not merely potential: it has already been realized. The woman's body is valuable because it has already been used. In the extreme case, the more it has served, the more it is worth…. [It] has become once again no more than a vehicle for relations among men. (186)

10 See Butler, de Lauretis, and Fuss.

11 Cf.

> The actor Robert De Niro walks "like" a crab in a certain sequence: but, he says, it is not a question of his imitating a crab; it is a question of making something that has to do with the crab enter into composition with the image, with the speed of the image. (Deleuze and Guattari, 1987: 274)

CH 12

1 It is not clear that such a fascination is a universal *human* concern; I do not even want to suggest that most men find animal sex fascinating, but rather, the more limited claim, that such a fascination is a masculine one, that for *some* men, animal sex and even insect sex hold immense fascination because they represent motifs, themes, and fantasies that are close to what might

be understood as a masculine imaginary, to a masculine mode of representation of self and other.

2   What seems rare is not the combination of scholarship and personal obsessional—this could be said to characterize much if not all theoretical and scientific discourse—but the open acknowledgement that the research is based on personal concerns.

3   For further details, and for reproductions and translations of some of his formative works on what might be understood as a sociology of the sacred, see Denis Hollier, ed., 1988.

4   See a quirkily personal book, Caillois, 1985.

5   The mantis species is probably among the earliest to appear on land:

> Mantidae were probably the first insects to appear on earth, given that the *Mantis protogea*, whose fossil prints were found in the oeningen Myocena, belongs to the paleodictyoptera group as defined by Scudder, and whose traces are manifest from the Carboniferous Age on. (Caillois, 1990: 69)

6   See here, Caillois, 1984; I have discussed this analysis at some length in Grosz, 1994.

7   Lingis, in his dazzling evocative account of deep-sea diving in "The Rapture of the Deep" (in Lingis, 1983) provides something of an indirect confirmation of both the superabundance or excessiveness of camouflage and display and the irrelevance of an audience, or even an eye observing the spectacle:

> Before the plumage and display behaviors of the bird-of-paradise, before the coiled horns of the mountain sheep, one has to admit a specific development of the organism to capture another eye...there is a logic of ostentation over and beyond camouflage and semantic functions. The color-blind *octopus vulgaris* controls with twenty nervous systems the 2-3 million chromatophores, iridophores and leucophores fitted in its skin; only fifteen of these have been correlated with camouflage or emotional states. At rest in its lair, its skin invents continuous light shows. The sparked and streaked coral fish school and scatter as a surge of life dominated by a compulsion for exhibition, spectacle, parade.
>
> The most ornate skins are on nudibranchia, blind sea slugs. In the marine abysses, five or six miles below the last blue rays of the light, the fish and the crabs, almost all of them blind, illuminate their lustrous colors with their own bioluminescence, for no witness. (Lingis, 1983: 9–10)

8   Caillois outlines a whole series of cultural associations regarding the mantis, which seem to place it in a privileged, if somewhat ambivalent social and theological position:

> ...sometimes the mantis is called an 'Italian girl' or a 'phantom', and less explicably a 'strawberry' or a 'madeleine'. More generally, an ambivalent attitude emerges: on the one hand the insect is regarded as sacred, whence its usual name of *prégo-Diéou* ("pray-to-God"), with its variants and corresponding expressions...; on the other hand the insect is considered diabolic, as testified by the symmetrical name of *prégo-Diablé* ("pray-to-the-Devil").

If we look now at the sayings used by children with respect to the mantis, we find two main themes: first, it is said to be a Prophetess who knows everything, and especially the whereabouts of the wolf, and secondly, it is assumed that it is praying because its mother died or drowned. On this last point the testimony is unanimous. (1990: 69–72)

9 Caillois will cite a series of remarkable case studies from the annals of psychoanalysis, particularly examples of oral persecution mania to make more explicit this link between the mantis, the *vagina dentata* and the *femme fatale*:

> Bychowski analyses a case of a victim who is convinced that he will be devoured by a prostitute before he has even approached her. I would be inclined more generally to link these fantasies with the development of most castration complexes that…commonly originate in the terror of the toothed vagina, given the assimilation of the entire body to the male member and likewise that of the mouth to the vagina are…classics of psychoanalysis. (1990: 78–79)

10 Rather ironically, Caillois's analysis at this point finds a linkage with Deleuze's early analysis of the structure of masochism in his analysis of Sacher von Masoch: he claims that masochism is not, as Freud suggests, an inverted homosexual desire for the father, who is disguised by the figure of the punishing mother, but rather, an attempt to psychically kill the father, insofar as it is the father that induces male and filial identifications in the son. See Deleuze, 1989. Caillois explicitly connects the appeal of the praying mantis to the sadomasochistic complex.

11 Caillois quotes Paul Eluard, who "admits to seeing the ideal sexual relationship in their love-making habits; the act of love, he says, diminishes the male and aggrandises the female, so it is natural that she should use her ephemeral superiority to devour him, or at least to kill him." (Caillois, 1990: 79) Freud makes a similar claim in his analyses of love relations and the "tendency to debasement in the sphere of love."

12 While remaining critical of the Sartrean analysis of sexual desire as fundamentally appropriative, sadistic, an imposition onto the other which confirms one's consciousness and sense of self, Lingis nonetheless affirms Sartre's refusal to reduce sexuality and sexual pleasure to functional or pragmatic projects or goals:

> It is not the dexterity of the hands that is most captivating but a hand trailing over the other with trembling and indecisive movements.…A sex organ is not a tool; it is essential that penis and clitoris in erection, the vagina lubricating, not be activated voluntarily, used by a reflective consciousness. No fine, prehensile organ assembled with striated muscles can be a sex organ, Sartre says; a sex organ can only be part of a vegetative system. (Lingis, 1985: 25)

13 Sexuality, desire, cannot be seen in terms of a function, purpose or goal, for this is to reduce it to functionality; materiality, as I have already suggested following Caillois, is always in excess of function or goal. This is one of the problems with the sex-manual approach: "how-to" books on sexuality presume a certain principle of the performance of a chore or task, not

the uncovering of desire, which cannot be summarized, put into a formula or learned by rote.

14 In Lyotard's text (1993), the organic body does function as something of a pure plenitude, a prelapsarian given (which, if it is produced, is the effect of physiology, anatomy, neurology, and biochemistry) or presence that is deflected by a secondary intervention, a structure not unlike that which is the object of Derrida's continuous criticisms.

15 The Moebius strip, incidentally, also a pervasive metaphor in some of Lacan's writings on the subject, is the driving model behind my own understanding of the mind/body relation in Grosz, 1994.

16 Lingis quotes from the French ex-prostitute, Xavière Lafort:

> Punishment is again a way of making a human being accept the inacceptable. But the S-M bond also ends up making you feel something for your pimps. This 'something' is nameless; it is beyond love and hatred, beyond feelings, a wild joy mixed with shame, the joy of taking it, enduring the blow, of belonging and of feeling freed or freedom. It must exist in all women, in all couples, in lesser or unconscious degrees. I can't really explain it. It's like a drug, like a feeling of living your life several times at once, in incredible intensity. The pimps themselves in inflicting these punishments experience this 'something', I'm sure…I am not saying that I want to go back to that life. But you always do miss it. It's cocaine. You never find such intensity in normal life. (quoted in Lingis, 1985: 84–85)

17 It is significant that in gay community responses to the AIDS crisis and the advocacy of "safe sex" sexual practices, there has been considerable effort devoted to publicizing the fact that "safe sex" does not necessarily imply more boring sex; that one need not court danger and possible death in the search for an ultimate sexual high: or rather, there are many bodily ways in which sexual and erotic relations remain intense and exciting without necessarily being life-imperilling.

18 It is not clear to me to what degree Lingis is prepared to limit the relevance and scope of his analysis of libido: while certainly much of what he says about the formlessness of sexual pleasure, the indeterminacy of the objectives of desire seems to me directly relevant to women and female sexuality, nonetheless it is also likely that much of his account, as (quasi-) autobiographical, is specifically limited to masculine experience.

19 See, for example, Shannon Bell, 1991, who claims that women too can, with the right information and practice, achieve ejaculatory orgasms. While I do not doubt that some women, and perhaps, under certain circumstances, all women, are capable of orgasmic ejaculations, it is not clear why this should be regarded as an improvement on or progression from non-ejaculatory orgasms.

20 In his paper "Khajuraho" (1983), Lingis makes a similar point:

> It turns the most unlikely things into analogies or figures of lust so as to be able to excite itself anywhere; it even, in the case of fetishes, can displace itself

entirely onto things remote from any possibility of interaction. It is as though the libidinous impulse is an exorbitant energy that tends not to satisfy itself and subside, like other desires and appetites, but to excite itself with its own function; everything gets infected with its trouble, even practical associations to work with tools, political relationships within institutions, pedagogical relationships over ideas, military alliances before the imminence of disaster and in the thirst for conquest. Not only can the pursuit of riches or the investiture with political authority function as a means to obtain partners of flesh and blood, but cupidity and calculation themselves become lascivious. (1983: 50)

CH 13

1 The history of the label "queer theory" has its problems, though it has some appeal. What I think works well in this formulation is an ambiguity about what the term "queer" refers to: that not only are the objects of speculation—lesbian, gay, and other forms of sexuality intolerable to the heterocentric mainstream—"queer," but perhaps more interestingly, the ways in which they are treated is "queer," the knowledges that deal with them are also queer.

But there is also a cost in using this term, a certain loss of specificity, and the capacity for cooption and depoliticization. In her introduction to the "Queer Theory" issue of *differences* (1991), Teresa de Lauretis provides a useful account of the genesis and function of the label "queer," its own self-understanding as distinctively defiant, transgressive, postmodern:

(249)

> Today we have, on the one hand, the term "lesbian" and "gay" to designate distinct kinds of life-styles, sexualities, sexual practices, communities, issues, publications, and discourses; on the other hand, the phrase "gay and lesbian," or more and more frequently, "lesbian and gay" (ladies first), has become standard currency.... In a sense, the term "Queer Theory" was arrived at in the effort to avoid all of these fine distinctions in our discursive protocols, not to adhere to any one of the given terms, not to assume their ideological liabilities, but instead to both transgress and transcend them—or at the very least problematize them. (v)

De Lauretis is of course perfectly correct in her claim that the phrase "Lesbian and Gay" by now has a pre-designated and readily assumed constituency, and a correlative set of identities. And with it, a series of easy presumptions and ready-made political answers. The label "queer" does problematize many of these presumptions; but its risks are greater than simply remaining tied to a set of stale and conventional assumptions. "Lesbian and Gay" has the advantage of straightforwardly articulating its constituency, while "queer" is capable of accommodating, and will not doubt provide a political rationale and coverage in the near future for many of the most blatant and extreme forms of heterosexual and patriarchal power games. They too are, in a certain sense, queer, persecuted, ostracized. Heterosexual sadists, pederasts, fetishists, pornographers, pimps, voyeurs suffer from social sanctions: in a certain sense they too can be regarded as oppressed. But to claim an oppression of the order of lesbian and gay, women's, or racial oppression is to ignore the very real complicity and phallic rewards of what might be called "deviant sexualities" within patriarchal and heterocentric power relations. It is of the same order as the claim that men too can be the victims of "female chauvinism": such a claim rests on the denial of a relentless and systematic distribution of values and benefits.

Moreover, underlying the incipient distinction between the labels "lesbian and gay" and "queer" is a series of often unspoken ontological and political assumptions. For example, the question of sexual difference is at the very heart of lesbian and gay theory and politics (the marking of "homosexual" necessarily designates a specific type of love object, male or female); while the proliferation of "queer" sexualities is bound to include bisexuality, heterosexual transvestism, transsexualism, and sado-masochistic heterosexuality. The proliferation of sexualities beyond the notion of two (the assertion of two has been difficult enough!) seems to underlie the rapidly expanding domain and constituency of queerness (n sexes). While I do not want to prevent this proliferation, nor to judge the transgressiveness or conservatism of these multiple sexualities, this field of queerness, it seems to me, can only ignore the specificities of sexed bodies at its own peril. Even if we are all composed of a myriad of sexual possibilities, and fluid and changeable form of sexuality and sexual orientation, nevertheless, these still conform to the configurations of the two sexes. A male sado-masochist does not function in the same way or with the same effect as a female sado-masochist. It *does* make a difference which kind of sexed body enacts the various modes of performance of sexual roles and positions.

2 How one could ever in fact compare different articulations of oppressive structures in order to find out who is more oppressed than whom is entirely unclear to me, particularly in view of the fact that, with the exception of a relatively small minority of white middle class, hetero, Anglo, young men, all of us can in some sense or other understand ourselves as oppressed.

3 In a whole series of current lesbian feminist texts, there seems to be the curious imperative to provide an account of lesbianism, or feminism, from which no category of women is excluded, in which all women are able to find some self-representation. This is a consequence of a drive to all-inclusiveness, which has had the effect, on the one hand, of creating discourses that naïvely and self-contradictorily claim to speak only for me, not representing anyone, and thus not coercing anyone into accepting a self-representation which is mine alone (see, for example Trebilcot, 1990). This kind of position not only refuses to accept the responsibility for the fact that no discourse or cultural production simply reflects the intentions of its author, insofar as they are read, responded to, and are of interest to others independent of intentions. They are read, and can be effective, only if they are

more than mere self-expression. If what I write is true only for myself, it is not true at all ("true for me" is self-contradictory). On the other hand, the opposite extreme is found in many feminist texts that either become embedded in and crippled by their own hyphenization and hybridization as lesbian-feminist-anti-racist-anti-classist-anti-agist…, their aspiration towards all-inclusiveness, or reduced to the kinds of generalizations that, while including everyone, have very little to say about anyone's specificities and differences. A choice has to be made either to refuse to efface specificity (in which case clearly not everyone can be included); or to refuse to efface generality or universality (in which case, no particular form of oppression can be adequately accounted for in its concrete articulations). For a particularly acute analysis of the difficulties of these two extremes, and the political necessity of acknowledging that all subjects are in fact placed in a position (whether they recognize it or not) of speaking on behalf of others, even if their words cannot express or include valid universal claims, see Alcoff, 1992.

4 Most notably, Foucault's inability to acknowledge that the institutions whose genealogies he so well documents—prisons, the insane asylum, the discourses on sexuality and self-production, and so on—are distinctively male dominated sites, and the privileged subjects whose histories of subordination and insurrection he documents are those of men. See Diamond and Quinby, eds., 1988.

5 On the question of morphologies, and the redundancy of the category of gender, see Grosz, 1994.

6 Deleuze's reading of Nietzsche makes it clear that the forces of the body are only ever a matter of more or less, a question of differential quantities, and through the differential relation between two quantities, the production of qualities. Nietzsche says:

> The attempt should be made to see whether a scientific order of values could be constructed simply on a numerical and quantitative scale of forces. All other "values" are prejudices, naiveties and misunderstandings. They are everywhere reducible to this numerical and quantitative scale. (Nietzsche, 1968: 710)

7 In her intriguing and brilliant paper, "Lesbian 'Sex,'" (1990), Marilyn Frye quotes some of the statistics of the sex researchers Philip Blumstein and Pepper Schwartz from their text *American Couples* (William and Morrow Co, New York, 1983) on rates of frequency of sexual activity amongst married, de facto heterosexual, gay, and lesbian couples. Their statistics suggest that 47% of lesbians in long term relationship had sex once a month or less while only 15% of married couples had sex once a month or less. Frye's profound insight in her commentary on these statistics is that it is not clear what "having sex" actually means, especially when it emerges that the 85% of married couples who "had sex" more than once a month on the average take less than 8 minutes for such activities. I will return to this crucial paper later in my discussion.

8 Butler argues that Foucault seems to want to say *both* that the regimes of sexuality are what produce sex; and at the same time, that there are bodies and pleasures that are somehow outside the law and the discursive apparatus, there as "raw materials" for the functioning of power. She claims that there is

> ...an unresolved tension within the *History of Sexuality* itself (he refers to "bucolic" and "innocent" pleasures of intergenerational sexual exchange that exists prior to the imposition of various regulative strategies). On the one hand, Foucault wants to argue that there is no "sex" in itself which is not produced by complex interactions of discourse and power, and yet there does not seem to be a "multiplicity of pleasures" *in itself* which is not the effect of any specific discourse/power exchange. (Butler, 1990: 97)

9 Hence the final paragraph to Foucault's text in which he counterposes the reorganization or realignments of bodies and pleasures to the regime of sexuality:

> we need to consider the possibility that one day, perhaps, in a different economy of bodies and pleasures, people will no longer quite understand how the ruses of sexuality, and the power that sustains its organization, were able to subject us to that austere monarchy of sex, so that we became dedicated to the endless task of forcing its secret, of exacting the truest of confessions from a shadow. (159)

10 It seems stuck within a model that can do nothing but endlessly vary itself around a central core that itself remains inviolable: the domination of the phallus, the structure of power accorded to the position of the father at the expense of the mother's body, the impossibility of a viable position for women as autonomous and self-defining subjects.

11 Most notably in her earlier work (1985a; 1985b). But also in her more recent writings:

> she does not set herself up as *one*, as a (single) female unit. She is not closed up or around one single truth or essence. The essence of a truth remains foreign to her. She neither has nor is being.... The/a woman can sub-sist by already being double in her self: both the one and the other. Not: one plus an other, more than one. More than. She is "foreign" to the unit. And to the countable, to quantification. There to the more than, as it relates to something already quantifiable, even were it a case of disrupting the operations. If it were necessary to count her/them in units—which is impossible—each unit would already be more than doubly (her). But that would have to be understood in another way. The (female) one being the other, without ever being either one or the other. Ceaselessly in the exchange between the one and the other. With the result that she is always already othered but with no possible identification of her, or of the other. (Irigaray, 1991a: 86.)

12 This is precisely Naomi Schor's and Margaret Whitford's arguments in their separate introductions to their anthology on Irigaray. See Burke, Schor, and Whitford, 1994.

13 Incidentally, there need be no commitment to the presumption of an

homogeneity of the objects or victims of homophobia—lesbians and gays may be as varied in these characteristics as any individuals, indeed, are likely to be members of more or less every constituency, every social category or group; but simply that whatever "identity" is bestowed on lesbians and gay men is the product of relentless forms of oppression, for they produce the homogeneity necessary to single out and define the objects of revulsion and inequity.

14 Indeed, there is a common reaction when someone comes out or is "outed" that they may not be believed—a reaction that is pretty well unimaginable in the case of other oppressions. If someone confessed to being Jewish or Islamic, there could be no disbelief!

BIBLIOGRAPHY

Alcoff, Linda. 1992. "On Speaking for Others." In *Cultural Critique* 20: 5–32.

Allen, Jeffner, ed. 1990. *Lesbian Philosophies and Cultures.* Albany: SUNY Press.

Allen, Judith and E Grosz, eds. 1987. *Australian Feminist Studies* 5, special issue on "Feminism and the Body."

Antonopoulos, Anna. 1992. "Feminism's Other: On the Politics and Poetics of Domesticity in Postmodern Texts." Unpublished paper presented at the Canadian Society for Women and Philosophy, York University, Toronto, September.

Aristotle. 1968–1970. *Physics.* (2 Volumes) Trans. P.H. Wicksteed and F.M Cornford. London: Heinemann.

Barthes, Roland. 1977. "The Death of the Author." In *Image-Music-Text.* Trans. Stephen Heath. London: Fontana Paperbacks, 142–48.

Battersby, Christine. 1992. "Hermaphrodites of Art

and Vampires of Practice: Architectural Theory and Feminist Theory." *Journal of Philosophy and the Visual Arts* 3.

Bell, Shannon. 1991. "Feminist Ejaculations." In *The Hysterical Male; New Feminist Theory*. Eds. Arthur and Marilouise Kroker. New York: St Martin's Press, 155–69.

Bennington, Geoffrey. 1994. *Legislations. The Politics of Deconstruction*. London and New York: Verso.

Bennington, Geoffrey and Jacques Derrida. 1993. *Jacques Derrida*. Chicago: University of Chicago Press.

Benveniste, Emile. 1961. *Problems in General Linguistics*. Bloomington: Indiana University Press.

Bergren, Ann. 1992. "Architecture, Gender, Philosophy." In *Strategies in Architecture*. Eds. John Whiteman, Jeffrey Kipnis, and Richard Burdett. Cambridge: MIT Press.

Bersani, Leo and Ulysse Dutoit. 1985. *The Forms of Violence. Narrative in Assyrian Art and Modern Culture*. New York: Schocken Books.

Bordo, Susan. 1988. "Anorexia Nervosa: Psychopathology as the Crystallization of Culture." In *Feminism and Foucault. Reflections on Resistance*. Eds. Irene Diamond and Lee Quinby. New York: Methuen.

———. 1989. "The Body and the Reproduction of Femininity: A Feminist Appropriation of Foucault." In *Gender/ Body/ Knowledge. Feminist Constructions of Being and Knowing*. Eds. Alison M. Jagger and Susan Bordo. New Brunswick and London: Rutgers University Press.

Boundas, Constantin V., ed. 1993. *The Deleuze Reader*. New York: Columbia University Press.

Boundas, Constantin V. and Dorothea Olkowski, eds. 1994. *Gilles Deleuze and the Theater of Philosophy*. New York and London: Routledge.

Braidotti, Rosi. 1989a. "Envy: Or With Your Brains and My Looks." In *Men in Feminism*. Eds. Alice Jardine and Paul Smith. New York: Routledge, 233–41.

———. 1989b. "The Politics of Ontological Difference." In Teresa Brennan, ed. *Between Feminism and Psychoanalysis*. London and New York: Routledge, 89–105.

———. 1991. *Patterns of Dissonance*. Cambridge: Polity Press.

———. 1994. "Toward a New Nomadism: Feminist Deleuzian Tracks; or, Metaphysics and Metabolism." In Constantin V. Boundas and Dorothea Olkowski, eds. *Gilles Deleuze and the Theatre of Philosophy*. New York and London: Routledge, 157–86.

Brennan, Teresa, ed. 1989. *Between Feminism and Psychoanalysis*, London and New York: Routledge.

Brodrib, Somer. 1992. *Nothing Mat(t)ers: A Feminist Critique of Postmodernism*. Melbourne: Spinifex Press.

Burke, Carolyn, Naomi Schor and Margaret Whitford, eds. 1994. *Engaging with Irigaray*. New York: Columbia University Press.

Butler, Judith. 1990. *Gender Trouble. Feminism and the Subversion of Identity*. New York: Routledge.

———. 1991. "Imitation and Gender Insubordination." In *Inside/ Out. Lesbian Theories. Gay Theories*. Ed. Diana Fuss. New York and London: Routledge, 13–31.

———. 1992. "The Lesbian Phallus and the Morphological Imaginary." *differences: A Journal of Feminist Cultural Studies* 4.1: 133–70.

———. 1993. *Bodies That Matter. On the Discursive Limits of 'Sex.'* New York: Routledge.

Butler, Rex and Paul Patton, eds. 1993. "Dossier on Gilles Deleuze." In *Agenda. Contemporary Art Magazine* 33, (Sept.): 16–36.

Caillois, Roger. 1938. *Le mythe et l'homme.* Paris: Gallimard.

———. 1984. "Mimicry and Legendary Psychasthenia." Trans. John Sheply. *October* 31: 12–32.

———. 1985. *The Writing of Stones.* Trans. Barbara Bray. Charlottesville: University of Virginia Press.

———. 1990. *The Necessity of Mind. An Analytic Study of Mechanisms of Overdetermination in Automatic and Lyrical Thinking and of the Development of Affective Themes in the Individual Consciousness.* Trans. Michael Syrotinski. Venice, CA: The Lapis Press.

Caine, Barbara, E. A. Grosz, and M. de Lepervanche, eds. 1988. *Crossing Boundaries. Feminism and the Critique of Knowledges.* Sydney: Allen and Unwin.

Casey, Edward. 1993. *Getting Back Into Place. Toward a Renewed Understanding of the Place-World.* Bloomington: Indiana University Press.

Certeau, Michel de. 1979. "Des outils pour ecrire le corps.'" *Traverses* 14–15: 1–11.

Chodorow, Nancy. 1978. *The Reproduction of Mothering. Psychoanalysis and the Sociology of Gender.* Berkeley: University of California Press.

Colombat, André Pierre. 1991. "A Thousand Trails to Work with Deleuze." *SubStance* 66 (20, 3): 10–23.

Colomina, Beatriz, ed. 1992. *Sexuality and Space.* Princeton: Princeton Architectural Press.

Cornell, Drucilla. 1991. *Beyond Accommodation. Ethical Feminism, Deconstruction and the Law.* New York: Routledge.

———. 1992. *Beyond Accommodation.* New York: Routledge.

———. 1992a. "Gender, Sex and Equivalent Rights." In *Feminists Theorize the Political.* Eds. Judith Butler and Joan W Scott. New York: Routledge, 280–96.

———. 1992b. "The Philosophy of the Limit: Systems Theory and Legal Reform." In *Deconstruction and the Possibility of Justice.* New York: Routledge, 68–91.

Clifford, Sue. 1988. "Common Ground." In *Meanjin* 47:4: 625–36.

Cooke, Philip. 1988. "Modernity, Postmodernity and the City." *Theory, Culture and Society* 5, 475–93.

Creech, James, Peggy Kamuf, and Jane Todd. 1985. "Deconstruction in America: An Interview with Jacques Derrida." *Critical Exchange* 17 (Winter): 1–33.

Creet, Julia. 1991. "Daughter of the Movement: The Psychodynamics of Lesbian S/M Fantasy." *differences* 5, 2: 135–59.

Critchley, Simon. 1991. "'Bois'—Derrida's Final Word on Levinas." In *Re-Reading Levinas.* Eds. R. Bernasconi and S. Critchley. Bloomington and Indianapolis: Indiana University Press, 162–89.

———. 1992. *The Ethics of Deconstruction. Derrida and Levinas.* Oxford: Polity Press.

Davidson, Cynthia, ed. 1992. *ANYwhere.* Rizzoli International Publications: New York.

De Landa, Manuela. 1986. "Policing the Spectrum." *Zone*, 1/2: 176–93.

De Lauretis, Teresa. 1987. "The Female Body and Heterosexual Presumption." *Semiotica* 67: 3–4.

———. 1988. "Sexual Indifference and Lesbian Representation." *Theater Journal* 40: 2.

———, ed. 1991. "Queer Theory" issue of *differences* 3, 2.

———. 1994. *The Practice of Love. Lesbian Sexuality and Perverse Desire.* Bloomington: Indiana University Press.

Deleuze, Gilles. 1983. *Nietzsche and Philosophy.* Trans. Hugh Tomlinson. New York: Columbia University Press.

———. 1988. *Foucault.* Trans. Séan Hand. Minneapolis: University of Minnesota Press.

———. 1989a. *Masochism. Coldness and Cruelty.* Trans. Jean McNeil. New York: Zone Books.

———. 1989b. *Cinema 2: The Time-Image.* Trans. Hugh Tomlinson and Robert Galeta. Minneapolis: University of Minnesota Press.

———. 1990. *The Logic of Sense.* Trans. Mark Lester with Charles Stivale. New York: Columbia University Press.

———. 1991. "Postscript on the Societies of Control." *October* 59, (Winter): 3–7.

———. 1993. *The Fold. Leibniz and the Baroque.* Trans. Tom Conley. Minneapolis: University of Minnesota Press.

———. 1994a. *Difference and Repetition.* Trans. Paul Patton. New York: Columbia University Press.

———. 1994b. "He Stuttered." In Constantin V. Boundas and Dorothea Olkowski, eds. *Gilles Deleuze and the Theatre of Philosophy.* New York and London: Routledge, 23–31.

———. 1994c. "Ariadne's Mystery." *ANY*, 5: 8–9.

Deleuze, Gilles and Felix Guattari. 1983. *Anti-Oedipus. Capitalism and Schizophrenia.* Trans. Robert Hurley, Mark Seem, and Helen R. Lane. Minneapolis: University of Minnesota Press.

———. 1986. "City/State." *Zone* 1/2: 194–99.

———. 1987. *A Thousand Plateaus. Capitalism and Schizophrenia*, Vol. 2. Trans. Brian Massumi. Minneapolis: University of Minnesota Press.

Deleuze, Gilles and Claire Parnet. 1987. *Dialogues.* Trans. Hugh Tomlinson and Barbara Habberjam. New York: Columbia University Press.

De Man, Paul. 1979. *Allegories of Reading. Figural Language in Rousseau, Nietzsche, Rilke and Proust.* New Haven and London: Yale University Press.

———. 1984. *The Rhetoric of Romanticism.* New York: Columbia University Press.

Derrida, Jacques. 1978. "Freud and the Scene of Writing." In *Writing and Difference.* Trans. Alan Bass. London: Routledge and Kegan-Paul,

———. 1979. *Spurs. Eperons.* Trans. Barbara Harlow. Chicago: University of Chicago Press.

———. 1983a. "Geschlecht. Sexual Difference, Ontological Difference." Trans. R. Berezdivin in *Research in Phenomenology* 13: 65–83.

———. 1983b. "The Principle of Reason: The University in the Eyes of its Pupils." *Diacritics* Fall: 3–20.

———. 1984a. *Signeponge/Signsponge.* Trans. Richard Rand. New York:

Columbia University Press.

———. 1984b. "Deconstruction and the Other." In *Dialogues with Contemporary Continental Thinkers—The Phenomenological Heritage*. Manchester: Manchester University Press, 105–26.

———. 1985. "Point de Folie—Maintenant L'Architecture." In Bernard Tschumi, *La Case Vide la Vilette*. London: Architectural Association.

———. 1986a. *Glas*. Trans. John P. Leavey Jr. and Richard Rand. Lincoln: University of Nebraska Press.

———. 1986b. "Architecture. Where Desire May Live." *Domus* 671 (April): 17–24.

———. 1987. *The Truth in Painting*. Trans. Geoffrey Bennington and I. McLeod. Chicago: University of Chicago Press.

———. 1988a. "Signature, Event, Context." In *Limited Inc*. Trans. Samuel Weber and Jeffrey Mehlman. Baltimore: The Johns Hopkins University Press.

———. 1988b. *The Ear of the Other. Otobiography, Transference, Translation*. Ed. Christie McDonald. New York: Schocken Books.

———. 1988c. "Why Peter Eisenman Writes Such Good Books." *Threshold* 4. Journal of the School of Architecture, University of Illinois at Chicago. Eds. M. Diana and C. Ingraham, 99–105.

———. 1989a. "Women in the Beehive." In *Men in Feminism*. Eds. Alice Jardine and Paul Smith. New York: Routledge, 189–203.

———. 1989b. "Rights of Inspection." Trans. David Wills. *Art and Text* 32: 19–97.

———. 1989c. "Psyche. Inventions of the Other." Trans. Catherine Porter. In *Reading De Man Reading*. Minneapolis: University of Minnesota Press, 25–66.

———. 1991a. "At This Very Moment in This Work Here I Am." In *Re-Reading Levinas*. Eds. Robert Bernasconi and Simon Critchley. Bloomington and Indianapolis: Indiana University Press, 11–48.

———. 1991b. "'Eating Well,' or the Calculation of the Subject: An Interview with Jacques Derrida." In *Who Comes After the Subject?* Eds. Eduardo Cadava, Peter Connor, and Jean-Luc Nancy. New York: Routledge, 96–119.

———. 1992a. "Ulysses Gramophone." In *Acts of Literature*. Ed. D. Attridge. New York: Routledge, 256–309.

———. 1992b. "Faxitexture." In *ANYwhere*. Ed. Cynthia Davidson. New York: Rizzoli International Publications, 23–33.

———. 1993. "Chora." In *Choral Works. A Collaboration Between Peter Eisenman and Jacques Derrida*. Ed. Jeffrey Kipnis. New York.

Diamond, Irene and Lee Quinby, eds. 1988. *Feminism and Foucault. Reflections on Resistance*. New York: Methuen.

Donzelot, Jacques. 1979. *The Policing of Families*. New York: Pantheon Books.

Douglas, Mary. 1991. "The Idea of a Home: A Kind of Space." *Social Research* 46 (Spring): 287–307.

Eisenman, Peter. 1993. "Folding in Time: The Singularity of Rebstock." *Columbian Documents of Architecture and Theory (D)* 2: 99–112.

Elam, Diane. 1994. *Feminism and Deconstruction. Ms en Abyme*. New York: Routledge.

Mary Fallon. 1989. *Working Hot*. Melbourne: Sybella Press.

Foucault, Michel. 1970. *The Order of Things*. Trans. Alan Sheridan. London: Tavistock.

————. 1972. "The Discourse on Language." In *The Archaeology of Knowledge.* Trans. A.M. Sheridan Smith. New York: Harper Colophon.

————. 1977a. *Language, Counter-Memory, Practice. Selected Essays and Interviews.* Ed. Donald Bouchard. Oxford: Basil Blackwell.

————. 1977b. *Discipline and Punish. The Birth of the Prison.* Trans. A. Sheridan. London: Allen Lane.

————. 1980a. *The History of Sexuality, Volume 1: An Introduction.* Trans. Robert Hurley. New York: Vintage/Random House.

————, ed. 1980b. *Herculine Barbin. Being the Recently Discovered Memoirs of a Nineteenth Century Hermaphrodite.* New York: Pantheon Books.

————. 1985. *The Use of Pleasure, Volume 2 of the History of Sexuality.* Trans. Robert Hurley. New York: Pantheon.

————. 1986. *The Care of the Self, Volume 3 of The History of Sexuality.* Trans. Robert Hurley. New York: Pantheon.

Fraser, Nancy. 1989. *Unruly Practices. Power, Discourse and Gender in Contemporary Social Theory.* Minneapolis: University of Minnesota Press.

Fraassen, Bas van. 1970. *An Introduction of the Philosophy of Time and Space.* New York: Random House.

————. 1980. *The Scientific Age.* Oxford: Clarendon Press.

Freedman, Hy. 1977. *Sex Link.* New York: NEL Paperbacks.

Freud, Sigmund. 1895. "Project for a Scientific Psychology." *Standard Edition of the Complete Psychological Works of Sigmund Freud* (hereafter *S.E.*). Oxford: The Hogarth Press, Vol. 1, 295–343.

————. 1905a. "The Three Essays on the Theory of Sexuality." *S.E.* Vol. 7, 135–243.

————. 1905b. "Fragment of an Analysis of a Case of Hysteria." *S.E.* Vol. 7, 1–122.

————. 1907. "Delusions and Dreams in Jensen's *Gradiva.*" *S.E.* Vol. 9, 1–93.

————. 1909. "Notes Upon a Case of Obsessional Neurosis." *S.E.* Vol. 10, 151–320.

————. 1910a. "Analysis of a Phobia in a Five Year Old Boy." *S.E.* Vol. 10, 5–149.

————. 1910b. "Leonardo da Vinci and a Memory of his Childhood." *S.E.* Vol 11, 59–137.

————. 1914. "On Narcissism: An Introduction." *S.E.* Vol. 14, 73–102.

————. 1915. "Repression." *S.E.* Vol. 14, 146–58.

————. 1919a. "'A Child is Being Beaten': A Contribution to the Study of the Origin of Sexual Perversions." *S.E.* Vol. 17, 179–204.

————. 1919b. "Beyond the Pleasure Principle." *S. E.* Vol. 18, 7–64.

————. 1920. "The Psychogenesis of a Case of Homosexuality in a Woman." *S.E.* Vol. 18, 147–72.

————. 1923. "The Ego and The Id." *S.E.* Vol 19, 13–66.

————. 1924. "Neurosis and Psychosis." *S.E.* Vol. 19, 149–53.

————. 1925a. "Some Psychical Consequences of the Anatomical Distinction Between the Sexes." *S.E.* Vol. 19, 248–58.

————. 1925b. "Negation." *S.E.* Vol, 19. 235–39.

————. 1927. "Fetishism." *S.E.* Vol. 21, 152–57.

————. 1940. "Splitting of the Ego in the Process of Defence." *S.E.* Vol. 23. 275–78.

Marilyn Frye. 1984. *The Politics of Reality: Essays in Feminist Theory.* Trumansburgh: The Crossings Press.

———. 1990. "Lesbian 'Sex.'" In *Lesbian Philosophies and Cultures.* Ed. Jeffner Allen. Albany: SUNY Press

Fuss, Diana. 1989. *Essentially Speaking. Feminism, Nature and Difference.* New York and London: Routledge.

Fuss, Diana, ed. 1991. *Inside/Out. Lesbian Theories. Gay Theories.* New York and London: Routledge.

Gale, Richard, ed. 1968. *The Philosophy of Time.* London: MacMillan.

Gallop, Jane. 1982. *The Daughter's Seduction. Feminism and Psychoanalysis.* Ithaca: Cornell University Press.

Gatens, Moira. 1990. "A Critique of the Sex/ Gender Distinction." In *A Reader in Feminist Knowledge.* Ed. Sneja Gunew. London and New York: Routledge.

———. 1991. *Feminism and Philosophy. Perspectives on Equality and Difference.* Cambridge: Polity Press.

Gauthier, Lorraine. 1989. "Truth as Eternal Metaphoric Displacement: Traces of the Mother in Derrida's Patricide." *Canadian Journal of Political and Social Theory* xiii, 1/2: 1–24.

Gordon, Colin. 1981. "The Subtracting Machine." *I & C* 8.

Greenacre, Phyllis. 1979. "Fetishism." In *Sexual Deviations.* Ed. I. Rosen. London and New York: Routledge, 191–207.

Grisham, Therese. 1991. "Linguistics as an Indiscipline: Deleuze and Guattari's Pragmatics." *Sub-Stance* 66 (20, 3): 36–54.

Grisoni, Dominique. 1982. "The Onomatopoeia of Desire." In *Theoretical Strategies.* Ed. Peter Botsman. Sydney: Local Consumption, 162–89.

Grosz, E. A. and Marie de Lepervanche. 1988. "Feminism and Science." In *Crossing Boundaries. Feminism and the Critique of Knowledges.* Eds. Barbara Caine, E. A. Grosz, and Marie de Lepervanche. Sydney: Allen and Unwin, 5–28.

Grosz, Elizabeth. 1990. *Jacques Lacan. A Feminist Introduction.* London and New York: Routledge.

———. 1994. *Volatile Bodies. Toward a Corporeal Feminism.* Bloomington: Indiana University Press; and Sydney: Allen and Unwin.

Guattari, Félix. 1993. "Space and Corporeity." *Columbian Documents of Architecture and Theory (D)* 2: 139–48.

Guillaume, Paul. 1971. *Imitation in Children.* Trans. Elaine Halperin. Chicago: University of Chicago Press.

Haraway, Donna. 1985. "A Manifesto for Cyborgs." *Socialist Review* 15, 2.

———. 1988. "Situated Knowledges." *Feminist Studies* 3.

Hardt, Michael. 1993. *An Apprenticeship in Philosophy. Gilles Deleuze.* Minneapolis and London: University of Minnesota Press.

Hawkins, Stephen. 1988. *A Brief History of Time.* London: Bantam Press.

Heidegger, Martin. 1978. "Letter on Humanism." In *The Basic Writings from Being and Time (1927) to The Task of Thinking (1964).* Ed. David Farrell Krell. London: Routledge and Kegan-Paul.

———. 1984. *The Metaphysical Foundations of Logic.* Trans. M. Heim. Bloomington: Indiana University Press.

Holland, Nancy J. 1992. "Derrida and Feminism." *APA Newsletter* 91: 2 (Fall): 40–43.

BIBLIOGRAPHY

Hollier, Denis. 1984a. "Mimesis and Castration 1937." *October* 31: 3–16.

———. 1984b. "How To Not Take Pleasure in Talking About Sex." In *enclitic* 8, 1–2 (Spring/Fall): 84–93.

———. 1988. *The College of Sociology 1937–39.* Trans. Betsy Wing. Minneapolis: University of Minnesota Press.

Hopkins, Juliet. 1984. "The Probable Role of Trauma in a Case of Foot and Shoe Fetishism: Aspects of Psychotherapy of a Six Year Old Girl." In *International Review of Psychoanalysis* 11: 79–91.

Husserl, Edmund. 1970. *The Crisis of European Sciences and Transcendental Phenomenology.* Trans. D. Carr. Evanston: Northwestern University Press.

Ingraham, Catherine. 1993. "Moving Targets." In *Columbian Documents of Architecture and Theory (D)* 2: 112–22.

Irigaray, Luce. 1981. *Le corps-à-corp avec la mère.* Montreal: Les editions de la pleine lune.

———. 1983. "Comment et où habiter?" *Cahiers du Grif* 26, Mars.

———. 1984. *Ethique de la différence sexuelle.* Paris: Minuit.

———. 1985a. *Speculum of the Other Woman.* Trans. Gillian C. Gill. Ithaca: Cornell University Press.

———. 1985b. *This Sex Which Is Not One.* Trans. Catherine Porter. Ithaca: Cornell University Press.

———. 1985c). "Is the Subject of Science Sexed?" *Cultural Critique* 1: 73–88.

———. 1985/6. "Language, Persephone and Sacrifice: An Interview." In *Borderlines* (Winter): 30–32.

———. 1991b. "Questions to Levinas." In *Irigaray Reader.* Ed. Margaret Whitford. Oxford: Basil Blackwell, 178–90.

———. 1991a. *Marine Lover of Friedrich Nietzsche.* Trans. Gillian C. Gill. New York: Columbia University Press.

———. 1992. *Elemental Passions.* Trans. Joanne Collie and Judith Still. New York: Routledge.

———. 1993a. *An Ethics of Sexual Difference.* Trans. Carolyn Burke and Gillian C. Gill. Ithaca: Cornell University Press.

———. 1993b. *Je, tous, nous. Toward a Culture of Difference.* Trans. Alison Martin. New York: Routledge.

Jacobus, Mary. 1986. *Reading Woman. Essays in Feminist Criticism.* New York: Columbia University Press.

Jardine, Alice. 1985. *Gynesis. Configurations of Women and Modernity.* Ithaca: Cornell University Press.

Jerde, Jon. 1988. "A Philosophy for City Development." In *Meanjin* 47: 4: 609–14.

Johnson, Barbara. 1988. *The Critical Difference. Essays in the Contemporary Rhetoric of Reading.* New York and London: The Johns Hopkins University Press.

Kafka, Franz. 1969. "The Penal Settlement." *Metamorphosis and other Short Stories.* Harmondsworth: Penguin.

Kamuf, Peggy. 1980. "Writing Like a Woman." In *Women and Language in Literature and Society.* Eds. Sally McConnell-Ginet, R. Borker, and N. Furman. New York: Praeger, 284–99.

———. 1988. *Signature Pieces. On the Institution of Authority.* Ithaca, Cornell University Press.

————. 1990. "Replacing Feminist Criticism." In *Conflicts in Feminism*. Eds. Marrianne Hirsch and Evelyn Fox Keller. New York and London: Routledge, 105–11.

Kamuf, Peggy and Nancy K Miller. 1990. "Parisian Letters. Between Feminism and Deconstruction." In *Conflicts in Feminism*. Eds. M. Hirsch and E. Fox Keller. New York and London: Routledge, 121–31.

King, Katie. 1990. "Producing Sex, Theory and Culture: Gay/Straight Remappings in Contemporary Feminism." In *Conflicts in Feminism*. Eds. M. Hirsch and E. Fox Keller. New York and London: Routledge, 82–101.

Kirby, Vicki. 1987. "On the Cutting Edge: Feminism and Clitoridectomy." *Australian Feminist Studies* 5: 35–56.

————. 1991. "Corpus Delicti: The Body at the Scene of Writing." In *Cartographies Poststructuralism and the Mapping of Bodies and Spaces*. Eds. R. Diprose and R. Ferrell. Sydney: Allen & Unwin, 88–102.

Kofman, Sarah. 1985. *The Enigma of Woman—Woman in Freud's Writings*. New York: Cornell University Press.

Kohon, Gregorio. 1987. "Fetishism Revisited." In *International Journal of Psychoanalysis* 68: 213–28.

Krell, David Farrell. 1990. *Of Memory, Reminiscence and Writing. On the Verge.* Bloomington and Indianapolis: Indiana University Press.

Kristeva, Julia. 1981. "Women's Time." In *Signs* 7, 1.

Kwinter, Sandford. 1986. "La Citta Nuova: Modernity and Continuity." In *Zone* 1/2: 80–127.

Lacan, Jacques. 1953. "Some Reflections on the Ego." In *International Journal of Psychoanalysis* 34.

————. 1977a. *Ecrits. A Selection.* Trans. Alan Sheridan. London: Tavistock.

————. 1977b. *The Four Fundamental Concepts of Psychoanalysis.* Trans. A. M. Sheridan. London: Tavistock.

Lacan, Jacques and W. Granoff. 1956. "Fetishism: The Symbolic, The Imaginary and The Real." In *Perversions, Psychodynamics and Therapy*. Ed. Michael Balint. London: Tavistock, 265–76.

Laplanche, Jean. 1989. *New Foundations For Psychoanalysis*. London: Karnac Books.

Le Doeuff, Michèle. 1989. *The Philosophical Imaginary*. Trans. Colin Gordon. Stanford: Stanford University Press.

Lewin, Bertram D. 1931. "The Body as Phallus." In *Psychoanalytic Quarterly* 2: 24–47.

Lingis, Alphonso. 1984. *Excesses. Eros and Culture.* Albany: SUNY Press.

————. 1985a. *Libido.* Albany: SUNY Press.

————. 1985b. "The Libidinal Origin of Meaning and the Value of the I." In *enclitic* Vol. IX, Nos. 1–2: 80–94.

————. 1989. *Deathbound Subjectivity.* Bloomington: Indiana University Press.

————. 1991. "Segmented Organisms." Paper presented to the Merleau-Ponty Circle, University of Colorado at Colorado Springs.

————. 1992. "The Society of Dismembered Body Parts." In *Pli. Warwick Journal of Philosophy*. Ed. Joan Broadhurst. Special issue on 'Deleuze and the Transcendental Unconscious': 1–20.

————. 1994a. *The Community of those Who Have Nothing in Common.*

Bloomington: Indiana University Press.

———. 1994b. *Abuses*. Berkeley: University of California Press

———. 1994c. *Foreign Bodies*. New York: Routledge.

Lorand, Sandor. 1930. "Fetishism in *Statu Nascendi*." In *International Journal of Psychoanalysis* 11, 4: 419–27.

Lyotard, Jean-Francois. 1978. "One of the Things at Stake in Women's Struggles." In *Sub-Stance* 20: 9–18.

———. 1993. *Libidinal Economy*. Trans. Ian Hamilton Grant. Bloomington: Indiana University Press.

McCarthy, Thomas. 1989–90. "The Politics of the Ineffable: Derrida's Deconstructionism." In *Philosophical Forum* XXI 1–2 (Fall-Winter): 146–168.

McNay, Lois. 1991. "The Foucauldian Body and the Exclusion of Experience." In *Hypatia* 6, 2: 124–139.

McNay, Lois. 1993. *Foucault and Feminism*. Oxford: Polity Press.

McNulty, Robert. 1988. "The Economics of Amenity." In *Meanjin* 47: 4: 614–25.

Massumi, Brian. 1992. *A User's Guide to Capitalism and Schizophrenia. Deviations from Deleuze and Guattari*. Cambridge and London: The MIT Press.

Massumi, Brian. 1993. "Everywhere You Want to Be. Introduction to Fear." In *The Politics of Everyday Fear*. Ed. Brian Massumi. Cambridge and London: The MIT Press: 3–38.

Merleau-Ponty, Maurice. 1963. *The Primacy of Perception*. Ed. James M. Edie. Evanston: Northwestern University Press.

———. 1964. *Signs*. Trans. Richard C. McCleary. Evanston: Northwestern University Press.

Miller, Nancy K. 1990. "The Text's Heroine: A Feminist Critic and Her Fictions." In *Conflicts in Feminism*. Eds. Marianne Hirsch and Evelyn Fox Keller. New York and London: Routledge, 112–20.

Moi, Toril. 1985. *Sexual/ Textual Politics. Feminist Literary Theory*. London: Methuen.

Money, John. 1968. *Sex Errors of the Body. Dilemmas, Education, Counselling*. Baltimore: Johns Hopkins University Press.

Morgan, Kathryn. 1991. "Women and the Knife: Cosmetic Surgery and the Colonization of Women's Bodies." In *Hypatia* 6, 2: 25–53.

Morris, Meaghan. 1992. "Great Moments in Social Climbing: Kong and the Human Fly." In *Sexuality and Space*. Ed. Beatriz Colomina. Princeton: Princeton Architectural Press, 1–51.

Nancy, Jean-Luc. 1993. *The Birth To Presence*. Trans. Richard Holmes and others. Stanford: Stanford University Press.

Nietzsche, Friedrich. 1968. *The Will to Power*. Trans. Walter Kaufmann and R.J. Hollingdale. New York: Vintage Books.

———. 1969. *On the Genealogy of Morals*. Trans. Walter Kaufmann. New York: Vintage Books

Nerlich, Graham. 1976. *The Shape of Space*. Cambridge: Cambridge University Press.

Plato. 1977. *Timaeus and Critias*. Trans. Desmond Lee. Penguin: Harmondsworth.

Probyn, Elspeth. 1991. "This Body Which Is Not One: Technologizing an Embodied Self." In *Hypatia* 6, 2: 349–61.

Rajchman, John. 1992. "Anywhere and Nowhere." In *ANYwhere*. Ed. Cynthia Davidson. New York: Rizzoli International Publications, 229–33.

———. 1994a. "Lightness: A Concept in Architecture." *Any* 5: 5–6.

———. 1994b. "The Earth is Called Light." *Any* 5: 12–13.

Reichenbach, Hans. 1958. *The Philosophy of Space and Time*. Trans. Maria Reichenbach and John Freund. New York: Dover Publications.

Rheingold, Howard. 1991. *Virtual Reality*. New York: Summit Books.

Rich, Adrienne. 1986. "Compulsory Heterosexuality and Lesbian Existence." *Blood, Bread and Poetry: Selected Prose 1979–1985*. New York: Norton, 23–75.

Richards, Janet Radcliffe. 1982. *The Sceptical Feminist*. Harmondsworth: Penguin.

Robinson, Sally. 1989. "Misappropriations of the Feminine." *Sub-stance* 59: 48–70.

Ronell, Avital. 1994. *Finitude's Score. Essays on the End of the Millenium*. Lincoln: University of Nebraska Press.

Jacqueline Rose. 1985. "Dora: Fragment of an Analysis." In *Dora's Case. Freud-Hysteria-Feminism*. Eds. Charles Berheimer and Claire Kahane. New York: Columbia University Press, 128–47.

Ruch, E.A. 1958. *Space and Time. A Comparative Studies of the Theories of Aristotle and Einstein*. Pretoria: University of South Africa Press.

Ryan, Michael. 1982. *Marxism and Deconstruction. A Critical Articulation*. Baltimore: Johns Hopkins University Press.

Sartre, Jean-Paul. 1961. *Anti-Semite and Jew*. New York: Schocken Books.

Saussure, Ferdinand de. 1974. *Course in General Linguistics*. New York: Fontana/Collins.

Sawicki, Jana. 1991. *Disciplining Foucault. Feminism, Power and the Body*. London: Routledge.

Scarry, Elaine. 1985. *The Body in Pain: The Making and Unmaking of the World*. Oxford: Oxford University Press.

Schilder, Paul. 1978. *The Image and Appearance of the Human Body. Studies in the Constructive Energies of the Psyche*. New York: International Universities Press.

Schor, Naomi. 1985. "Female Fetishism: The Case of George Sand." In *The Female Body in Western Culture*. Ed. Susan Rubin Suleiman. Cambridge: Harvard University Press, 363–72.

Sky, Alison. 1988. "On Site." *Meanjin* 47, 4: 644–56.

Spacks, Patricia M. 1975. *The Female Imagination*. New York: Knopf.

Spitz, René. 1965. *The First Year of Life. A Psychoanalytic Study of Normal and Deviant Development of Object Relations*. New York: International Universities Press.

Spivak, Gayatri Chakravorty. 1982. "Displacement and the Discourse of Woman." In *Displacement. Derrida and After*. Ed. Mark Krupnick. Bloomington: Indiana University Press, 169–93.

———. 1984/5. "Criticism, Feminism and the Institution." *Thesis Eleven* 10/11: 175–89

———. 1987. *In Other Worlds*. New York: Routledge.

———. 1989. "Feminism and Deconstruction, Again: Negotiating with Unacknowledged Masculinism." In *Between Feminism and Psychoanalysis*. Ed. Teresa Brennan. London and New York: Routledge, 206–23.

———. 1992. "French Feminism Revisited: Ethics and Politics." In *Feminists Theorize the Political*. Eds. Judith Butler and Joan W. Scott. New York: Routledge, 54–85.

Ströker, Elisabeth. 1987. *Investigations in the Philosophy of Space*. Trans. Algis Mickunas. Ohio University Press.

Studlar, Gaylyn. 1988. *In the Realm of Pleasure. Von Sternberg, Dietrich and the Masochistic Aesthetic*. Urbana: Illinois University Press.

Suleiman, Susan, ed. 1986. *The Female Body in Western Culture. Contemporary Perspectives*. Cambridge: Harvard University Press.

Treblicot, Joyce. 1990. "Dyke Methods." In *Lesbian Philosophies and Cultures*. Ed. Jeffner Allen. Albany: SUNY Press, 15–29.

Tschumi, Bernard. 1983. "Illustrated Index: Themes from the Manhattan Transcripts." *Architectural Association Files* 4 (July): 65–74.

Turner, Bryan S. 1984. *The Body and Society. Explorations in Social Theory*. Oxford: Basil Blackwell.

Ulmer, Gregory. 1985. *Applied Grammatology: Post(e)-Pedagogy from Jacques Derrida to Joseph Beuys*. Baltimore: The Johns Hopkins University Press.

Virilio, Paul. 1986. "The Overexposed City." *Zone 1/2*: 14–39.

———. 1993. "The Law of Proximity." *Columbian Documents of Architecture and Theory (D)* 2: 123–38.

Whitford, Margaret. 1991. *Luce Irigaray. Philosophy in the Feminine*. London: Routledge.

Whitford, Margaret, ed. 1991. *The Irigaray Reader*. Oxford: Basil Blackwell

Wigley, Mark. 1987. "Postmortem Architecture. The Taste of Derrida." *Perspecta* 23: 157–72.

———. 1993. *The Architecture of Deconstruction. Derrida's Haunt*. Cambridge: The MIT Press.

Wilson, Elizabeth. 1994. *Dislocations. Feminism between Psychology and Cognition*. Unpublished dissertation, University of Sydney.

Wilson, James G. 1973. *Environment and Birth Defects*. New York: Academic Press.

Woolf, Virginia. 1963. *A Room of One's Own*. Harmondsworth: Penguin.

Yencken, David. 1988. "The Creative City." *Meanjin* 47, 4: 597–609.

Young, Iris Marion. 1990. *Throwing Like a Girl and Other Essays in Feminist Philosophy and Social Theory*. Bloomington: Indiana University Press.

Zeman, Jirí, ed. 1971. *Time in Science and Philosophy. An International Study of Some Current Problems*. Amsterdam, London, and New York: Elsevier Publishing Company.

INDEX

(269)